W9-BHM-699

EDUCATION LIBRARY
UNIVERSITY OF KENTUCKY

Nascent Entrepreneurship and Learning

Nascent Entrepreneurship and Learning

Mine Karataş-Özkan

Lecturer in Entrepreneurship, University of Southampton, UK

Elizabeth Chell

Research Consultant and Professor of Entrepreneurial Behaviour, Small Business Research Centre, Kingston University, UK

Edward Elgar
Cheltenham, UK • Northampton, MA, USA

Edvc.
HB
615
.K3665
2010

© Mine Karataş-Özkan and Elizabeth Chell 2010

All rights reserved. No part of this publication may be reproduced, stored in a retrieval system or transmitted in any form or by any means, electronic, mechanical or photocopying, recording, or otherwise without the prior permission of the publisher.

Published by
Edward Elgar Publishing Limited
The Lypiatts
15 Lansdown Road
Cheltenham
Glos GL50 2JA
UK

Edward Elgar Publishing, Inc.
William Pratt House
9 Dewey Court
Northampton
Massachusetts 01060
USA

A catalogue record for this book
is available from the British Library

Library of Congress Control Number: 2009938386

Mixed Sources
Product group from well-managed
forests and other controlled sources
www.fsc.org Cert no. SA-COC-1565
© 1996 Forest Stewardship Council
FSC

ISBN 978 1 84720 760 9

Printed and bound by MPG Books Group, UK

Contents

Figures

Tables

1. Introduction

1.1 SCOPE AND AIM OF THE BOOK

This book examines the process of nascent entrepreneurship from a learning perspective. The overall aim of the research is to generate insights into nascent entrepreneurs' learning and managing experiences by exploring their perspectives in relation to the enterprise culture and education discourses in the United Kingdom (UK). Embedded in a social constructionist paradigm, a process-relational stance is taken to entrepreneurship. This recognises the dynamic and emergent processes through which business opportunities are realised and constructed in the context of social interactions with numerous stakeholders.

The social constructionist position, in which this research is grounded, calls for the need to understand human experiences in their socio-cultural context, with an acknowledgement of human agency and active perceptual constructions of people in a society. Nascent entrepreneurs' biographies, motivations and characteristics or capitals that make up their profiles are examined at the micro-individual level, combined with meso-level considerations, including social processes of business venturing. The research also analyses how these micro-individual and meso-relational processes relate to macro-field forces of enterprise culture, moving beyond an individual or team understanding of nascent entrepreneurship.

The book is supported by an empirical investigation of two case studies of the business venturing process. The first case pertains to the formation of a creative venture (that is a brand communications agency, which uniquely includes in-house production of advertising vehicles with marketing strategy business) by a team of five nascent entrepreneurs. This group of friends set up the company outside the local university's incubator centre while they were students in different areas of arts, design and technology at the local university. The second case account is about a solo entrepreneur's business venturing story, which *is* characterised by a venturing process supported by the local university's incubator centre.

In methodological terms we have adopted *naturalistic inquiry* as the research design, which is compatible with the social constructionist position taken. The triangulation of participant observation, in-depth interviews and documentary analysis has been carried out in order to address the research questions. Because of the longevity (two years) and intensity of the fieldwork and the resulting richness of data generated, the first case constitutes the principal case account in this research. The second case study provides very useful and rich material to juxtapose the salient themes and patterns in general and to reach towards a multi-layered understanding of nascent entrepreneurship and that of underpinning processes of learning and managing in particular.

A multi-layered conceptualisation of nascent entrepreneurship has been offered in this book, with the following key themes at each layer. The layers include three levels of analysis: micro-level analysis, which includes scrutinising nascent entrepreneurs' individual experiences by examining their motivation, dispositions and resources that they draw on and capitals, using the term 'capital' in Bourdieu's (1986) conceptualisation,[1] that they want to attain in life; meso-relational level analysis, which refers to the analysis of relational experiences of entrepreneurial learning and managing by looking into relational dynamics of 'venture communities' that they form as a part of their entrepreneurial becoming; and macro-level analysis, which denotes an examination of how the 'field' of enterprise culture – with its associated policies, intervention and support programmes – and institutions impact on their development of entrepreneurial learning and managing.

Our key argument is that it is not sufficient to study nascent entrepreneurship and the concurrent process of entrepreneurial learning at the individual (entrepreneur) or collective (team or organisational) levels and examine the socio-behavioural aspects of learning. Entrepreneurial learning should be understood by inter-relating personal (micro), relational (meso) and macro-contextual aspects of nascent entrepreneurship. These three layers, together with eight aforementioned sub-themes, form the basis for multi-layered understanding of nascent entrepreneurship from a learning perspective. This study takes this gap in our knowledge as the starting point and intends to move the discussion further by undertaking a multi-layered examination of nascent entrepreneurs' learning and managing.

The contributions of this book are multiple. Firstly, it provides an investigation of social construction processes of nascent entrepreneurship, from a learning perspective, which is identified as an under-researched area by many scholars in the field. Secondly, the research provides rich empirical material in the form of case accounts to exemplify such processes. Thirdly, a multi-layered framework of nascent entrepreneurship has been developed in this research, which moves beyond individual or collective understandings of entrepreneurship, by taking an inter-disciplinary approach and applying Bourdieu's conceptual tools in a comprehensive way in the entrepreneurship field. Finally, a number of research implications for academics and practical insights for practitioners including nascent entrepreneurs, enterprise educators and mentors are offered in Chapter 10.

1.2   ORGANISATION OF THE BOOK

Chapter 2 presents a review of the policy context in the UK in relation to enterprise culture by examining the underlying philosophies, assumptions and institutions from a historical perspective. Enterprise culture debates have been presented in order to emphasise the political, economic and social factors in the UK that have resulted in enterprise education and support agendas. The role of universities has been not insignificant, with particular reference to university incubators. The vagueness of the notion of enterprise and its political and ideological use in government pronouncements is worth noting (Chell, 2007).

Chapter 3 locates the current research in relation to developments in entrepreneurship and organisation studies. It places emphasis on how entrepreneurship has been conceptualised in academic discourses over time. In line with the research aims and questions, three major perspectives, which are in tune with social constructionist and constructivist perspectives in studying social phenomena, have been identified when charting the literature on entrepreneurship. These include processual perspectives, relational perspectives and process-relational perspectives on entrepreneurship.

Approaching entrepreneurial behaviour and process from a variety of angles and methodological positions, processual studies centre around the functions and activities associated with perceiving business opportunities and creating ventures to pursue them. Thus a processual way of looking at entrepreneurship entails the examination of emerging characteristics of the entrepreneurial process. From processual perspectives, the dynamic process through which business opportunities are realised becomes the central focus of entrepreneurship studies (Fletcher, 2003).

Relational perspectives highlight the human relationships involved in the process. Entrepreneurial activities are realised and constructed through social processes. This understanding of entrepreneurship builds on the Schumpeterian (1934) notion of contributing to economic change through new combinations of products or processes. Entrepreneurs bring about new ideas, products, or processes by working in relation to a team, small community or network of people (Johannisson, 1990; Fletcher, 1997, 2003). This leads to process-relational perspectives, which combine the processual view of emergence with a relational dimension in order to generate deeper insights. The relational part is in essence about relating to each other through language, narrative, discourse as well as enactment.

The process-relational position adopted in this research project takes account of the following conceptualisation of entrepreneurship, which is based on the studies of Stevenson and Gumpert (1985), Stevenson and Jarillo (1990), Hart, Stevenson and Dial (1995), Chell (2000, 2001, 2007, 2008) and Fletcher and Watson (2003):

> Entrepreneurship is the process through which people with ideas for product, service or process relentlessly and relationally pursue business opportunities without regards to alienable resources currently available and with an intention and motivation to create wealth and accumulate capital.

Chapter 4 follows with a discussion on nascent entrepreneurship and entrepreneurial learning. Aldrich (1999) defines nascent entrepreneurs as those who initiate serious entrepreneurial activities that are intended to culminate in a viable business start-up. They are in the process of beginning their entrepreneurial venture with the potential and capacity to become successful entrepreneurs (Westhead and Wright, 1998); therefore they have very limited experience or practical understanding of the concepts and processes involved. Thus, the intrinsic elements of the entrepreneurial process of business venturing include entrepreneurial learning and managing. These, we anticipate, will be highly evident in the case of nascent entrepreneurs. As such, they will develop meanings and understandings of venturing through a constant process of negotiations and exchanges with clients, competitors, mentors, financial organisations, regional development agencies and members of a variety of networks. From this analysis we bring together key ideas from the extant literature on entrepreneurial learning.

Chapter 5 discusses the methodological approach taken in crafting the research. The social constructionist paradigm and Bourdieu's relational methodology are explained with reference to their application in the research underpinning the book. The social constructionist position in which this research is grounded calls for the need to understand human experiences in their socio-cultural context (Berger and Luckmann, 1966; K.J. Gergen, 1985; Burr, 1995), with an acknowledgement of human agency and active perceptual constructions of the members of a society (Martin and Sugarman, 1996; Chell, 2000, 2008; Nicholson and Anderson, 2005). The individual entrepreneurs' biographies, choices, motivation and the 'capitals' (Bourdieu, 1986), some of which they draw on and some others that they make determined effort to attain, have been examined in the project. Entrepreneurial learning literature (for example Cope and Watts, 2000; Cope, 2003, 2005; Rae, 2003, 2004a, 2004b; Politis, 2005), which reveals complexities of the learning process and yields rich insights into entrepreneurs' transformative learning experience in their cultural and organisational context, is reviewed in order that we may locate the current research as a continuation of these 'interpretive' studies (Burrell and Morgan, 1979) that aim to explain the dynamics and subtleties of the process.

Chapter 6 presents the research design based on 'naturalistic inquiry' (Lincoln and Guba, 1985) and an overview of social constructionist paradigmatic assumptions, research questions, associated methods of data collection and analysis, and criteria applied for establishing the trustworthiness of this qualitative study. The research data were collected primarily through participant observation and in-depth interviews. Observation and interview data were supplemented by documentary evidence provided by participants. Observation data were stored and analysed using Spradley's (1980) participant observation framework. Meeting talks and interviews were analysed from transcripts using qualitative data analysis techniques that Miles and Huberman (1994) and Patton (2002) provide in their source books. Bourdieu's (1986, 1990, 1998) conceptual tools including dispositions and different forms of capital at micro-individual level, *habitus* at the meso-relational level and field at the macro-level were instrumental in defining broad categories of data during the analysis. This allowed the data to be accessible at individual case level and particularly cross-case level.

Chapter 7 presents the first case study, labelled using the pseudonym 'KBrandArt'. The first case venturing process relates to the formation of a creative venture (that is a brand communications agency, which uniquely includes in-house production of advertising vehicles) so-called 'KBrandArt'. The case material was generated by observing the venture team meetings and daily and strategic conduct of the business by five nascent entrepreneurs, who set up the company outside the local university's incubator centre while they were students in different areas of arts, design and technology at the local university. This case material includes face-to-face interviews and documents from their organisational texts (mainly business plans, meeting notes, internal memos and press releases). The 'Creative Industries' (CI) context, as defined by two government documents (Department of Culture Media and Sport, 1998, 2001), sets the common macro-level ground for both case accounts.

Chapter 8 presents the second case account, 'R-Games', which is about a solo entrepreneur's business venturing story. Her story is characterised by a venturing process supported by the local university's incubator centre.

Chapter 9 offers a multi-layered framework of nascent entrepreneurship. Nascent entrepreneurship is conceptualised from a multi-layered perspective by taking into account the interplay of micro-, meso- and macro-level qualities of the process. The key argument is that individual nascent entrepreneurs (micro-level) actively and relationally form their new ventures as a part of a broader venture community (meso-relational level), which is embedded in the macro-field of enterprise culture with its institutions and education programmes.

The salient themes of the book are pulled together in the conclusion in Chapter 10. It is the idea that the current research is a part of these several movements in knowledge. This study would, we hope, enable us to make a contribution by studying such an under-researched area in diverse settings and offering rich case study material and ultimately to generate significant insights to venture community members, academics who research and teach the subject, and policy-makers at national and international levels.

NOTE

1. Bourdieu's (1986) concept of capital is broader than the notion of capital in economics. It is used in a more encompassing sense to represent 'resource' that can assume monetary and non-monetary as well as tangible and intangible forms. This is delineated in Chapter 5 of the book.

2. Setting the discursive context: enterprise culture debates in the UK

2.1 INTRODUCTION TO THE CHAPTER

Political discourse in many advanced liberal economies has been dominated by references to 'enterprise' for the best part of a quarter of a century (du Gay, 2004, p. 38). The enterprise culture is founded on the premise that entrepreneurship has a transformative function, which drives the economy (Jack and Anderson, 1999). This belief that new enterprises fuel employment and wealth creation, combined with a shift from the orthodoxy of Keynesian economics to a market-driven ideology, has cemented entrepreneurship into political discourse (Ogbor, 2000; Swedberg, 2000; Perren and Jennings, 2005).

The chapter seeks to examine the political discourse of enterprise culture that has prevailed in the UK since the early 1980s, by analysing the underpinning philosophies and assumptions from a historical perspective. To this end, the chapter is organised as follows: the first section discusses the political usage of the term 'enterprise culture', by showing how successive politicians have played on the ambiguity of interpretation in order to serve several purposes at different times. The second section considers the role of higher education institutions (HEIs) in the further development of the enterprise agenda. The part played by university incubators provides a deeper insight into the context for nascent entrepreneurship. The chapter concludes with a summary of the key debates.

2.2 ENTERPRISE CULTURE DEBATES

The notion of enterprise culture has been at the forefront of political debate for three decades, with successive UK governments having committed themselves to making the UK a country of enterprise (Gavron, Cowling, Holtham et al., 1998). During the course of the 1980s, the idea of an enterprise culture emerged as a central motif in the political thought and practice of the Conservative government in the UK (Keat, 1991). However, there is a continuing political enthusiasm for encouraging enterprise and entrepreneurship in the UK (Ram and Smallbone, 2003). As pointed out by Gibb (2002a), enterprise has been at the core of the UK government's 'competitiveness initiative' for several years (Blair, 1998 in Gibb, 2002a; Department of Trade and Industry, 1998). Gibb (2002a, p. 235) maintains that there is a crucial difference between the 2002 Labour government's version and that of the Thatcher government. The difference is that the Thatcher government's attempts to create an enterprise culture were based on free market economics and bringing about a range of external structural changes (Morris, 1991).

Specifically, these interventions entailed: dismantling the welfare state, reducing the power of trade unions, deregulation, introduction of the market mechanism, privatisation, cuts in taxation, reducing the role of the state and enlarging that of the individual, reducing the public sector borrowing requirement, introducing firm monetary and fiscal discipline thus bringing inflation under control, and promoting self-employment (Carr and Beaver, 2002). By implementing these policies, questions were raised about the moral underpinnings of the Thatcherite enterprise culture and the need to develop a deeper understanding of the values and attitudes implicit in the concept of enterprise within the organisational psyche and society more widely (Keat, 1991; Gavron et al., 1998; Carr and Beaver, 2002, p. 106). Therefore, the Thatcherite project of economic reconstruction has been redefined as 'one of cultural reconstruction – the attempt to transform Britain into an enterprise culture' (Keat, 1991, p. 1).

Morris (1991) provides a detailed account of the historical development of the notion of 'enterprise culture' by showing how its meaning fluctuated through a series of policies from 1974 until the beginning of the 1990s. In 1974, the Centre for Policy Studies (CPS) was founded to study free market economics. In its publications from this time until around 1985, 'enterprise' was understood largely in terms of commercial and industrial initiative and advocacy of the extension of the market model to new areas (Morris, 1991, p. 23). These studies therefore focused on the removal of various economic and fiscal barriers in order to allow for the development of the culture of enterprise rather than defining the characteristics of the enterprise itself (Morris, 1991). Since 1985, there was an increase in emphasis on individualism (including personal property and individual responsibility) and the ethos of the market as individual choice. This ideological emphasis manifested itself in the establishment of an Enterprise Policy Unit in 1987, whose aim was the creation of a full enterprise culture, concentrating on enterprise, educational issues, business concerns and taxation. In a 1987 policy document (cited in Morris, 1991), the CPS defined 'enterprise culture' as follows: 'Enterprise culture is defined as the full set of conditions that promote high and rising levels of achievement in a country's economic activity, politics and government, arts and sciences, and also distinctively private lives of the inhabitants'. Further, enterprise was associated with risk-taking in all areas of life; individual commitment and creativity were to be manifest at all levels of 'work and play' in order to foster initiative (Morris, 1991, p. 24). The emphasis on motivation, creative ambition and excellence was considered to be a significant point as these could be gained through education. Therefore, it would appear that the idea that 'enterprise is teachable' is rooted in these developments and forms a central plank of enterprise and entrepreneurship education to the current day.

A seminal lecture by Lawson (1984, cited in Morris, 1991) advocated the view that 'Britain must create an enterprise culture by changing psychology in order to change the business culture'. He contended that the effects of all the measures to free the market could be thwarted by the particular British historico-cultural and psychological realities; so what is required is education in enterprise and specific policies to counter these realities. A new scheme called 'Enterprise in Higher Education' (EHE) was introduced in 1987 by the then Department of Employment, the aim of which was 'to increase dramatically the supply of more highly qualified people with enterprise' (MSC, 1987 cited in Morris, 1991, p. 30). Thus, the definition of enterprise was extended to include: 'generating and taking ideas and putting them to work, taking decisions, welcoming change and helping to shape it and create wealth'.

The changing meaning of enterprise in the late 1980s paved the way for the introduction of concepts such as 'social entrepreneurship' or 'social enterprise'. In his 1986–87 speeches, Lord Young argued that the basis of national unity was a cluster of shared values and only enterprise values could provide this basis. As expressed by Morris (1991, p. 31):

> The values of personal responsibility and confidence, together with the desire to improve one's own circumstances, are the foundation for what he calls 'enterprise in the community'. That is the creation of communities based on self-respect and respect for others, which is manifest in good citizenship.

This period is referred to by Morris (1991) as 'partnership in cultural engineering' in which a conscious attempt was made to create the conditions to effect massive cultural and psychological transformation of British society in order to bring about an enterprise culture.

Analysing the political speeches delivered between 1985 and 1988, Fairclough (1991) deciphered the 'enterprise discourse', which had been shaped and reshaped in relation to shifting strategies, and reached the conclusion that 'enterprise discourse is best conceived of as a rather diffuse set of changes affecting various aspects of the societal order of discourse in various ways' (Fairclough, 1991, p. 39). Fairclough's (1991) analysis starts with the dictionary meanings of 'enterprise', as he outlines three senses of the word: engagement in bold, arduous or momentous undertakings; disposition or readiness to engage in undertakings of difficulty, risk, danger, or daring spirit; and private business as a collective noun. He refers to these as 'activity', 'quality' (in the sense of personal quality), and 'business' senses. He notes the ambivalence potential of enterprise in Lord Young's speeches since any occurrence of the word is open to being interpreted in any of the three senses or any combinations of them. Establishing the links to wider strategic objectives of the speeches, Fairclough (1991) points out that the strategic exploitation of the ambivalence of the word 'enterprise' in the political speeches of the time is a significant element in achieving the higher purposes – particularly contributing to revaluation of a somewhat discredited private business sector, by associating private enterprise with culturally valued qualities of 'enterprisingness'.

Fairclough (1991) observes that almost all of Young's definitions of enterprise give it the quality sense. The differentiating point is the contrast between qualities that are specific to business activity and more general personal qualities. By giving examples of definitions from four speeches, he depicts a scale, which moves from business to general qualities. What is more important is the varying communication objectives, situations and audiences of speeches. For example, the following definition occurs in a speech whose focus is tackling unemployment: 'Enterprise encompasses flexibility, innovation, risk taking and hard work – the qualities so essential to the future of our economy and our nation' (Lord Young as quoted in Fairclough, 1991, p. 41). Another definition, which was provided in a speech two months later, was addressing the issue of inner city policy and 'enterprise in the community': 'Enterprise . . . means an acceptance of personal responsibility and a confidence and desire to take action to improve your own circumstances' (Lord Young as quoted in Fairclough, 1991, p. 41).

The expression 'enterprise culture', which occurs throughout these speeches, is widely used as a label for core components of government policy and strategy and is itself very vague, not only because 'enterprise' is vague between the three senses, but also because the relationship between the two elements of such nominal compounds is itself open to multiple interpretations (Fairclough, 1991). Providing a fairly representative sample of the speeches as a whole, he sums up the following usages: enterprise and employment, initiative and enterprise, enterprise and individual responsibility, self-reliance and enterprise, skills and enterprise, professionalism and enterprise, and talents and enterprise.

Looking into the configurations of the meanings, he notes that just as establishing particular salience hierarchies among the senses of a word can serve strategic purposes, so it can establish wider configurations between the discourses of enterprise and skill on the one hand, or between the discourses of enterprise and individual responsibility on the other. The analysis leads us to the following: firstly, the narratives (or vocabularies or discourses) of 'enterprise' and 'skill' blend enterprise with a particular vocationally oriented conceptualisation, wording and ideology of education and training, and that of its relationship to work and other dimensions of social life; and secondly, the narrative of 'enterprise' and 'individual responsibility' combines enterprise with personal morality.

Finally, Fairclough (1991, p. 47) suggests that the total configuration that results is the linguistic aspect of a major strategic conjunction in government policies: between a promotion of 'enterprise' in the workplace and beyond, consumerism and a vocationally geared education system.

Another work, which examined government pronouncements of enterprise culture during the 1980s, is that of Selden (1991). He looked into the speeches and published papers of Lord Young and Lord Lawson. As in the article of Fairclough (1991), he starts with the ambivalent nature of the terms 'enterprise', 'enterprising' and 'entrepreneur'. Joining the views of Morris (1991) and to some extent Fairclough (1991), he suggests the need to take a more encompassing approach in understanding enterprise discourse. The general human qualities that the term 'enterprise' connotes should not be restrained within a narrowly economic discourse. Seeing the industrial revolution as the first true moment of the enterprise culture, and relating the enterprise culture to the basic pillars of capitalism, Selden (1991) demonstrates the increasing emphasis placed on individualism in the speeches and readings of enterprise culture particularly in late 1980s:

> This is based on the fundamental premise of the enterprise argument: only by allowing the individual to act in an economically self-interested manner can sufficient wealth be created to allow individuals to care for others. . ... The entrepreneurial discourse is here in danger of undoing its binary logic. The terms are clearly in uneasy relation: 'wealth creation versus wealth consumption, standard of living versus caring, civilized society'. We cannot have a caring, civilised society, unless we allow individuals selfishly to reach the standard of living that makes helping others possible. There is no way of knowing at what stage the creation of wealth overflows into the socially altruistic consumption of wealth. It is necessary to legitimise individual greed in order to effect civilized ends. The priority of self-interest over helping others remains . . ... We must all accept the values of the enterprise culture. We must accept that helping ourselves comes before helping others. The enterprise discourse asks us to accept Hamlet's advice and to stop being the primarily social beings some of us feel we are. If we keep acting as though we are essentially entrepreneurial beings, we may actually start believing it; 'for' as Hamlet says 'use almost can change the stamp of nature' (Selden, 1991, p. 70).

Referring to Selden's (1991) paper, Chell (2004b) provides a critique of the Thatcherite period, by arguing that Thatcherism 'attempted to imbue "enterprise" with the sense that it is both natural and cultural – a binary opposition'. The argument of the era was centred on the notion that people are enterprising, because 'enterprising' was associated with 'good citizenship' (holding the qualities of being responsible, hard working and confident) and yet the Thatcherite revolution was about the restoration of a natural and spontaneous form of existence (Chell, 2004b). This suggests a sense of sloughing of culture, returning to a presumed natural state of being that emphasises greed, self-interest and brutishness. Indeed, it is a philosophy redolent of Thomas Hobbes, when he stated infamously in Leviathan: 'No arts; no letters; no society; . . . and the life of man, solitary, poor, nasty, brutish, and short' (Hobbes (1651/1962) pt I, 13). Thatcher famously asserted that 'there is no such thing as society'.

Returning to Fairclough's (1991) examination of the political discourse of the day, this 'quality' view was connected with business along the lines of the skills and knowledge required to create wealth and 'go it alone'; that is, make the leap into self-employment (Chell, 2004b, p. 5). Therefore, the philosophy of the era implied that 'entrepreneurship' was confined to self-employment and furthermore it was viewed as a natural progression by enterprising individuals. Enterprise education was played down and reproduced as vocational education and training, which put the emphasis solely on 'enterprising' qualities (Chell, 2004b) and developing knowledge of tools and techniques for enterprise.

Burrows (1991, p. 5) also problematises the use of the term 'enterprise culture' by suggesting that enterprise culture 'possesses only a small residual explanatory status in accounts of the materiality of the restructuring of Western economies'. Carr and Beaver (2002) acknowledge this problem that 'enterprise culture is presented as a simple justificatory discourse for the enormous changes and industrial shifts, which countries, such as the UK, have experienced in recent years'. However, they argue, it is equally problematic to perceive the attempts to create an enterprise culture in the UK solely in justificatory terms. Carr and Beaver (2002, p. 105) support the view that a connection between the public notions of the enterprise culture, as expressed by the government officials and the everyday experience of small business owners, is fundamental in resolving these issues. In spite of the government policy of individualism, Burrows and Curran (1991) argued that there was little connection between the attempts to create an enterprise culture and individual business activity in terms of its development and day-to-day activity. This was because of a disconnection between policies and small business practice.

The post-1997 era is characterised by a more focused and inclusive approach taken by the Labour government. The emphasis has been on the encouragement of positive attitudes towards entrepreneurship (Atherton, 2004) by mainly elevating its 'socially beneficial' aspects, and dispelling the perception of entrepreneurship as an individualistic pursuit of personal wealth, as endorsed in the Thatcherite era (Chell, 2004b). The following remark by Stephen Byers, the trade and industry secretary of the time, demonstrates that New Labour problematised the enterprise culture discourse of Thatcherism:

> The problem was that it (the enterprising culture) got confused with the 'loadsamoney' culture. Starting a business was seen as an unattractive thing to do because it was very selfish. The difference now is that we argue you can have enterprise and wealth together with social justice and fairness (Financial Times, 15 November 1999, emphasis added).

This reflects a re-emergence of enterprise culture with a more refined and inclusive view of what enterprise and entrepreneurship constitute. As a part of this realignment, 'science entrepreneurship' and recently 'social entrepreneurship' have been developed. The policy activity has focused on business start-up and addressing the needs of disadvantaged groups in society. The following statement, which was made in the 2001 Competitiveness White Paper, entitled 'Opportunity for All in a World of Change' (DTI, 2001, p. 35), reflects the encouragement of new enterprise creation:

> Entrepreneurship has become a critical part of the social, political and economic agenda around the world. Britain needs a business climate which supports the rapid creation of many more new and innovative enterprises, so vital to the dynamism of our economy.

Interpreting the public policy initiatives, Gibb (2002a) describes the 'enterprise culture' in the UK along these lines: the emergence of more small businesses, associated higher rates of small business creation, more fast growth firms and technology-based businesses, social entrepreneurship, enterprise in established public and private sector organisations and a basis for tackling social exclusion by supporting disadvantaged groups to start new businesses (Gibb, 2002a, p. 235). The earlier government discourse (Small Business Service, 2002) evidences some aspects of the enterprise culture. The aim is 'to accelerate the drive to make the UK the best place to start and grow a business by 2005' (SBS, 2002). To this end, the seven core strategies are put as follows: i) building an enterprise culture; ii) encouraging a more dynamic start-up market; iii) building the capability for small business growth; iv) improving access to finance for small businesses; v) encouraging more enterprise, in disadvantaged communities and underrepresented groups; vi) improving small businesses' experience of government services; and vii) developing better regulation and policy (SBS, 2002, pp. 3–6). Essentially, however, this was driven by a small business agenda and not specifically entrepreneurship or innovation.

Carr and Beaver (2002) define enterprise culture 'as a set of institutionally embedded relations of government, established during a particular historical period, which aim to influence and transform the mindset and conduct of a population'. Their definition acknowledges the contextual and historical qualities of the concept and also places emphasis on changing people's mindsets and actions. However, the processual characteristics are dismissed. The question of how government policies and initiatives can take individuals through an enculturation process in order to develop enterprising characteristics, such as initiative, risk-taking, flexibility, creativity, independence, leadership, daring spirit and responsibility (Gibb, 1987) is missing. This is related to the continuing and growing need to base academic research and policy on rigorous, grounded and insightful thinking, which provides an effective representation of actual experience (Atherton, 2004; Chell and Oakey, 2004).

Acknowledging the need for flexibility to ensure that the economy could respond quickly and efficiently to global economic changes, the government White Paper entitled 'Realising our Potential' (2003), states that young people should be educated and trained to equip them with enterprising skills. In the aforementioned document, the UK government set targets for embedding enterprise education and training in schools and providing the pupils with the opportunity to experience enterprise learning, helping to develop the entrepreneurial knowledge, skills and positive attitudes for enterprise capability, financial capability, and economic and business understanding. Enterprise advisers were recruited across the country in order to work with schools and give extra support to the enterprise education agenda.

Another government document (SBS, 2004, p. 5), entitled 'A Government Action Plan for Small Business', emphasises the crucial role of the government in generating business 'churn' and in creating the competitive forces that provide the link between new business formation and growth, and productivity growth in the economy as a whole. In the chapter entitled 'building an enterprise culture', the government's objectives are articulated in the following way (SBS, 2004, p. 20):

> The government's main objective in building an enterprise culture is to provide people with sufficient understanding to enable them to make an informed choice between employment and enterprise. A secondary objective is to

enable people to make informed decisions about supporting enterprise by, for example, providing formal financial backing or encouraging a family member setting up in business. These choices should be based on full information and a rational appraisal of the opportunities, risks and rewards of enterprise (SBS, 2004, p. 20).

For new enterprises to flourish there needs to be a culture where people with the initiative, skills and drive to start and run a successful business have the confidence to do so and consider it to be a realistic choice. Therefore, raising this awareness as a legitimate option, by emphasising that enterprising qualities can be gained, is the starting point. However, this does not come out of the above statement. The emphasis is on informing people about different career options and providing them with some tools to evaluate their decisions. What is more problematic in the above utterance is that enterprise is seen as an alternative route to employment. Through this definition, the Small Business Service (SBS) confines itself to the understanding that enterprise culture is about setting up a new enterprise or supporting an enterprise. This stance does not quite fit with an inclusive definition of an enterprise culture and enterprising qualities as noted by Gibb (1998, 2002) and Chell (2004a):

Being enterprising is about having or developing a set of skills that a person can deploy to achieve a particular end – solve a problem effectively and if possible efficiently. An enterprising person is a useful person to have in any team, company or walk of life. Being enterprising is not about making money *per se* nor is it necessarily about starting up a business. Leading a not-for-profit organisation, for example, might require someone with enormous talent, resourcefulness, initiative and drive – a person who is probably admired for their capability which might be summed up as enterprising (Chell, 2004a).

Although there is a political consensus as to the significance of entrepreneurship and an acknowledgement of the need to be more focused and to provide a more supportive environment for enterprise and entrepreneurship, the political discourse of the post-1997 era indicates an 'over-loaded' notion of 'enterprise'.[1] There is a sense in which many of these so-called enterprise qualities may equip a person with 'life skills'. Moreover, there are notable differences from that of the Thatcherite era; in contrast to individualism 'team-enterprise' is stressed; and also 'enterprise education' is promoted as a vehicle of change and development (Chell, 2004b). There is a growing emphasis on founding a new venture and ensuring its sustainability by putting together a team with the appropriate skill sets, marketable opportunity and resources. This team approach is even extended to that of a wider network of people who may benefit from each other by accessing useful information and resources. The current collectively oriented 'network approach' is favoured by many scholars (Gray et al, 1985; Atherton, 2004; Chell, 2004b). These changes in understanding also reflect the active and temporal social construction processes involved in shaping the enterprise culture in the UK. The changes of emphasis to more focused policies on entrepreneurial activity and innovation in general, and on technology and knowledge transfer in particular, are in recognition of the emergent knowledge economy. The re-orientation towards new industries as old industries were swept away by Thatcher in the 1980s is an important part of this socio-economic and political transformation in the UK.

A further recent development has been the creation of a new government department, the 'Department for Business, Enterprise and Regulatory Reform' (BERR). BERR brings together functions formerly with the Department of Trade and Industry and the Better Regulation Executive, formerly with the Cabinet Office. Whilst it is too early to evaluate its impact, its goals appear to be consistent with New Labour's repositioning of the enterprise economy, by creating a facilitating environment for new business and economic developments. Thus the 2008 government continues to identify innovation, business taxation, skills, migration, planning and transport as areas of initial focus for the new department. In delivering these goals, simplifying business support and delivering stronger regional economies through enhanced economic performance, the UK's enterprise activity and facilitating environment should be strengthened (BERR White Paper, 2008). The restructuring of the Regional Development Agencies (RDAs) and enhanced regional government also play an important role because they set the agenda for what local clusters of industry types and firms should form the basis of the new and reinvigorated regional economies of the UK.

The 2008 government stresses the importance of better regulation for businesses through BERR. This can be attributed to increasing consciousness for supporting businesses for more effective and sustainable management (BERR, 2008). Sustainability of enterprises is a highly significant concern in the governmental and business domains. One of the key contributing factors to sustainable development of new enterprises is equipping people who have entrepreneurial motivation with knowledge and skills through a lifelong journey for enterprise education, starting in primary schools, continuing in universities, and embedded in the workplace. It also means equipping employees and owners with the tools to unlock their entrepreneurial talent (BERR White Paper, 2008; Chell, 2008). In addition to BERR, the Department for Innovation, Universities and Skills (DIUS) was set up in 2007 with an objective to embed innovation in all sectors of the economy by enhancing the interaction between universities as institutions offering research and a skills base, and industry that can utilise this research and skilled workforce in fostering innovation activity (DIUS, 2008).

At the national level, the most recent development has been the announcement of the creation of the Department for Business, Innovation and Skills (BIS) in June 2009 by merging BERR and DIUS. Through this single department, government commits to combine BERR's functions in facilitating the enterprise culture and environment, analysing the strengths and needs of British industry, and building strategies for industrial strength and expertise in better regulation, with DIUS's expertise in maintaining world class universities, expanding access to higher education, investing in the UK's science base, and shaping skills policy and innovation through bodies such as the Technology Strategy Board (BIS, 2009). This new development has been criticised by academics who raised concerns that there is no new government department with 'education' or 'universities' in its title (Curtis, 2009). Dismantling the newly established departments BERR and DIUS and creating a single department whose remit is so broad has generated concern in the higher education sector about the feasibility of the implementation of the new department's strategies and scrutiny of its activities by pertinent committees (Attwood, 2009).

2.3   THE ROLE OF HIGHER EDUCATION INSTITUTIONS (HEIs)

The need to encourage collaboration between universities and the business sector is a discernible part of the government's policy and prevailing discourse to drive forward a knowledge-based economy (Hartshorn, 2002) and an enterprising society (Carr and Beaver, 2002) in the UK. The role of the university sector in regional and national economic development has been reportedly flourishing (Greenwood and Lewin, 2001; Chell and Allman, 2003; Taylor and Karataş-Özkan, 2008). The focus of much policy attention in this area has been on the added value that business and university collaboration should bring to the economy. This focus has been sharpened in the current discourse of knowledge-based economy where knowledge creation and sharing activities are acknowledged as the drivers of economic growth and sustainable development (Bayliss, 2001; Harris, 2001; Dooley and Kirk, 2007).

Thus knowledge generation and knowledge transfer through research, teaching and consultation activities have been subsumed by UK universities. The 'transfer of knowledge from the university sector to the business community', the so-called 'third leg activity', aims to meet the needs of business and the community, contributing to economic and social development both regionally and nationally (HEFCE, 2002). This new role suggests a blurring of the traditional boundaries between the university and business. This new order envisages that academics and business practitioners (end-users and stakeholders) work in a co-generative process of knowledge production with a view to resolve their problems, to generate new business opportunities (Greenwood and Levin, 2001; Morris, 2002) and to bridge the knowing-doing gap, which they encounter (Luna and Velasco, 2003; Van Raaij and Weimer, 2003; Nicolaidis and Michalopoulos, 2004).

The Lambert Review (2003) heralded the idea that the relationship between the university and business sectors should be transforming 'with many universities casting off their ivory tower image and playing a much more active role in the regional and national economies'. The United States (US) higher education institutions experienced this transformation in the early 1980s by broadening their traditional mission of teaching and research to include a more active participation in regional economic development (Mian, 1997; Johnson, 2003). This was underpinned by changes in the legal framework and the role of federal government in the funding of university research and the commercialisation of university technology. The passing of the Bayh-Dole Act in 1980 gave academic institutions the property rights to federally funded inventions (Mowery, 2001). The Act and subsequent changes in patent laws facilitated entrepreneurial activity by providing universities with greater incentives to license their technologies and made the commercialisation process easier (Shane, 2004). Coupled with the growth of the biomedical technology sector, this change in the legal framework resulted in dramatic growth in technology transfer and commercialisation activities at a wide range of universities in the US, patenting, licensing and generating spin-outs at a faster rate. Above all, this accelerated a positive attitude towards entrepreneurial activity amongst researchers and scientists at universities, which brought about a cultural change in universities. The creation of support mechanisms for university spin-outs, the formation of university incubators and establishment of venture capital funds are concrete examples to such a cultural and structural transformation.

In a parallel vein, but perhaps at a slower rate, similar changes were occurring in the UK (Quince and Wicksteed, 2000). The 1977 Patents Act gave universities the right to intellectual property produced by their staff (Shane, 2004). Another initiative, the University Challenge Fund, which was established in 1998 to provide seed stage financing to university spin-outs, is similar to the Advanced Technology Program (ATP) and Small Business Innovation Research (SBIR) funds in the US. Although the UK did not follow the legislative lead of the US, UK universities enjoy weak, but beneficial Bayh-Dole type effects from the governmentally-influenced polycentric development of university technology transfer (Wright, Birley and Mosey, 2004; Hoorebeek, 2005; Brennan and McGowan, 2006). Commercialisation through university technology transfer is a concept that is not yet fully embraced by UK universities. Despite the policy emphasis and support provided by recent governments and private sector organisations alike, as mentioned in the preceding section, which have helped to raise the profile of the Science, Engineering and Technology (SET) industry and supply of the funding available, UK universities fall far behind their US counterparts. Moreover, the Research Assessment Exercise (RAE) has been presented as another framework to encourage Bayh-Dole type effects within the UK university sector. However, the RAE in its current form has proven to be ineffective, and in fact hindered commercialisation activity at UK universities, as there is an increased pressure on academics to produce publications rather than engage in entrepreneurial activity (Chell, Karataş-Özkan, Read and Wilson, 2007).

In other European countries a similar trend has been observed, together with a demand for universities as potentially attractive partners for business (Mora and Valentin, 2000; Czarniawska and Genell, 2002; Taousanidis, 2002; Webster, 2003). The nature of European universities is changing, as reduced public funding reflects public debate on their role in society. Linked to this is the commercialisation of university research and academic entrepreneurship. In many European countries, there is also a structural and cultural shift that recognises the rising role of universities in spinning out technology and knowledge generated by universities (Wright, Clarysse, Mustar and Lockett, 2008). Selective outsourcing of research and development activities and the need for 'enterprise education' have also triggered more collaborative relationships, aligning the instrumental interests of the business sector with those of universities. In the UK, universities have been developing different ways and mechanisms to engage in collaborative activities with businesses. University incubators, technology and innovation centres, science parks and knowledge-transfer partnership schemes can be cited as examples of these developments. In partnership with local and regional agencies as well as businesses, many universities have established science-based clusters, technology centres or business incubation and partnership centres across the country.

There are also rapid transformations occurring at a more abstract level. There are significant shifts in sites, processes and relational dynamics of knowledge production and transfer. In this context, additional demands are placed on the business and university sectors as well as the government agencies to develop their co-generative capacities (Lambert, 2003). The question of 'how' finds some answers in the Lambert Review in the form of a number of recommendations across a wide range of issues. The review suggests that the most effective forms of knowledge transfer involve human interaction and it puts forward a number of ways to bring together people from businesses and universities. It argues that it is crucial to develop effective ways and methods of social exchange between the two communities. Echoing the review, the need to work more systematically and productively with community and business practitioners is acknowledged by some scholars across all sectors of the economy, including the public, private and non-profit sectors (Matlay, 2000; Hughey, 2003; Kitson et al., 2009).

In parallel with the UK government's pronouncement of bringing universities and businesses together and establishing a strong enterprise culture by embedding enterprise education throughout universities, the lifelong learning agenda has recognised the need for individuals to engage throughout their lives in a personal process of learning and retraining. For example Hartshorn (2002) acknowledges that career choices for graduates and others with higher level skills and knowledge have not traditionally included business creation and growth. She emphasises the need for increased motivation and movement of knowledgeable and highly skilled people into business ownership in order to achieve the societal and economic aspirations set by the government. In addition to the increasing demand for generic, transferable skills (enterprising qualities), it is recognised that programmes should be customised to the varying needs of potential entrepreneurs. This entails a change in understanding as to what is taught in the business schools and also how it is taught. Linked with the 'collectively-oriented approach' and 'team entrepreneurship', educational policies and practice should address the issue of going beyond limited management skills training courses. These courses are limited because they do not offer insights into the entrepreneurial process and cannot equip people who have entrepreneurial motivation with the necessary knowledge and skills to set up a new venture.

The enterprise education agenda should be critically examined. The question of 'can entrepreneurship be taught', which is often raised, is related to the enigmatic nature of entrepreneurship (Jack and Anderson, 1999). The 'entrepreneurs are born' thesis can no longer be maintained (Gartner, 1988; Gray, 1998; Chell, 2004b; Karataş-Özkan, 2006; NESTA, 2008a). Entrepreneurship can be 'taught' by carefully designing programmes that are underpinned by the notion of entrepreneurship as a process, which involves both art and science. Jack and Anderson (1999) maintain that graduating enterprise students should be innovative and creative to satisfy the need for entrepreneurial novelty; they should also develop skills to become competent and multifunctional managers. In enterprise education this becomes a question of how to nurture the cultural and behavioural changes that are needed for this development of the 'enterprising manager', represented as entrepreneurs (Hjort, 2003b). Therefore, the intended outcome of the educational processes is 'reflective practitioners' who are equipped with knowledge and skills fit for an entrepreneurial career. The enterprise educators, who form a significant component of the educational processes, are required to be trained accordingly in order to operate effective enterprise education programmes (Hytti and O'Gorman, 2004).

Linked with the need to develop enterprise policies that reflect the actual experiences of entrepreneurs as discussed in the previous section, there is a need to move away from the conventional focus of entrepreneurship education on new venture management, business plans and growth and innovation, to a broader understanding of the way entrepreneurs live and learn (Gibb, 2002b; Mahroum, 2008; NESTA, 2008a). The challenges are numerous as noted by Gibb (2002b, p. 135). First, how can we create 'the way of life' of the entrepreneur? This entails bringing in practitioner knowledge and insight to the programmes. Second is about the recognition, and questioning in fact, of the values and beliefs underpinning what is taught and how it is taught (methods of education) to create a conducive environment for entrepreneurial learning. Connected with this is the third challenge, which is the pedagogical issue of developing behaviours, skills and attributes. A careful appraisal and use of the wide range of available pedagogical approaches is essential. Fourth is the challenge associated with the recognition that learning does not take place solely in an 'instructional' context. The key issue is to create an environment in which participants can learn to learn in the way that will be demanded of them in entrepreneurial circumstances (NESTA, 2008). This includes managing their time, tasks and relationships with lecturers, mentors and fellow students effectively so that they can cope with more complex tasks and relationships with various stakeholders (such as financiers, customers, suppliers, competitors and employees). How more tailored entrepreneurship education and support programmes such as 'university incubators' address these issues and what kind of a context they create for nascent entrepreneurs are the concerns of next section.

2.3.1 University Incubators

The incubators are viewed as one of the means of fulfilling the government's objectives of linking universities more closely with the business community. The notion of incubation is usually associated with business support and advice activities that aim to foster the creation and development of small and medium enterprises (SMEs) or corporate ventures in the large established organisations. As provided by Barrow (2001), an incubator offers a full array of business assistance services tailored to the client companies; it has an incubator manager on site who co-ordinates staff and outside professionals to deliver those services. Although there is such a common understanding of the concept, subtle differences exist in its application (Albert and Gaynor, 2001; NESTA, 2008b). The most comprehensive study, which analyses the existing literature on incubators and incubation, is the one conducted by Albert and Gaynor (2001). Covering a wide range of studies, they argue that the literature on incubators can be broken down into descriptive, prescriptive or evaluative research. Expanded from the work of Albert and Gaynor (2001), Table 2.1 provides a chronological review of the definitions of incubation and incubators.

While it has already been acknowledged that there are different views as to what constitutes incubation or incubator, it is nevertheless possible to identify some core ideas, which characterise the notion of incubator in recent years. The historical analysis of the concept illustrates the shift in emphasis from the physical facilities to the business development process, which is linked to the notion of equipping the entrepreneurs or the entrepreneurial teams with business knowledge and helping them to get access to the relevant people, information and other resources, with an ultimate objective of contributing to an enterprise culture.

The more recent concept of incubator goes beyond the simple provision of a shared office or workspace facility. The focus is on the added value that it brings to nascent entrepreneurs in terms of strengthened business skills, access to business services, improved operating environment and opportunities for business networking. University incubators, or universities themselves as 'incubators without walls' (Lockett, Vohora and Wright, 2002), are increasingly envisaged as the centres of innovation and business creation and growth. Resources, such as human (i.e. the capable incubation team), physical (i.e. office spaces or labs) and social (i.e. relationships and networks), are crucial to the process of new venture creation (Lockett et al., 2002). Business incubators can act as facilitating environments in which incubated businesses can learn from each other and benefit from 'clustering' effects. The evidence suggests that incubation adds value to a firm, with incubated businesses significantly less likely to fail in their first years than the average (NESTA, 2008b). A desirable benefit of this approach is to establish long-term relations between universities and small businesses, thus delivering the government's policy to make the academic and business communities work collaboratively (Karataş-Özkan, Murphy and Rae, 2005).

In the UK, incubation development is rooted in government policy to establish an infrastructure of support for small firms and new venture creation. Specific policy measures and organisations such as Business Link and the SBS, have been developed to promote and support entrepreneurship.

Table 2.1   Historical development of the concept of incubation/incubator

Author(s)	Definition of incubation/incubator
Albert (1986)	An enterprise incubator is a collective and temporary place for accommodating companies which offer space, assistance and services suited to the needs of companies being launched or recently founded.
Smilor and Gill (1986)	A technology incubating programme is an innovative system designed to assist entrepreneurs in the development of new technology-based firms, both start-ups and fledglings.
Allen and Bazan (1990)	An incubator is a network or organisation providing skills, knowledge and motivation, real estate experience, provision of business and shared services.
Allen and McCluskey (1990)	An incubator is a facility that provides affordable space, shared office services and business development assistance in an environment conducive to new venture creation, survival and early stage growth.
Duff (1994)	A business incubator offers a range of business development services and access to small space on flexible terms to meet the needs of new firms.
Enterprise Panel (1996)	An incubator is a property with small units which provides an instructive and supportive environment to investors and entrepreneurs at start-up and during the early stages of businesses.
Tornatzky et al. (1996)	A technology business incubator gives the investor/entrepreneur the place and time to develop the product, as well as access to the skills and tools needed to create a successful business.
Kumar and Kumar (1997)	The process of incubation refers to a set of activities designed to facilitate new firm formation via entrepreneurship and technology transfer.
Albert and Gaynor (2001)	Incubators, created by either private or public bodies, are support mechanisms for enterprise creation, with varying objectives: local and economic development, rejuvenation of deprived areas, creation of employment, technology transfer and support for minority groups.
Totterman and Sten (2005)	A business incubator is a framework that supports new potential companies in their development process by giving them credibility, but also by helping them to build promising support and business networks.

Kirby (2002) groups them as the measures targeted at raising awareness, facilitating entry and facilitating growth. Hannon, Atherton and Chaplin (2002) argue that the Labour government has demonstrated commitment to enterprise by placing emphasis on incubators' potential for job and wealth creation; role in enhancing and accelerating new firm growth; and transfer of knowledge from the university sector. DTI initiatives, such as the University Challenge Initiative, Science Enterprise Challenge and Higher Education Innovation Fund (HEIF), have reinforced this view of the role of incubators, supporting universities to engage in entrepreneurial activities by seeking opportunities for new venture start-ups, spin-outs and supporting corporate ventures in particular (Hague and Oakley, 2000).

According to Kirby (2002), although the managed workspace movement dates back from the 1970s, the first incubators did not begin to appear until the 1980s. In 1996, the Enterprise Panel identified just 25 incubators (Enterprise Panel, 1996). Reflecting the rapidly growing incubation industry in the UK, UK Business Incubation (UKBI) identified more than 200 incubators in 2002 (UKBI, 2002). According to the latest mapping survey (UKBI, 2008), the business incubation industry in the UK is still evolving but has reached a level of maturity where business incubation environments now have a more specialist focus on new sectors, or on specific community groups, in order to cater for the needs of businesses and provide tailored support. More business incubators have become sector specific. The most cited sectors included high tech industries, creative industries, knowledge-based businesses, bioscience/biotechnologies, advanced manufacturing and energy. The number of business incubation environments in the UK seems to have stabilised, with approximately 265 incubators. A slight decrease in numbers between 2005 and 2008 has been observed and this trend is similar to other European countries such as Sweden, Finland and Germany (UKBI, 2008).

According to the mapping survey (UKBI, 2008), only 23 per cent of business incubation clients are incubatees. The impact of business incubation is far-reaching and has a vital effect within the wider business community. Origins of the majority of clients (incubatees and other supported client businesses) include local community (90 per cent), spin-out from university, HEI, R&D centre or corporate (63 per cent), inward investment (37 per cent) and large corporates (20 per cent). Financial engagement by incubators with their client businesses is another interesting aspect explored in the earlier survey (UKBI, 2002). It has been found that taking an equity stake is the most common way of strengthening the financial basis of clients and potentially of getting a significant return. University incubators appear to be more likely to take an equity stake (61 per cent compared to 32 per cent overall).

2.4 CONCLUSIONS TO THE CHAPTER

In this chapter, we have reviewed the policy context of the enterprise culture in the UK by examining the underlying philosophies and assumptions from a historical perspective. The ambiguity in the use of the term 'enterprise' is noted in order to illustrate how policy-makers construct their realities and interventions to serve the needs of a particular era. While we criticise this equivocal use in terms of lack of focus and outcome-driven conceptualisations of enterprise culture, we have tried to reconcile different approaches in order to show the instrumentality of the enterprise culture impacting on the economy, on society and on our lives as entrepreneurship scholars and educators.

The shift in emphasis from enterprise culture in the Thatcherite era to more focused policies on innovation, university-industry collaboration, technology, and knowledge transfers in the Labour period have been noted in the chapter. Furthermore, the role of higher education institutions draws attention to the overall policy context of linking academia and the business community. In parallel with the development of an enterprise education agenda and that of Science Enterprise Centres (SECs), university incubators are fertile arenas for discussing and understanding the entrepreneurial contexts in which nascent entrepreneurs can develop themselves. As suggested in a recent NESTA (2008b) report, a strong entrepreneurial culture at the national and local levels is required for business incubators. A new incubator should be carefully tailored to meet its locality's requirements, necessitating careful feasibility studies and efforts to build local coalitions of support for the proposed scheme. Furthermore, incubators should be well designed as settings that will facilitate the painless exit of successful firms to new premises, once they have outgrown the incubator's capacity and can stand on their own feet.

The next chapter presents academic discourses on entrepreneurship, mapping out different disciplinary perspectives and offering readers a coherent and integrative framework of concepts and theories that underpin the current research.

NOTE

1. Drakopoulou-Dodd and Anderson (2001) make a similar observation and argue that the Blairite enterprise policies are remarkably similar in their ideological underpinning to those of the Thatcherite 1980s. The authors note that the failure of enterprise culture policies to impact upon the life and work of small firm owner-managers is due to culturally-based differences. It is not due to substantive differences in the material 'ways of doing' ascribed to enterprise adherents and small firm owner-managers.

3. Academic discourses on entrepreneurship

3.1 INTRODUCTION TO THE CHAPTER

'What is identified as entrepreneurship depends on what is described as entrepreneurship, which, in turn, depends on what people do as they perform entrepreneurship, or the other way around. Different people like to start in different ends – practice or concepts – as they approach what is entrepreneurship' (Steyaert and Hjort, 2003, p. 11).

According to Steyaert and Hjort (2003, p. 5), there are many forms of entrepreneurship concerned with differences in focus, definition, scope and paradigm. Addressing such multiple forms of entrepreneurship is not an end in itself, but rather a starting point from which to work. To do so, we seek to map out sociological and social psychological perspectives to entrepreneurship in this chapter, with the aim of scoping the current research. The studies included in this review are based on different paradigmatic, and therefore, methodological standpoints. The examination of entrepreneurship literature from paradigmatic perspectives was previously undertaken by Pittaway (2000, 2003, 2005) and Grant and Perren (2002). Their findings suggest the preponderant influence of functionalism in entrepreneurship research, despite a growing recognition and encouragement to study entrepreneurship from alternative – mainly interpretivist – perspectives (Chell, 1985; Bouchikhi, 1993). The power of alternative paradigms and also inter-disciplinary approaches to contribute to knowledge and understanding of entrepreneurship is well acknowledged (Chell et al., 1991; Grant and Perren, 2002; Steyaert, 2004; Jennings, Perren and Carter, 2004). Besides the call for more attention to multi-paradigmatic and multi-disciplinary issues, Steyaert and Katz (2004, p. 181) suggest that entrepreneurship should be studied as a societal phenomenon rather than purely as an economic reality with a view to the generation of practical knowledge.

Entrepreneurship research is influenced considerably by Joseph Schumpeter, whose economic perspective saw the entrepreneur as driven by the pursuit of innovation, from combining existing or new resources by which actions he or she would produce economic disequilibrium (Schumpeter, 1934). This, in turn, created economic pressure to which other firms could adjust, respond competitively or perish (Hjort, 2003b, p. 50). Schumpeter termed this process 'creative destruction'; this may be said not only to comprise the destruction of the old, but also the creation of a new economic and social space (Steyaert, 2005). In essence, this perspective does not lend itself to purely economic rationalisation of entrepreneurship but conceived entrepreneurship as a social phenomenon.

Recently Goss (2005) has explored the sociological implications of Schumpeter's insights by offering an interactionist reading of Schumpeter that dissolves the duality of structure and agency, and develops a theory of entrepreneurial action where social interaction and emotions are key variables. Rather than defining an entrepreneur as an 'heroic economic superman' who possesses qualities of 'rationality and 'self-centredness' (Schumpeter, 1934, p. 85) and entrepreneurial process as a systemic function, it is argued that we should view entrepreneurship as a form of social action, whereby entrepreneurs may be thought of as social agents that learn by doing and develop their entrepreneurial identities in interaction with others in a socio-economic context. Entrepreneurial activities are embedded within social practices. For example, entrepreneurs 'draw others in' (such as competitors and financiers) to a new sector (Schumpeter, 1934), creating the momentum necessary for 'new combinations' to become embedded within social practices (Goss, 2005, p. 215). One can relate Goss's (2005) work to Giddens's (1984, 1990, 1991) structuration theory, which highlights 'rules and resources' as structures drawn upon by actors to reproduce and transform social order (Chell, 2008). The duality of structure refers to the way in which the same structures enable and constrain human action.

In his application of Giddens's ideas in entrepreneurship, Downing (2005) suggests that entrepreneurs' personal theory and actions and the development of new organisations they create, can be understood by analysing their interactions with a community of stakeholders. Social order and transformation is rooted in joint sense-making and identity creation work amongst people. Therefore, Downing (2005) suggests that entrepreneurship should be investigated as a social activity, which is a multidirectional process where stakeholders are active. Social structures shape agentic behaviour, and that agentic behaviour, reflexively produces and reproduces structure (Giddens, 1984, 1990, 1991). Chell (2008, p. 246) provides a useful critique of Giddens's structuration theory. She argues that the nature of the agent is underdeveloped in structuration theory. She maintains that structuration theory fails to theorise about the cognitive and social capabilities of the agent, the nascent entrepreneur in this study. Recognising this, in this study we analyse the agentic aspects of the entrepreneurial process at the micro-individual level, as introduced in

Chapter 1, by examining in-depth the biographies, motivations and capitals of nascent entrepreneurs; and offer a multidimensional framework, whereby the interaction of micro-individual, meso-organisational, and macro-contextual dimensions of the entrepreneurial process is highlighted (Karataş-Özkan, 2006).

The academic discourses on entrepreneurship are moving as we develop ourselves as researchers and widen our understandings and conceptions of entrepreneurship. This study draws mainly on sociological perspectives to entrepreneurship, taking a social-constructionist paradigmatic stance as will be elaborated in Chapter 5. In this chapter, a variety of sociological and social psychological perspectives have been reviewed in conjunction with the research questions and paradigmatic position taken in the current research. They are grouped under 'processual', 'relational' and 'process-relational' perspectives and are explicated below. These should not be viewed as mutually exclusive categories. It is not intended to create artificial boundaries in evaluating previous studies. The intention is to map out and extend current boundaries of thinking concerning entrepreneurship, thereby synthesizing and developing existing studies into a coherent and integrative framework. It illustrates a developmental approach, which indicates a natural progression from processual approaches to process-relational approaches with a keener view pertaining to the socially constructed nature of entrepreneurship. The chapter is structured around these three approaches and concludes with a summary and the position we adopt in this study, as illustrated by Figure 3.1. We have chosen to take a process-relational perspective in this research, which is evidently underpinned by social constructionist ideas and characterised by combining the processual view of 'organisational emergence' with 'relational' dimensions of business venturing. This choice aligns with the research questions and the overall paradigmatic approach applied in the research as discussed in more detail in Chapter 5.

3.2 PROCESSUAL APPROACHES TO THE STUDY OF ENTREPRENEURSHIP

Since the mid-1980s, there has been a shift towards more dynamic and processual accounts of entrepreneurship (for example Chell 1985, 2000, 2008; Chell et al, 1991; Gartner, 1985, 1988, 1990; Olson, 1985; Low and MacMillan, 1988; Stevenson and Jarillo, 1990; Bygrave and Hofer, 1991; Bhave, 1994; Bruyart and Julien, 2000; Shane and Venkataraman, 2000; Jack and Anderson, 2002; Neergard, 2003; Downing, 2005; Goss, 2005). Approaching entrepreneurial behaviour or process from a variety of

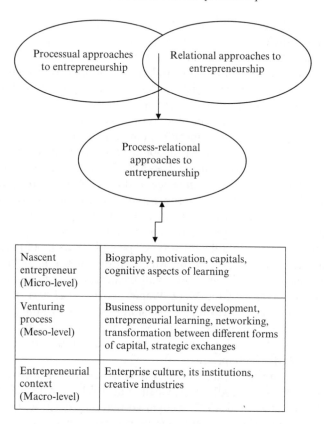

Figure 3.1   Processual, relational and process-relational approaches to entrepreneurship

angles, these studies focus on the functions and activities associated with perceiving opportunities and creating ventures to pursue them.

One popular conceptualisation of entrepreneurship is Stevenson and Jarillo's (1990), which takes an opportunity-centred perspective. Stevenson and Jarillo define entrepreneurship as a process by which individuals – either on their own or inside organisations – pursue opportunities without regard to the resources they currently control. Similarly, Bygrave and Hofer's (1991) definition includes all functions, activities and actions associated with perceiving opportunities and creating organisations to exploit them. Recounting the idea of emergence of a new venture creation as the essence of entrepreneurial process, Bygrave (1993, p. 257) suggests that it is the 'entrepreneurial event' which should be the focal point in researching entrepreneurship and he acknowledges its human and emerging attributes: 'It is initiated by an act of human volition, it is on the level of the individual firm, it is a change of state, it is a discontinuity, it is a holistic and dynamic process'. However, Chell (1985, 1997, 1998) takes the view that it is the identification and pursuit of opportunities for capital accumulation and growth, which can occur at any point in the life cycle of the business. Therefore, she has focused on the economic outcomes of an ongoing process, which is beyond 'business founding'. In a more recent study Chell (2007) offers a more encompassing approach and defines entrepreneurship as 'the pursuit of opportunity without regard to alienable resources currently controlled with a view to the creation of social and economic value'. The significance of this definition in this context is two-fold. First, entrepreneurial process is about economic as well as social value creation. Second, it is an emergent and ongoing process that entails constructing business opportunities constantly and managing the process of growth. In a slightly different way, Cope and Watts (2000) argue that the rich and complex process by which entrepreneurs learn to negotiate the management of a growing small business is de-emphasised in the literature. Aligning with the Merz, Weber and Laetz (1994) stance, they maintain that a firm's growth or expansion through constant recognition of business opportunities is a valid indicator of the continuing process of entrepreneurship within firms well beyond the initial founding event (Cope and Watts, 2000, p. 115).

Locating entrepreneurial processes in a contextual framework, some scholars (Chell, 1985, 2007, 2008; Chell et al, 1991; Gartner, 1985, 1990; Bird, 1989; Gartner et al, 1992) recognised that they occur within a larger context – a framework of events, circumstances, situations, settings and niches. Entrepreneurs interpret these situations and co-ordinate their actions. These co-ordinations are historically and socially located, reproduced in certain relational processes and not others. Hence, the academic discourse starts to give voice to the relational qualities of the entrepreneurial process in addition to its processual characteristics.

3.3   RELATIONAL APPROACHES TO THE STUDY OF ENTREPRENEURSHIP

The relational perspectives on entrepreneurship are mainly portrayed by studies that indicate how networking is central to the entrepreneurial process. Networking has been described as a social construction process that is characterised by the individual's creation and use of relationships (Johannisson, 1995). According to Dubini and Aldrich (1991, p. 305), entrepreneurship is inherently a networking activity because a crucial part of the process, that is mobilising resources to pursue opportunities, requires entrepreneurial contacts, knowledge and confidence. To expand on this, Chell and Baines (2000, p. 196) state that networking comprises social processes over and above the normal economic trading relationship. The central idea is that entrepreneurs try to set up an elaborate web of relationships over the firm's life span (Jarillo, 1989) in a variety of forms. Conceiving entrepreneurial networks as comprised of sets of interacting persons, Johannisson (1995, 1998, 2002) stresses that continuous entrepreneurship requires perpetual venturing as opportunities arise, thus lending further support to the idea that entrepreneurship and networking are strongly linked and remain a significant aspect of the venturing process.

Using the idea of 'embeddedness' to explain how networking contributes to economic and social activity, its organising and its outcomes, Johannisson, Ramirez-Pasillas and Karlsson (2002, p. 298) argue that networks constitute forms of 'voluntary co-operation that involve information sharing and/or mutual learning and exchange between their members as well as social control'. The social control dimension of networking has been taken up by Varamaki and Vesalainen's (2003) study, where they underline the significance of planning, promoting or building up co-operative arrangements as a device for generating and controlling future arrangements. One of the case studies presented in Chapter 7 illustrates this, as the key members of the venture team steer a formal networking activity in the region. It is seen as a reflection of the concern to take ownership of the newly created set of relationships and shape and reshape the future ones.

Networks and networking are considered to provide excellent opportunities to investigate the 'social' in entrepreneurship, because it is recognised that networking contributes to entrepreneurial capacity by extending the individual's asset base of human, social, financial and technical capacity. As such, the enacting of entrepreneurship, through opportunity identification and exploitation, takes place through networking (Jack, Drakopoulou-Dodd and Anderson, 2008). The idea is that entrepreneurial actions do not occur in a vacuum, but are conditioned by ongoing structures of social relations (Granovetter, 1973, 1985; Johannisson, 1990; Johannisson and Monsted, 1997; Bygrave and Minniti, 2000). Aldrich and Zimmer (1986) also took this view, by suggesting that entrepreneurship is embedded in a social context, channelled and facilitated or constrained and inhibited by an individual's position in a social network (Jack and Anderson, 2002, p. 469). A social constructionist view enables us to appreciate and understand how entrepreneurs use networks, and the strong and weak ties of which they are composed, to make sense of the world they live and operate in, but also to enact the environment, and through networking activity make that environment work effectively and efficiently for them, hence supporting the development and growth of the new venture (Granovetter, 1973; Jack et al., 2008, p. 152).

With an emphasis on the wider social environment within which entrepreneurship emerges, exist and evolves, Zafirovski (1999) offers a multi-level sociological approach. Such a setting comprises contextual networks (Johannisson, Alexanderson and Semeseth, 1994), personal and entrepreneurial networks (Johannisson, 1995, 1998), as well as macro-social structure and culture. Zafirovski (1999, p. 354) illuminates the importance of culture in a powerful way:

> A key assumption of the sociology of enterprise is that entrepreneurship, development and related economic activities are primarily complex social processes, and only secondarily physical, technological or psychological ones. They cannot be treated as independent and imputed with an intrinsic law of their own because they are embedded in the social framework. From the sociological perspective, rather than a logic of the state of nature, technological production, chemical laboratory, or psychological impulses, there is an underlying logic of social processes, relations and changes – the logic of social structure and culture conducive to 'humanistic entrepreneurship' as opposed to undersocialized economic animals or robots.

Arguably, this view shifts the focal point from entrepreneurship as actions of an elitist group of entrepreneurs to the everyday processes of new organisation formation where multiple actors and stakeholders are made researchable. The assumption behind the everydayness of entrepreneurship is that 'entrepreneurship is a matter of everyday activities rather than actions of elitist groups of entrepreneurs' (Steyaert and Katz, 2004, p. 180). We can widen our understanding and conceptions of entrepreneurship by bringing entrepreneurship out of a selected and selective circle of entrepreneurs and entrepreneurial companies. These authors argue that entrepreneurship can occur in a variety of interactions across large segments of a population (Holmquist, 2003; Lindgren and Packendorff, 2003). Rehn and Taalas (2004) call this 'mundane entrepreneurship' and argue that entrepreneurship is not reserved for specific actors and actions. Entrepreneurial activities involve specific entrepreneurial actions, such as developing a sound business opportunity and harnessing resources to fulfil this opportunity; however, this is not reserved for 'heroic entrepreneurs', whom they define in terms of the greatest wealth creators. By examining the everydayness of entrepreneurship through social interactions amongst a team of entrepreneurs and other stakeholders, their stories can be told. Exploring these stories entails moving away from the dominant functionalist economic discourse, which conceptualises entrepreneurship as an economic specialty towards profit and wealth maximisation, towards opening up alternative perspectives within which to conceive entrepreneurship.

This 'mundane entrepreneurship' perspective may be contested however, without returning to the 'heroic view of the entrepreneur' as critiqued by Ogbor (2000) and others. Mundane entrepreneurship conflates practical management of business with entrepreneurship – a process, which Schumpeter was also at pains to distinguish – and the entrepreneur with the small business owner manager, the tradesperson and/or the petite bourgeoisie. Thus, individuals who pursue opportunities with a view to creating economic and social outcomes, also produce novelty in their products and services. This is the nub of the entrepreneurial act. Building a team, garnering resources and so forth may be necessary management skills should the individual want to found a business around an opportunity, but they are not *per se* entrepreneurial skills (Chell, 2008).

3.4 PROCESS-RELATIONAL APPROACHES TO THE STUDY OF ENTREPRENEURSHIP

A processual way of looking at entrepreneurship requires the examination of emerging characteristics and features of the entrepreneurial process. From processual perspectives, the dynamic process through which business opportunities are realised becomes the central focus of entrepreneurship studies (Fletcher, 2003). Relational approaches highlight the human relationships involved in the process. Entrepreneurial activities are realised and constructed through social processes. The relational approaches build on the Schumpeterian (1934) notion of contributing to economic change through new combinations of products or processes, with entrepreneurs bringing about new ideas, products, and processes by working in relation to a team, small community or network of people (Johannisson, 1990; Fletcher, 1997, 2003). Thus, process-relational perspectives on entrepreneurship combine the processual view of 'emergence' with the 'relational' dimension in order to generate deeper insights. The relational part is in essence about relating to each other through language, narrative, and discourse as well as enactment.

Process-relational approaches are relatively well established in organisation studies (Hosking and Morley, 1991; Czarniawska, 1997, 1998; Hosking and Ramsey, 2000; Watson, 2003, p. 1306). Underpinned by the social constructionist assumptions (K.J. Gergen, 1985), Watson (2003) suggests that a process-relational approach to study organisations has been grounded in the belief that processes of social construction create 'the organisation' involving a multiplicity of goals, interests and understandings

within the 'quasi' or 'virtual' entity. Such a multiplicity of goals and interests require 'strategic exchanges' in organisational life (Watson, 1994a).
In the same vein, Jack and Anderson's (2002) work on social embeddedness of entrepreneurship, focuses on the strategic and reflexive nature of
social relationships. The need for such a process-relational approach also
stems from the perceived limitations of the functionalist and structuralist
approaches in explaining entrepreneurship (Giddens, 1984). Building on
Watson's (1994a, p. 27) interpretation of Giddens, an entrepreneur's initiative (agency) may not only be constrained by the circumstances in which
it occurs (structure); it may alternatively also be enabled. Therefore, the
circumstances in which entrepreneurs find themselves shape their thinking
and acting, but entrepreneurs also shape those circumstances. They engage
with each other through a number of networking activities, which they
influence and are influenced by. These activities are driven by economic
motives of wealth creation, which we define as 'economic becoming'.

This focus on the cognitive and the behavioural aspects of the entrepreneurial process omits effects, that is, the feelings and emotions that accom-
pany any and every behavioural act. Goss (2005), for example, offers a
different reading of Schumpeter's ideas. His perspective does justice to
such a process-relational approach by integrating 'social interaction' and
'emotions' into the picture. He argues that 'as long as human beings engage
one another socially and experience the emotions thereby produced, there
will be scope for entrepreneurial action' (Goss, 2005, p. 216).

The translation of these ideas into entrepreneurship studies is relatively
recent. At the European Academy of Management (EURAM) conference,
Fletcher and Tansley (2003) presented a variety of social constructionist
approaches permeating entrepreneurship literature over the last ten years
and argued that researchers approaching their entrepreneurial research
with a constructionist orientation should be receptive to concerns about
the inter-relationship between process, context, language, discourse and
interaction in shaping entrepreneurial outcomes. Their process-relational
stance enables them to conclude that individuals relationally enact entrepreneurial practices in different contexts in ways that facilitate entrepreneurial becoming. At the same conference, Fletcher and Watson (2003)
defined entrepreneurship as 'a distinctive approach to making a living
in which people with ideas for a product or service create, develop and
realise those ideas as part of their social becoming'. In order to emphasise its relational and processual qualities, they describe how entrepreneurs 'make and remake themselves' as they engage, imaginatively and
creatively through economic exchange with the people who are willing
to make or remake themselves (Fletcher and Watson, 2003). Taking on
board Steyaert's (2003) recent definition of the entrepreneurial process

as a creation of a living world with economic outcomes, Fletcher and Watson's (2003, p. 3) perspective explains how people work together to bring about economic change, through new combinations of technological products or processes. Hence, attention is drawn to how groups of people collectively organise themselves in venture communities or partnerships, and act together by coming to acknowledge and realise their creative ideas as a part of this process of creation of a living world during which they are constantly evaluating information, talking through different scenarios, bringing to their interaction previous understandings, experiences and history of relationships (Fletcher and Watson, 2003).

This understanding takes the discussion beyond the founding event as the centre of entrepreneurship and indicates that it is a continual process which is always in movement and coming ever afresh into existence (Steyaert, 1998). Therefore, people may enact entrepreneurial practices at any stage of the lifespan of the venture as they develop themselves relationally and identify new entrepreneurial possibilities by negotiating and conversing about the new business ideas.

Using 'theatricality' as a conceptual tool to understand the continual entrepreneurial process, Anderson (2003) highlights the process of creating that is not fixed in time or space, but draws on one's earlier experiences in life and reflects a transformation, which is about enacting a future:

> 'Of course when we talk of entrepreneurship we usually mean the process of becoming, thinking, planning, conspiring, doing the things, which may lead to entrepreneurship. In consequence it seems fair to say that entrepreneurship, as we use the term, is this process of becoming. But becoming is not fixed in time or space; the aspiration may have germinated in childhood; the idea may have resulted from fleeting thought and gathering the physical, mental resources and courage may have taken half a lifetime. To appreciate entrepreneurship we need to appreciate it as processual, as a process of becoming. So entrepreneurship as a process of becoming is transitive, transitory and ephemeral. It fits in the spaces between the here and then and reflects a transformation.'

The 'creativity' quality linked to the transformative nature of the entrepreneurial process is strongly advocated in some entrepreneurship writings (Hjort, Johansson and Svengren, 2004; Steyaert, 1998; Hjort, 2003a, 2003b; Steyaert and Hjort, 2003). For example, Steyaert (1998, p. 22) reinforced the need to engage in studies that approach entrepreneurship as a creative process in which it is accepted that 'entrepreneurs are creators of new realities walking on the boundary between destabilising existing situations and actualising implicit possibilities into new contexts'. This is in accordance with Johannisson (2002, p. 5), who argued that entrepreneurship is concerned with the 'creative envisioning of that which does not yet exist'. Furthermore, Johannisson (2002) comments that 'entrepreneurial venturing is reflected in the multiple social constructions, where individual and collective forces interplay creatively to enact a future'. Moreover, it draws attention to that awesome element of the entrepreneurial process, the uncertain abyss into which the entrepreneur ultimately peers.

Entrepreneurial creativity is about producing innovative ideas and turning them into value-creating profitable business activities. Some argue for entrepreneurship as a process of getting products and services to the market and innovation as the creative part. Harryson (2008), for example, conceptualises entrepreneurship as a process through relationships navigating from creativity to commercialisation. The creativity phase, which is generally typified as opportunity recognition, requires a creator with visionary leadership; and the commercialisation phase, typically referred to as opportunity exploitation, requires innovation through understanding of social needs and market requirements. Sternberg and Lubart (1999) define creativity as the ability to produce work that is both novel and useful. According to their definition, entrepreneurship can be described as a form of creativity, because new businesses are original and useful (Lee, Florida and Acs, 2004); and most aspects of the entrepreneurial process require creativity. The creativity dimension of entrepreneurship is the one that changes our everyday practices (Spinosa, Flores and Dreyfus, 1997) and it entails a boundary spanning activity. Hence, entrepreneurship can be thought of as harnessing creative energy and moving forward with a sound business idea toward a business opportunity that is anchored in value for the end users.

The research conducted by Bouwen and Steyaert (1990) on the process of creating an entrepreneurial firm is another illuminating example of process-relational studies of entrepreneurship. Using the metaphor of 'texture' their conceptualisation of entrepreneurship is a powerful one:

> The creation of a new organisation can be conceived as creating organisational 'texture'. The metaphor emphasises the simultaneity of processes and outcomes. The entrepreneur, in interaction with his immediate co-workers, weaves the 'weft' and 'warp' into a particular organisational texture. The social network and the task are interwoven continuously. Our interest in organising, that is, the making of organisation . . . organisation is not a 'given' social reality. Rather, there is a lot of 'dialoguing' among the parties, steered to some extent by the motivation and competences of the entrepreneur (Bouwen and Steyaert, 1992).

Their research is based on fieldwork undertaken in six start-ups and six older firms over a series of months. Considering the entrepreneur as the main actor, they pay particular attention to the entrepreneur's motivation to start his own business and his basic competences that contributed to the organisation. They studied how the entrepreneur's personal motivation was to some degree transferred to the other co-workers and they call this process of sharing 'organisational motivation'. The entrepreneur's original competences are configured as the organisation's task domain, which forms the 'genetic pool' of the organisation (Bouwen and Steyaert, 1990). The dominant logic reflected the entrepreneur's and other co-workers' conceptualisation of the business and critical resource allocation decisions and this has evolved during the process of creating the organisation as new and complementary logics emerged. They call this the 'dialogue process' as the core business organisation is formed through the processes of the development of social networks, the development of a task domain and the dialoguing between these issues (Bouwen and Steyaert, 1990, p. 640). Studying these dialoguing processes around networking and task creation in a firm, they make few remarks about learning as another quality of the so-called 'organisational dialogue' process. They do not elaborate on this quality in their article. However, they come to a conclusion that they offer an approach of organising so that entrepreneurs and their co-workers can ask themselves a set of questions to deepen their understanding of their own behaviour and organisational processes, which is a part of their entrepreneurial becoming.

Providing a social constructionist framework, Downing (2005) elaborates on the narrative processes in the co-production of organisations and identities. As discussed in Chapter 2, processes of social construction reflect the narrative dramatic means by which actors co-ordinate actions, projects and identities. Entrepreneurship should be understood by examining the ways in which entrepreneurs interact with their stakeholders to form, sustain and enhance new organisations and they apply such concepts of 'innovation', 'risk taking' and 'creativity' to the social process of 'new world making' (Czarniawska and Wolff, 1991; Downing, 2005, p. 196). Downing's (2005) article provides a 'SENSE framework'. SENSE stands for Storylines, Emplotment, Narrative Structuring Enactment. It illustrates linkages between how one group of actors might select events or actions from storylines, how these enable actors to tacitly locate a plot, and how they then become elaborated in narrative structure. The SENSE framework has not been developed from empirical research and this is manifest in its descriptive nature. One should be critical in evaluating such social constructionist perspectives to entrepreneurship, unless they explain how these social construction processes occur among entrepreneurs and stakeholders by drawing on real-life examples. However, the framework highlights significant issues pertaining to the social constructionist nature of entrepreneurial process and can be applied in further studies.

3.5   CONCLUSIONS TO THE CHAPTER

The central argument of this section is that entrepreneurship is a social process whereby individuals create a new venture to actualise their ideas for a product, service or process by pursuing business opportunities in order to create wealth. The way we research, write and teach entrepreneurship should be based on such conceptualisations of entrepreneurship based on examination of the real world of nascent entrepreneurs so that creating a new venture can be learnt, while the skill sets and foundations for entrepreneurial managing can be developed by focusing on the 'science' part without 'interfering' with the crafting process. One needs to consider the underlying motivations for entrepreneurial endeavours. The intrinsic motivation of entrepreneurs is not only wealth creation but also the need to position themselves as 'creators' and 'owners'. This requires the acknowledgement of human willpower and belief for personal and social change, which can also be viewed as an existential challenge.

In this chapter we have presented a discussion on academic discourses of entrepreneurship pertaining to the nature of the current research study. The overall aim has been to relate to the previous movements of the discipline and locate this research as a part of these movements. It is also intended to create a platform for debate in the analysis of case studies by reengaging with the arguments put forward in this section. In line with the first research question, which seeks to generate insights into the nature of the business venturing process, the entrepreneurship literature has been charted along three approaches: processual, relational and process-relational. A processual way of looking at entrepreneurship requires the examination of emerging characteristics and features of the entrepreneurial venturing process. From processual perspectives, the dynamic process through which business opportunities are realised becomes the central focus of entrepreneurship studies. Relational perspectives point out the human relationships involved in the process. Process-relational perspectives take it one step further and refine the notion of entrepreneurship by combining the processual view of 'emergence' with the 'relational' dimension in order to generate deeper insights. The relational part is in essence about relating to each other through language, narrative and discourse as well as enactment. Embedded in the social constructionist approach, a process-relational perspective is taken in this research. It proposes the view that entrepreneurship is a social process whereby individuals create a new venture to actualise their ideas for a product, service or process by pursuing business opportunities persistently in order to create wealth as a part of their personal, social and economic becoming and transformation. It is crucial to understand the transformative nature of the process by looking into the learning experiences of nascent entrepreneurs. To this end, the next chapter is devoted to addressing the following questions by drawing on the literature. Who are nascent entrepreneurs? How are they different from entrepreneurs? How does their venturing experience converge with and diverge from 'business venturing' as discussed so far? How do nascent entrepreneurs learn and manage while engaged in business venturing?

4. Nascent entrepreneurs: characteristics of nascent entrepreneurs and entrepreneurial learning

4.1 INTRODUCTION TO THE CHAPTER

There has been a dearth of research investigating the processes of entrepreneurial learning and managing as experienced by nascent entrepreneurs. Entrepreneurial learning is an emerging domain within the discipline of entrepreneurship. Drawn from a number of epistemological perspectives, the following studies largely examine entrepreneurial learning at the individual entrepreneur level (Young and Sexton, 1997; Cope and Watts, 2000; Rae and Carswell, 2000; Honig, 2001; Minniti and Bygrave, 2001; Rae, 2002, 2004a, 2004b; Cope, 2005) or at the small firm level (Deakins and Freel, 1998; Penn, Angwa, Forster et al., 1998; Anderson and Skinner, 1999; Chaston, Badger and Sadler-Smith, 1999a, 1999b). The learning experience of entrepreneurial teams has received little attention despite the literature on the characteristics or formation of entrepreneurial teams or venture teams (Stewart, 1989; Kamm, Shuman, Seeger and Nurick, 1990; Birley and Stockley, 2000; Vyakarnam, Jacobs and Hadelberg, 1999; Ucbasaran, Westhead, Wright et al., 2001).

This chapter takes this gap in our knowledge as the starting point and develops the discussion by considering nascent entrepreneurs' learning and managing in two ways. At the micro-level, this includes scrutinising nascent entrepreneurs' individual experiences by examining their motivation, dispositions and capitals, in Bourdieu's sense, such as the cultural and social capital that they draw on and capitals that they want to attain in life, such as economic capital. At the meso-relational level this refers to the relational experiences of entrepreneurial learning and managing by examining the teams or 'venture communities' that they form as a part of their entrepreneurial becoming. To this end, the chapter is structured in two sections. First, a conceptualisation of nascent entrepreneurs is made, with a focus on their characteristics and key forms of capital that are developed in the process of business venturing. Second, entrepreneurial learning and managing are discussed as intertwined processes.

4.2 NASCENT ENTREPRENEURS

There is a well-established literature that recognises there are different types of entrepreneurs and types of owner managers (Chell, Haworth and Brearley, 1991; Allinson, Chell and Hayes, 2000; Chell, 2000; Pittaway, 2000; Malach-Pines, Sadeh, Dvir et al., 2002). However, few studies differentiate entrepreneurs on the basis of being at different stages of business venturing or engaging in different forms of venturing (Chell et al., 1991; Chell, 2008; Wright, Robbie and Ennew, 1995; Westhead and Wright, 1998; Ucbasaran, Wright and Westhead, 2003). Westhead and Wright (1998) examined the differences between novice, serial, habitual and portfolio entrepreneurs. The authors define nascent entrepreneurs as those who are in the process of beginning their entrepreneurial venture with the potential and capacity to become successful entrepreneurs. Hence they have very limited experience or practical understanding of the concepts and processes involved.

In Delmar and Davidsson's (2000) work, an individual is considered to be 'a nascent entrepreneur if he or she had completed at least one business gestation activity by the time of the interview'. This approach is limited to an examination of the characteristics of four sub-groups of nascent entrepreneurs within a sample of 405 Swedish nascent entrepreneurs, and as such the emphasis is more on the stages of the entrepreneurial process and activities involved.

Taking the conceptualisation back to activities, Aldrich (1999, p. 77) defines a nascent entrepreneur as 'someone who initiates serious activities that are intended to culminate in a viable business start-up'. Networking, resource mobilisation and entrepreneurial enactment constitute those 'serious activities' (Reynolds, 1994 cited in Aldrich, 1999) throughout the process of nascent entrepreneurship. The stages of nascent entrepreneurship are outlined by Reynolds (1994 in Aldrich, 1999) as involving three transitions and four periods which are illustrated in Figure 4.1.

Transition 1 is instigated when someone starts thinking about setting up a new business and actually engages in entrepreneurial activities to pursue this objective (Aldrich, 1999). If they do so on their own and if the new venture can be considered as an independent start-up, they are called 'nascent entrepreneurs' (Wagner, 2004). If they are sponsored by an existing business, they are described as 'nascent corporate entrepreneurs'. The second transition takes place when the gestation process is complete and

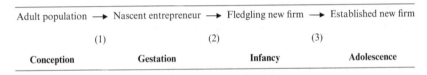

Source: Adapted from Reynolds (1994 cited in Aldrich, 1999).

Figure 4.1   Stages of nascent entrepreneurship

Table 4.1   Entrepreneurial activities undertaken by nascent entrepreneurs

Activity
1. Serious thoughts about business
2. Looked for facilities/equipment
3. Initiated savings to invest
4. Invested own money in the new firm
5. Organised start-up term
6. Wrote business plan
7. Bought facilities/equipment
8. Sought financial support
9. License, patent, permit applied for
10. Developed first model/prototype
11. Received money from sales
12. Achieved positive monthly cash flow
13. Devoted full time to new business
14. Received financial support
15. Other start-up behaviours initiated
16. Rented/leased facilities/equipment
17. Created a new legal entity
18. Hired employees to work for wages

Source: Adapted from Reynolds (1994 in Aldrich (1999).

when the new venture begins to operate as a business. The third transition refers to the passage from infancy to adolescence, that is to say, the fledgling new firms successfully shifts to an established firm (Reynolds and White, 1997; Wagner, 2004).

According to Reynolds' (1994 cited in Aldrich, 1999, p. 77) conceptualisation, someone is called a nascent entrepreneur if they not only say they are currently giving serious thought to starting a new business but also are engaged in at least one of 17 possible entrepreneurial activities as listed in Table 4.1 above.

These activities reflect the chaotic, complex and lengthy nature of business venturing. Chell and Oakey (2004) draw attention to the lengthiness of the process, which starts from the conception (emergence of an idea) and develops as a gestation period toward a realised founding. Taking a resource-based view (RBV), they amplify nascent entrepreneurship in a context of science enterprise formation and put forward a research agenda. Highlighting the paucity of empirical research that explains how nascent entrepreneurs learn and develop an effective understanding of the new venture process, their main lines of argument, which are not specific to science enterprise formation and pertinent in this research, hinge on the importance of taking the 'nascent entrepreneurial unit' (NEU) as the level of analysis and focusing on how it organises itself to create and pursue business opportunities, garner resources, develop networks and acquire new knowledge and skills. Three different modes of organising have been identified, by Lichtenstein, Dooley and Lumpkin (2006), as constitutive aspects of nascent entrepreneurship. These include vision, strategic organising and tactical organising. Drawing on an in-depth case study of a nascent entrepreneur examined for two years, the authors suggest that the first mode, vision, involves the development of the business opportunity the entrepreneur is hoping to capitalise on. The second mode, strategic organising, concerns the stream of decisions, actions and interventions enacted by the entrepreneur. The tactical moves pertain to particular events and timeframes indicative of an entrepreneurial start-up (Lichtenstein et al., 2006, p. 154). These different modes of organising in the process of nascent entrepreneurship will be explored in the case accounts of the current research.

The process-relational approach to entrepreneurship enables a focus to be maintained on the relational qualities of the new venture development as a process, with development of the nascent entrepreneurial team and their entrepreneurial learning and managing experience as they engage in those activities of opportunity creation, resource marshalling, networking and using outside assistance. Thus, Chell and Oakey (2004) note some key issues to be addressed, which include what the core resources are that a NEU requires and how to access them. It has been recognised that nascent entrepreneurs usually rely on their experience, as they go through several stages of the business venturing process, which is viewed as a resource that is invested in the business (Honig, 2001; Chell and Oakey, 2004). Prior experience in business and self-employment may be helpful in that it allows time for skills development, but it is not sufficient to generate entrepreneurship capability (Chell, 2008) to undertake business venturing successfully. Other resources, which are seen as significant ingredients for nascent business venturing, include less tangible resources that give reputation, external networks, internal team competences (Kamm et al., 1990; Birley and Stockley, 2000) and early stage assistance for both survival and growth. This view resonates with the argument put forward by Ucbasaran, Wright and Westhead (2003). Using a human capital perspective (Becker, 1975) in explaining the dynamic entrepreneurial process, the authors argue that the nature and extent of an entrepreneur's human capital is crucial in accessing and leveraging social, financial, physical and organisational resources (Ucbasaran et al., 2003). They investigate how habitual entrepreneurs acquire resources during their entrepreneurial careers and how these add to their existing human and social capital endowment, enabling them to access additional resources, and possibly adding value to the entrepreneurs' subsequent activities. Nascent entrepreneurs' asset base of human, social, market, financial and technical capacity collectively contributes to entrepreneurial capacity (Jack, Drakopoulou-Dodd and Anderson, 2008). Education and social learning are fundamental in building entrepreneurial capacity (Chell, 2008, p. 240). Domain-relevant skills, technical skills, knowledge of the industry, and that of business/market are developed at the ideation and opportunity recognition stage of business creation. Nascent entrepreneurs should learn and absorb these skills for business development.

4.3   ENTREPRENEURIAL LEARNING AND MANAGING

How nascent entrepreneurs attain different forms of capital (such as cultural, social and economic capital) by developing the required entrepreneurial skill sets and knowledge, constitutes the focal question of this section. Entrepreneurial learning is an emerging movement of entrepreneurship, which has attracted more attention very recently. This attraction culminated in a special issue of *Entrepreneurship Theory and Practice* in July 2005 whereby the editors drew attention to the infancy of the study of learning in entrepreneurial contexts (Harrison and Leitch, 2005). Drawn from a number of epistemological perspectives, the existing studies largely examine entrepreneurial learning at the individual level (Reuber and Fischer, 1993; Young and Sexton, Upton, Wacholtz et al., 1997; Cope and Watts, 2000; Rae and Carswell, 2000; Bishop, Crown and Weaver, 2001; Cope, 2001, 2003a, 2003b, 2005; Honig, 2001; Minniti and Bygrave, 2001; Rae, 2002, 2004a, 2004b, 2005; Taylor and Thorpe, 2004; Parker, 2006) or at the small firm level (Deakins and Freel, 1998; Penn, 1998; Anderson and Skinner, 1999; Sadler-Smith et al, 1999). The learning experience of entrepreneurial teams has received little attention despite the literature on the characteristics or formation of entrepreneurial teams or venture teams (Stewart, 1989; Kamm et al., 1990; Birley and Stockley, 2000; Vyakarnam et al., 1999; Ucbasaran, Westhead, Wright et al., 2001). Taking this criticism one step further could be the argument that a multi-level approach has not been taken whereby individual entrepreneurs' learning (micro-level) can be examined in relation to the development of entrepreneurial learning at the meso-relational level by becoming a part of 'venture communities', which are embedded in certain socio-cultural and economic milieus (macro-level). The current study aims to address this gap in our understanding.

Until recently the focus of the entrepreneurial learning literature has been mostly on the cognitive processes concerned with entrepreneur's way of gathering, processing and evaluating information (Young and Sexton, 1997; Bishop et al., 2001; Honig, 2001; Minniti and Bygrave, 2001). A related critique that can be directed towards previous studies on entrepreneurial learning is that they take a rather static perspective on the process of entrepreneurial learning, where 'process' merely refers to the logic of explicating the causal relationship between entrepreneurs' previous experiences and the performances of subsequent ventures (Politis, 2005). There is a consensus by the scholars in the field that little attention is devoted to how entrepreneurs, through experience, develop entrepreneurial knowledge that enables them to create entrepreneurial opportunities to organise and manage new ventures (Cope, 2001, 2003a, 2003b, 2005; Rae, 2002, 2004a, 2004b; Harrison and Leitch, 2005; Politis, 2005). Making this gap central to this study, we relate back to the previous works and aim to position this research in a continuing space of writing and talking about entrepreneurial learning in order to improve our understanding of the area.

Drawing on doctoral research (Cope, 2001) which explored the learning process of individual entrepreneurs and its impact on both their personal development and that of their firms, Cope and Watts's (2000) study developed a dynamic learning perspective by applying critical incidents technique (Flanagan, 1954; Chell, 1998) and showed how the entrepreneur learns from these incidents within the wider context of business and personal growth. One lesson taken from their work is the importance of critical incidents for accelerating the process of learning and growing self-awareness, and hence they are established as seminal moments within this process of change. Cope and Watts touch on the contextual nature of critical incidents and the need to understand and interpret them in relation to the circumstances in which they occur. However, it is difficult to infer the significance of context on the learning process from their study. Similarly, drawing on an empirical study of individual entrepreneurs in a wide range of industries and at different stages of their entrepreneurial career, Rae's

(2002) work developed three themes of entrepreneurial learning: personal and social emergence, contextual learning, and negotiated enterprise. The notion of negotiated enterprise is based on Watson's (2001a) conceptualisation of the 'negotiated order of an organisation' where he contends that it is 'the pattern of activities which has arisen or emerged over time as an outcome of the interplay of the variety of interests, understandings, reactions and initiatives of the individuals and groups involved in the organisation'. As regards entrepreneurial learning, Rae (2002, 2004a, 2004b) argues that the business emerges through a constant process of negotiations and exchanges just as do the personal and social identity of entrepreneurs.

Concurring with Watson's (2001a) argument, this research aims to address how nascent entrepreneurs – as a part of a broader network – bring in their own resources, understandings, and knowledge to the ventures they form, (that is the negotiated order), and how these elements shape this negotiation of order and are shaped by negotiations. Using the term 'organisational emergence' to highlight the social, processual and constructive aspects of new business venturing, Fletcher (2003) encourages entrepreneurship researchers to generate further insights into the underlying processes of venturing to facilitate new movements in entrepreneurial understanding. These underlying processes embrace the dynamic processes of personal, social and economic identity formation as nascent entrepreneurs make sense of the world through interactions within their *habitus* and field. In Watson's (2002) terms, this is called 'active use of discursive resources'.

Nascent entrepreneurs become actively engaged in learning to develop better understandings and actions during the business venturing process. This active engagement encompasses 'investment of the self', particularly the extreme levels of emotional and financial commitment and 'personal exposure' associated with small business ownership, which makes the study of entrepreneurs such a unique context within which to explore the phenomenon of learning' (Cope, 2003, p. 430). Again building on his doctoral work (Cope, 2001), Cope (2003) develops a deeper discussion of entrepreneurial learning and critical reflection by focusing on the discontinuous events, which have the capacity to lead to 'higher-level learning', rather than the incremental accumulation of more routinised, habitual learning, which results in 'lower-level learning'. Both types of learning relate primarily to the development of the cognitive capability of the entrepreneur. This would explain how a nacent entrepreneur engages with socio-economic phenomena, scans and interprets information in her or his environment, and synthesises this information by developing capabilities of opportunity recognition, formation and exploitation. This purposeful effort is in a part a reflection of a repertoire of learnt capabilities that are honed through experience and social interaction processes (Chell, 2008).

'Investment of self' and 'personal exposure' are two main areas that should be considered pertinent to entrepreneurial learning. Cope (2003, p. 430) suggests that many entrepreneurs commit significant personal resources to creating and managing a venture and in doing so expose both themselves and other stakeholders to the considerable financial, emotional and social risks associated with owning a business. This provides a different perspective compared to a widely endorsed view within the entrepreneurial learning literature that entrepreneurs are action oriented and yet much of their learning is experientially based (Cope and Watts, 2000; Rae and Carswell, 2000). Cope (2003) highlights the emotional element of entrepreneurial learning whereas prior research on the whole emphasises actions, behaviours and experiential aspects only. 'Learning by doing' is marked by many scholars (Kolb, 1984; Boud, Cohen and Walker, 1993) as it encompasses such activities as trial and error, explicit problem solving, discovery, and reactive or proactive response to opportunities and problems (Young and Sexton, 1997; Cope and Watts, 2000; Cope, 2003). As Gibb (1997: 19) points out, in an entrepreneurial context:

> 'The predominant contextual learning mode . . . is that of . . . learning from peers; learning by doing; learning from feedback from customers and suppliers; learning by copying; learning by experiment; learning by problem solving and opportunity taking; and learning from mistakes.'

Entrepreneurs tend to learn continuously as they set up and manage their venture. However, it is argued that entrepreneurs can experience distinctive forms of 'higher-level' learning from encountering, overcoming and reflecting on significant opportunities and problems during the entrepreneurial process (Cope, 2003, p. 432). Through two case studies, Cope (2003) illustrates that these distinctive forms of higher-level learning prove to be fundamental for both personal and business growth. The author acknowledges the need for further research on the social and affective dimensions of the learning process with discontinuous events, which refer to such events that led to crises and disruption in the business venturing process. In order to illuminate the concept of 'discontinuous events', he gives an example from one of his case studies. An entrepreneur encounters one of the most serious crises possible, potential bankruptcy. This crisis was self-imposed, as the entrepreneur acknowledges that he made a serious and very basic marketing mistake that he thought he was not capable of making, a mistake which effectively ruined the company. He made the marketing mistake just before the Christmas holidays. The holiday period enabled him to think through and take preventative action.

He was able to engineer a solution that allowed him to walk away from the situation, while leaving his partner with a failing company that was heading for bankruptcy. The entrepreneur describes this discontinuous event as a 'moral dilemma' as everything was on the line and he had to put his wife and family first (Cope, 2003, p. 442).

One should take a critical stance in applying such concepts in this research. Translating these ideas to nascent entrepreneurship requires a careful consideration of the level of intensity in their entrepreneurial experience. As conceptualised in section 4.2, nascent entrepreneurs are those who are at the beginning of their entrepreneurial career and therefore the extent and nature of these 'discontinuous events' or even 'critical incidents' may be rather limited. However, there is still some merit in examining the 'significant occurrences' that they perceive during the entrepreneurial process. This recognition heralds the idea that people, in general, tend to reflect on memorable events that happen in their lives and such a reflective process can give rise to fundamental forms of learning (Cope, 2003).

Further critique of Cope's (2003a, 2003b) perspective is that the conceptualisation of such crises and failures as 'discontinuous events' is under-theorised. In line with the process-relational approach to studying entrepreneurship, they can be interpreted as 'turning points' or 'critical incidents' (Chell, 1998) in one's entrepreneurial career and form a part of the entrepreneurial process. Learning by doing can be combined in this study with the notion of 'learning in performance' during the course of the entrepreneurial process, as put forward by Ramsey (2005, p. 219), from a social constructionist standpoint in studying nascent entrepreneurs' learning processes. As discussed in Chapter 3, entrepreneurial process is studied from a process-relational perspective in this research, which highlights 'the process of creating a new organisation' that is transformative as it draws on one's earlier experiences in life and reflects a transformation, which is about enacting a future (Anderson, 2003, 2005). Therefore, the questions remain: how do nascent entrepreneurs learn as they develop their performances by attending to certain issues, problems, actions and events? Do they develop a performative capacity during the process of nascent entrepreneurship? The answers to these questions will be sought in the case accounts of the research.

The reflective and iterative nature of the process of entrepreneurial learning is acknowledged by Bishop et al. (2001) in their 'individual entrepreneurial learning model', which has three principal components: development of a skill set, self-regulation and task evaluation. They suggest that the iterative processes that occur within each component as well as among components determine the behaviour of the entrepreneur. Linking entrepreneurial learning to venture growth and development, they argue that 'the skills and abilities within an entrepreneur's skill set are acquired, developed and applied based upon the multiple complex tasks to be performed as identified via motivation and self-regulation processes. The selection of tasks is achieved through an evaluation of what resources will be needed to achieve the skill levels necessary to reach the performance goals set within the self-regulation processes. The entrepreneur's goals are determined, in concert with the motivational decision to perform the tasks, through the processes of self-observation, self-evaluation and self-reflection' (Bishop et al., 2001, p. 19). Although the authors recognise the multidimensionality of the process, their conceptualisation denotes a linear understanding of the entrepreneurial process. In this study, however, it is viewed as chaotic, complex and emerging because entrepreneurial activities, in which nascent entrepreneurs are engaged, are complex by nature.

Representing entrepreneurial learning as a 'calibrated algorithm of an iterated choice problem', Minniti and Bygrave (2001) place emphasis on how entrepreneurs internalise information from successes and failures as the focal point of entrepreneurial learning. They argue that most learning takes place by filtering signals obtained by experimenting with different competing hypotheses, where some actions are reinforced and others are weakened as new evidence is obtained. Over time, entrepreneurs repeat those actions that have generated better outcomes. Similar to Bishop et al. (2001), Minniti and Bygrave (2001) take a rather static approach to entrepreneurial learning by focusing on the outcome being 'entrepreneurial knowledge', which is defined as the ability to obtain information (and other resources) and how to deploy them. Therefore, the authors posit that entrepreneurial learning is a process involving repetition and experimentation that increases the entrepreneurial confidence in certain actions and improves the content of her or his stock of knowledge. Such an outcome-oriented approach offers a limited understanding as it neglects the dynamic and contextual nature of the entrepreneurial process. Given this limitation, the contribution of Minniti and Bygrave (2001, p. 7) lies in their recognition of failure being as informative as success and their idea of 'cumulative knowledge'. Contrary to economic models in which agents are rational, the authors argue that entrepreneurs have myopic foresight; they process information, make mistakes, update their decisional algorithms and, possibly through this struggle, improve their performance. An entrepreneur's history is therefore influential and the entrepreneurial knowledge developed is cumulative: 'What is learned in one period builds upon what was learned in an earlier period' (Minniti and Bygrave, 2001, p. 7).

Defining entrepreneurial learning as 'learning that occurs during the venture creation process', Pittaway and Cope's (2006) work investigates student reflections on new venture planning courses exploring how or whether they promote entrepreneurial learning. The departure point is the creation of an uncertain and ambiguous context which forces students to step outside taken-for-granted assumptions about the educational process. Adding ambiguity and uncertainty to an educational process serves the purpose of replicating the circumstances in which an 'entrepreneur' founds a business (Pittaway and Cope, 2006). Having generated student reflections and used narrative analysis to interpret such rich data, the authors conclude that it is possible to identify how entrepreneurs learn and to create experiential designs that stimulate important aspects of entrepreneurial learning. The authors maintain that there are important aspects such as financial exposure and creation of discontinuities, which cannot be created in a classroom context by using simulations. However, they illustrate the important role of emotional exposure – through time-restrained exercises – experiential learning and problem-based orientation in generating reflective practice.

The following elements can be summarised as distinguishing characteristics of entrepreneurial learning: the significant role of financial and emotional exposure (Cope, 2003; Pittaway and Cope, 2006); action-orientation; its experiential and iterative nature (Cope and Watts, 2000; Rae and Carswell, 2000); the importance of critical incidents (Chell, 1998) or 'learning episodes' (Rae, 2002) which include 'discontinuous events' or crises (Cope, 2003); problem solving; and finally, reactive and proactive responses to opportunities and problems (Chell et al., 1991; Young and Sexton, 1997; Pittaway and Cope, 2006). These conclusions lead to a number of pedagogic and policy implications for entrepreneurship and enterprise education as pointed out in Chapters 2 and 3 where we highlighted the need for a critical examination of the enterprise/entrepreneurship education agenda and offered an approach to teaching entrepreneurship by carefully developing programmes that are underpinned by the notion of entrepreneurship, which involves both art and science. Such education programmes should aim to generate 'reflective practitioners' that are equipped with knowledge and skills fit for an entrepreneurial career.

A more comprehensive and recent theoretical approach to entrepreneurial learning is provided by Cope (2005) based on his doctoral study and subsequent works, as covered above. He suggests a framework that has three interconnected groups of elements as illustrated by Figure 4.2. The first elements are the dynamic temporal phases of entrepreneurial learning, which serve to demonstrate the connections between two pertinent stages of learning: learning prior to start-up and learning during the entrepreneurial process. He explains this aspect through three concepts: entrepreneurial preparedness, learning history and learning task. Building

Dynamic temporal phases of entrepreneurial learning:
Entrepreneurial preparedness, learning history and learning task

Interrelated processes of entrepreneurial learning:
Entrepreneurial learning from critical experiences
Affective dimension of critical experiences
Importance of routinised learning
Relationship between reflection, learning and action

Overarching characteristics of entrepreneurial learning

Generative process of entrepreneurial learning
Affective and social nature of entrepreneurial learning

Figure 4.2   Illustration of Cope's (2005) learning perspective of entrepreneurship

on Harvey and Evans's (1995 cited in Cope, 2005) work, from a dynamic learning perspective Cope (2005, p. 378) argues:

> . . . it is constructive to envisage 'entrepreneurial preparedness' as a concept that encapsulates the immense complexity of accumulated learning that individuals bring to the new venture creation process.

Entrepreneurial preparedness is inextricably linked to the idea of 'learning history' because preparing for entrepreneurship has personal and interactive dimensions that occur throughout an individual's life rather than concentrated during the immediate prestart-up phase (Cope, 2001). It is a part of one's evolving 'learning history', which is in tune with Minniti and Bygrave's (2001) perspective of 'cumulative knowledge'. According to Minniti and Bygrave (2001), cumulative knowledge is formed by repetition and experimentation that increases the entrepreneur's confidence in certain actions and such acquired knowledge generates routines and decisional procedures. Therefore, 'history matters' in their view; however, it reflects rather a static and functional approach to entrepreneurial learning. Moving away from such a static approach, Cope's (2005) concepts of 'entrepreneurial preparedness' and 'learning history' acknowledge the dynamic, reflexive and interactive nature of the learning process:

> 'To be fully prepared as possible for entrepreneurship, individuals must look outward in order to interact with, learn about, the wider environment and

recognise fully the opportunity that confronts them. Prospective entrepreneurs must also look forward, in order to visualise how to make their business grow and succeed. . . . It is a dual, interactive process, where the individual develops a clear appreciation of their own strengths and weaknesses and those of their potential business in relation to wider environment.'

In order to evaluate their strengths and weaknesses nascent entrepreneurs must reflect on their past experiences, in other words this process also entails looking inward. 'Learning task', which is the final concept Cope (2005) puts forward to explain the first element of the framework, is shaped by the unique range of experiences, skills and abilities deriving from the complexity and diversity of each individual's learning history and becomes crucial when entrepreneurs enter into the new venture creation process. How entrepreneurs learn to become effective managers of people and resources is Cope's (2005) definition of a 'learning task' from a dynamic learning perspective. Quoting Rae and Carswell (2000) he argues: 'A better theoretical grasp of entrepreneurial learning is imperative, as it is through learning that entrepreneurs develop and grow, and have the potential to become more capable business owners' (Cope, 2005). This assertion implies a 'small business owner-manager' type of approach whereby the entrepreneur's task is viewed as running the business successfully once it is set up.

The view of 'entrepreneurship' that we adopt in this book highlights the relentless pursuit of business opportunities with a view to growing the business and therefore accumulating wealth and capital (Chell, 2001). The focus is on entrepreneurship in the present study rather than small business management, around which Cope's work (2000, 2003a, 2005) revolves. The process-relational approach to entrepreneurship (Chell, 2001; Anderson, 2005) on the whole calls for viewing the entrepreneur as proactive in the learning process and envisioning future opportunities, while reflecting on past and current situations and conducting the day-to-day management of the business in relation to a number of stakeholders. This is what 'entrepreneurial managing' refers to in the current study. Contrary to Sexton et al.'s (1997, p. 3) view, which is that 'entrepreneurs are content, not process oriented', developed by drawing on their study of the learning needs of growth-oriented entrepreneurs, Cope (2005, p. 380) claims that we should understand not only what entrepreneurs must and do learn about during the establishment and management of entrepreneurial ventures, but also the specific processes of learning. These processes stimulate learning content structured around five broad areas: learning about oneself, learning about the business, learning about the environment and entrepreneurial networks, learning about small business management, and learning about the nature and management of relationships. Cope's approach to entrepreneurial learning is both content and process oriented. We recognise the content elements of entrepreneurial learning; however, we focus on the process of learning in this study, by highlighting the transformation between different forms of capital in the process, such as transformation of cultural and social capital to economic capital, or the transformation of symbolic capital (such as gaining legitimacy of the entrepreneur and venture) to social and economic capital. We will delineate these sub-processes of entrepreneurial learning through case studies, presented in Chapters 7 and 8.

Aligning with Cope's (2005) perspective, Politis (2005) puts the emphasis on the role of experience in developing entrepreneurial knowledge. Departing from a review and synthesis of the available research on learning in entrepreneurial contexts, she makes a useful distinction between the experience of an entrepreneur (entrepreneurial learning as a process) and the knowledge acquired as a result of that experience (entrepreneurial knowledge as the outcome of the process). She describes entrepreneurial learning as an experiential process that facilitates the development of necessary knowledge for being effective in setting up and managing ventures (Politis, 2005, p. 401) by drawing attention to transformational processes. Her conceptual framework of entrepreneurial learning is depicted in Figure 4.3 as follows:

Confronting the difficult task of describing or defining what 'learning' involves, Politis (2005) argues that in entrepreneurial contexts it pertains to learning how to recognise and act upon opportunities and learning how to overcome traditional hurdles when organising and managing new ventures, that is to say, coping with the liabilities of newness. Highlighting the role of 'experience' as an important source of entrepreneurial learning, she acknowledges the significance of the experiential process where experience is transformed into entrepreneurial knowledge. The intermediate processes involve exploration of new possibilities and exploitation of pre-existing knowledge, which in turn impact upon the development of entrepreneurs' ability to identify and exploit entrepreneurial opportunities and tackle with the common obstacles facing new ventures. Her framework calls for drawing a distinction between the events experienced by an entrepreneur and the acquired knowledge when studying entrepreneurial learning (Politis, 2005, p. 415). In this theoretical work, she does not offer any insights as to how to achieve this. Rather than making such a distinction, it is important to understand the dynamics of the relationship between the events experienced and understandings/insights or knowledge developed by nascent entrepreneurs.

Referring back to Figure 4.1, nascent entrepreneurs are at the phase

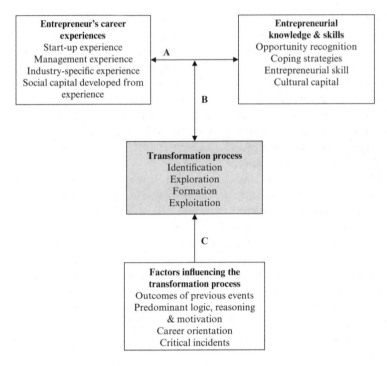

Source: Adapted from Politis (2005).

*Figure 4.3   A conceptual framework of entrepreneurial learning as an
              experiential process*

of 'gestation', and this 'newness' is an important dimension to take into
account. Learning and managing are interrelated in the context of nascent
entrepreneurship as nascent entrepreneurs tend to learn various aspects of
business venturing, such as the management of self presentation, opportunity and resource development processes, and manage the entrepreneurial
activities concurrently.

Drawing on Weick's (1979) definition of organising, Gartner et al.
(1992, p. 23) view the process of 'entrepreneurial managing' as 'the process
of changing the equivocality of interactions among a number of different
individuals into the non-equivocal interactions of an organisation'. This
implies creating a structure that is a negotiated order of an enterprise
(Watson, 2001a) whereby individual members attempt to reduce ambigui-
ties through interplay of a variety of interests and understandings in order
to promote and sustain co-ordinated effort. As suggested by Gartner et al.
(1992), the notion of entrepreneurship, as a type of organising performed

by nascent entrepreneurs, who relationally and relentlessly pursue business opportunities, calls for an examination of how specific patterns of interactions are generated. This is grounded in a social constructionist approach where the formation of organisations is seen fundamentally as an 'enacted phenomenon' which is a particular form of social reality construction (Berger and Luckman, 1966; Chell, 2000). Nascent entrepreneurs encounter a wide range of equivocal situations in the process of business venturing. Through their interaction with their wider network and involvement in defining the routines of the emerging organisation, entrepreneurs reduce the equivocality (Gartner et al., 1992). For example, as their business mentors are providing support as to how to go about constructing their business plan, financiers are evaluating the business plan, suppliers are providing quotations, customers are facing a prototype and individuals are considering employment in the firm, nascent entrepreneurs are moving towards more certain interpretations (Weick, 1995). However, this is not a linear process. It is emerging, complex and iterative just as the interlinked process of learning is.

As noted at the outset of the section, entrepreneurial learning is still an emerging subject domain within the discipline of entrepreneurship. It is useful to draw on pertinent organisational learning literatures to inform current understanding of entrepreneurial learning process. Chapter 5 will convey how social constructionism allows a participatory world-view and offers new and rich possibilities for interests in learning processes, relations and social interactions (Reason, 1994). Gherardi (1999) criticises common constructions of organisational learning that reflect a positivist approach and recommends constructionist epistemology. She has been one of the few researchers who takes a social constructionist view to learning in organisations and challenges the traditional technical views of learning. Organisational learning is ascribed to the members' collective construction of knowledge. The attention is on the processes through which individual or local knowledge is transformed into collective knowledge as well as the process through which this socially constructed knowledge influences, and is part of, local knowledge (Huysman, 2000, p. 136). Easterby-Smith, Crossan and Nicolini (2000, p. 787) call this movement the revolution that 'overturned the previously dominant model, which implicitly conceptualised learners as individual actors processing information or modifying their mental structures, and substituted it with an image of learners as social beings who construct their understanding and learn from social interaction within specific socio-cultural and material settings'. We echo this view of learning in the current study; it has informed our overall approach to studying nascent entrepreneurs' learning experiences when creating new organisations.

4.4   CONCLUSIONS TO THE CHAPTER

In the previous chapter, the entrepreneurial process of business venturing has been emphasised from a social constructionist premise that places
emphasis on the social processes by which new ventures come into existence. Highlighting the multi-layered nature (micro, meso-relational and
macro-levels) of the investigation in the current work, we have aimed
to further the debate by moving to the second research question which
is concerned with the intrinsic processes of entrepreneurial learning and
managing as experienced by nascent entrepreneurs.[1] To this end, we have
reviewed the literature pertaining to nascent entrepreneurs and entrepreneurial learning and managing supported by the pertinent organisational
learning literature.

Adopting Aldrich's (1999, p. 77) definition of nascent entrepreneurs
as those who initiate serious activities that are intended to culminate in a
viable business start-up, how they go through such a transformative experience lies at the heart of the discussion. In this chapter, the entrepreneurial
learning literature has been reviewed, by noting that it is a recently emerging
domain in entrepreneurship research. These studies largely examine entrepreneurial learning at the experienced individual entrepreneur level or small
firm level. The social constructionist and interpretivist perspectives have
been endorsed in this review. The fundamental qualities of entrepreneurial
learning involve the role of context, financial and emotional exposure,
action-orientation, its experiential and iterative nature, the importance
of critical incidents and finally proactive responses to opportunities and
relentless struggle against perceived difficulties. The 'entrepreneurial managing' pertains to finding ways to take the venture forward (Mangham and
Pye, 1991) by enacting what nascent entrepreneurs are learning as a part
of their personal, economic and social becoming through accomplishing
everyday tasks, dealing with uncertainties and engaging in other entrepreneurial practices in interaction with the members of their wider network
and stakeholders and thereby adapting and modifying these practices. This
links us to the notion of 'venture communities' developed in the research,
which represents the meso-relational level of analysis. These levels of analysis and theoretical constructs used at each level are illuminated in the next
chapter which discusses the social constructionist paradigm and Bourdieu's
relational methodology that underpins the current research.

NOTE

1.   See Table 6.3 in Chapter 6 for the research questions and levels of analysis.

5. Methodological approach: social constructionist paradigm and Bourdieu's relational methodology

5.1 INTRODUCTION TO THE CHAPTER

> In wrestling with the ways in which these [research] philosophies forestructure our efforts to understand what it means to 'do' qualitative inquiry, what we face is not a choice of which label – interpretivist, constructivist, hermeneuticist, or something else – best suits us. Rather, we are confronted with choices about how each of us wants to live the life of a social inquirer (Schwandt, 2000, p. 205).

The purpose of this chapter is to lay down the research paradigm underpinning the research. It starts with the definitions of 'paradigm' and an introduction of Burrell and Morgan's (1979) four-grid paradigmatic approach. The social constructionist paradigm is then discussed as the underlying paradigm in the current research. This is followed by the elaboration of the terms 'ontology', 'epistemology' and 'methodology' in relation to the nature of this research. The chapter concludes with Bourdieu's (Bourdieu, 1977, 1986, 1990, 1998; Bourdieu and Wacquant, 1992) frameworks, which are used in investigating nascent entrepreneurship and learning.

5.2 RESEARCH PARADIGMS

Lincoln and Guba (1985, p. 15) argue that 'paradigms represent a distillation of what we think about the world'. The term 'paradigm' derives from Kuhn's (1970) thesis where he referred to a set of beliefs, values, assumptions and techniques, which serves as 'a regulatory framework of metaphysical assumptions shared by members of a given community' (Kuhn, 1970, p. 175). He views this web of belief as underpinning scientific communities and their practices (Lowe, 2004, p. 209). In this respect Lowe (2004) maintains it is possible to see the web represented as a network, which comes to life in the knowledge and practices of specific groups of scientists. Joining this discussion about Kuhn's concept of paradigm, Johnson and Duberley (2000, p. 68) emphasise the shared way of thinking

and working by a 'practitioner community', which is characterised by consensus. They maintain that 'each paradigm therefore has its own distinctive language, which offers a unique means of classifying and construing
the objects encountered during scientists' engagements with the world'
(Johnson and Duberley, 2000, p. 69). This engagement is shaped by the
researcher's biography as well as that of people in the organisation or
community under study (Hertz, 1997; Brown, 2000; Patton, 2002).

Denzin and Lincoln (1998, p. 4), who described the researcher as the
'bricoleur', who produces a bricolage, that is a pieced-together, close
knit-set of practices that seek solutions to problems in certain situations,
reinforce this point in the following way:

> The bricoleur understands that research is an interactive process shaped by his
> or her personal history, biography, gender, social class, race and ethnicity, and
> those of the people in the setting. There is no value-free science. The bricoleur
> also knows that researchers all tell stories about the worlds they have situated.
> Thus, the narratives, or stories, scientists tell are accounts couched and framed
> within specific storytelling traditions, often defined as paradigms.

The debate on paradigms and their role in the research process was given
momentum by the publication of Burrell and Morgan's seminal work
entitled *Sociological Paradigms and Organisational Analysis* (Hassard and
Kelemen, 2002, p. 336). Outlining a number of key debates concerning
the production of knowledge in organisation studies, Burrell and Morgan
(1979) define paradigm by emphasising meta-theoretical assumptions
upon which a frame of reference is constructed:

> Paradigms are [the] . . . approaches grounded in fundamentally different meta-
> theoretical assumptions that are used to construct the frame of reference, mode
> of theorising and method of investigating of the theorists who operate within
> them.

Their thesis is therefore based on the premise that all researchers bring to
their study a frame of reference, a whole series of assumptions about the
nature of social world and the way it might be investigated. These assumptions suggest distinct views of the social world, which create different
ways of examining human behaviour (Chell and Pittaway, 1998a). Burrell
and Morgan (1979) contend that these meta-theoretical assumptions can
be organised into four paradigms: the functionalist, the interpretive, the
radical humanist and the radical structuralist. These four sociological
paradigms represent the major belief systems of academics and others,
who practise organisational analysis.

How were they produced? At the centre of Burrell and Morgan's four paradigm framework lies their view that all theories of organisations are constructed upon a philosophy of science and a theory of society. Both mainstream and alternative schools of thought are situated in terms of their relative position on a map of intellectual terrain produced through relating 'theories of social science' to 'theories of society' (Hassard and Kelemen, 2002, p. 336). The philosophical underpinnings are presented along a dimension of objectivity to subjectivity based on interrelated sets of core assumptions regarding ontology, epistemology, human behaviour and methodology (Morgan and Smircich, 1980).

Ontology concerns the nature of being, 'reality' (Burrell and Morgan, 1979; Morgan and Smircich, 1980; Lincoln and Guba, 1985; Easterby-Smith, Thorpe and Lowe, 2002). Epistemology is about what we can know. It concerns the nature of knowledge: the distinction between knowing and believing or opining (Chell and Pittaway, 1998a, p. 2). Researchers who work within a positivist paradigm view knowledge in absolute terms as either true or false and establish such knowledge through deterministic scientific inquiry. On the other hand, researchers in non-positivistic paradigms see knowledge as relativistic – it can only be understood from the perspectives of those involved (Pittaway, 2000). The human behaviour dimension is concerned specifically with free will or determinism, that is, whether human beings freely choose between different courses of action or whether their behaviour is determined by causal factors that ultimately can be identified. In the anti-positivist (or anti-functionalist in Burrell and Morgan's terms) paradigm there is a belief of the autonomous individual who has free will and choice and that this contrasts sharply with the deterministic view (Pittaway, 2000; Johnson and Duberley, 2000). This has significant implications concerning the role of the researcher and the relationship between the researcher and the participants. Methodology pertains to the question of how we can generate knowledge. It concerns use of methods to generate knowledge of human behaviour or the social world (Easterby-Smith et al., 2002). The researchers' ontological and epistemological assumptions and human behaviour positioning guide their choices of methods to create knowledge and inevitably the type of knowledge. A positivist view of the world conveys a belief of the social world as an external and objective reality; this calls for methods of investigation that primarily rely on the analysis of variables and causal relationships through empirical testing in the pursuit of law-like generalisations or concepts that describe the reality of the social world (Denzin and Lincoln, 1998, 2000; Johnson and Duberley, 2000). A non-positivist world-view entails the examination of experiences of individuals, who create, interpret and manipulate their reality. The knowledge generated will be concentrated on what is unique to individual experiences rather than what is universal or general.

Given this philosophical underpinning, the second dimension of Burrell and Morgan's four-grid paradigmatic framework is the nature of society. The assumptions vary along a dimension of social order (maintenance of the status quo) to an assumed norm of constant change and conflict. According to the positivist approach, society is believed to be stable where social order is the norm. Stability is maintained through structures that are acknowledged by the majority and endure through consensus. On the contrary, within an anti-positivist paradigm, the nature of society is believed to be one where deep conflict exists (Alvesson and Deetz, 1996, 2000) and conflict is both structural and functional (Chell and Pittaway, 1998a). There is an assumption of organisations as social and historical creations accomplished in conditions of struggle and domination that often hide and suppress meaningful conflict (Deetz, 1996, p. 202). The emancipation of human beings from the structures which inhibit them is the central concern of the sociology of knowledge (Steffy and Grimes, 1992; Alvesson and Willmott, 1996). Along these two major dimensions (the subjective-objective dimension and the radical change-regulation dimension), four paradigms are shown in the Figure 5.1.

The functionalist paradigm is characterised by objectivity and the sociology of regulation. The aim is to explain the relationships between variables that lead to universal principles. A deterministic view of human behaviour prevails and human beings are considered to be adaptable to

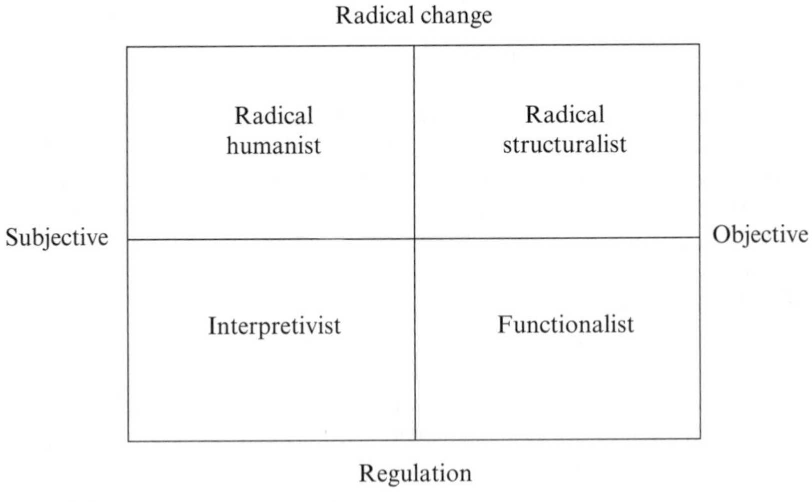

Radical change

Radical humanist	Radical structuralist
Interpretivist	Functionalist

Subjective   Objective

Regulation

Source: Adapted from Burrell and Morgan (1969).

Figure 5.1   Burrell and Morgan's (1979) four paradigms

the system rather than having the capacity to think and question or having free will and choice (Burrell and Morgan, 1979; Morgan and Smircich, 1981; Alvesson and Deetz, 1996). The implication is that research is conducted in a deductive way, that is the researcher begins with reviewing literature, identifies variables, develops hypotheses and tests them through empirical research. Researchers located in the interpretive paradigm, on the other hand, take a stance characterised by subjectivity and social order. The view is that researchers should understand the world as it is and seek for an explanation of that world from the realm of the individual or individual consciousness (Hassard, 1991; Chell and Pittaway, 1998a, p. 3). The radical humanist paradigm is typified by a subjectivist view, but with an ideological orientation toward radically changing constructed realities. Finally, the radical structuralist paradigm is characterised by an objectivist stance, with an ideological concern for the radical change of structural realities (Gioia and Pitre, 1990, p. 586).

Burrell and Morgan's (1979) grid can be criticised on a number of counts, including paradigm commensurability (Jackson and Carter, 1991; Willmott, 1993) and the dimensions of contrast. Deetz (1996) challenges their framework by questioning their interpretation of the first dimension (objectivity-subjectivity), and by raising the inadequacy of the second dimension (change-regulation) in the light of recent movements in organisation studies. He argues that the most problematic legacy of Burrell and Morgan's (1979) framework is the perpetuation of the subjective-objective controversy. He suggests that it does not provide a useful way of thinking about research paradigm differences. Similarly, the author claims that the second dimension of change-regulation does not reflect contemporary ways of looking at alternative research programmes. Acknowledging the 'linguistic turn' (thus locating research differences in discursive moves and social relations rather than procedures and individuals), Deetz (1996, p. 195) puts forward two alternative dimensions of contrast. The first dimension puts emphasis on the origins of concepts and problem statements as part of the constitutive process in research and suggests a dimension of comparison based on 'local/emergent' versus 'elite/a priori'. The second dimension that Deetz (1996) suggests focuses on the relation of research practices to the dominant social discourses within the organisation studied and/or the research community: 'Research orientations can be contrasted in the extent to which they operate within a dominant set of restructurings of knowledge, social relations, and identities (a reproductive practice), called here a "consensus" discourse, and the extent to which they work to disrupt these structurings (a productive practice), called here "dissensus" discourse' (Deetz, 1996, p. 195). The intention is to develop insights into meaningful differences and similarities among different research paradigms and activities rather than classification. How social constructionism has developed as a research paradigm is the concern of the next section.

5.2.1 Social Constructionism

As a well-established approach in sociology and to some extent in social psychology as well as in organisation and management studies, social constructionism challenges some of the central assumptions of mainstream social science (Rosen, 1991, p. 5; Shotter, 1993a, 1993b). Gergen's (1994) synthesis of the intellectual antecedents of social constructionist perspectives explains how the force of ideological, literary-rhetorical and social critique challenged the orthodoxy of objectivity, rationality and truth (Perren and Grant, 2000, p. 394). Its main proposition is that members of any social system enact their particular worlds through social interaction where ideas, concepts and beliefs are discussed and shared with others. Reality is thus a social product, which cannot be understood apart from the co-constructed meanings of the social actors involved in its enactment (Berger and Luckmann, 1966; Gergen, 1985; Rosen, 1991, Shotter, 1993b; Sarbin and Kitsuse, 1994; Hosking and Ramsey, 2000).

To help throw light on the intellectual roots of social constructionism, Burr (1995) provides a discussion about its history. She argues that social constructionism is a recent movement which has emerged from the combined influences of a number of North American, British and continental writers from the disciplines of sociology and social psychology dating back more than 30 years. This argument could be accepted to the extent that its fundamental assumptions have been refined in those so-called recent works. However, according to Berger and Luckmann (1966) its origins could be traced back to the German intellectual and philosophical context, where its root proposition derived from Marx, that man's consciousness is determined by his social being. The social constructionist approach, therefore, is recognised as 'a challenge to the primacy and priority of the individual, in effect, placing relationship, the social, as prior and primary' (Stacey, 2001, p. 55).

Social constructionism is well established in sociology, mainly owing to the works of Schutz (1967) and Berger and Luckman (1966), according to Sarbin and Kitsuse (1994). Through their works the idea was developed that social objects are not given in the world, but constructed, negotiated, reformed and fashioned and organised by human beings in their efforts to make sense of happenings in the world. Central to social constructionism is therefore the premise that human beings are active social beings and they constitute their social world through social practices. In Sarbin and Kitsuse's (1994, p. 2) terms: 'human beings are agents rather than passive organisms or disembodied intellects that process information. It is undeniable that human actors process information, but processing is carried out in the context of cultural practices'. These cultural practices carry important weight in social constructionism and they are produced and sustained through the use of stories. Members of a collectivity convey their constructions of the social world through stories, or narrative, to fellow members. These narratives are shaped by, and reflect, the perspectives of the narrators, who produce them (Sarbin and Kitsuse, 1994). This leads us to the notion of multiple realities at the ontological level, as will be elaborated in section 5.3. Multiple perspectives are fostered in social constructionism as there is an explicit acknowledgement of the differential perspectives in the observation and interpretation of social phenomena. Clearly, this counters the positivist assumption of a uniform and objective social reality. The social constructionist commitment to the conception of social phenomena as a multiplicity of actively constructed and emergent realities puts additional demands on researchers. In the first instance, the researcher's constructions are viewed as narratives, which are shaped by, and express, the social, moral, political, philosophical and other concerns of the researcher. Therefore, an awareness of, and reflection on, these concerns as well as awareness of how researchers are situated with regard to their research participants, are crucial in social constructionist research. This raises the issue of 'reflexivity' which has been the topic of an enduring debate in the social constructionist genre (Sarbin and Kitsuse, 1994; Hosking and Ramsey, 2000).

The following quote from Hosking and Green (1999) summarises the argument presented in this section. Focusing on the multiplicity of perspectives discursively formed through language, they differentiate between social constructionist approaches which put emphasis on the social, individual and reflexivity:

> There are many social constructionisms. They share an emphasis on language as communication (rather than representation) and view communication as formative i.e. as 'forming' or constructing persons and worlds. Constructionisms differ (a) in their centring of emphasis on socially constructed 'products' or processes, and (b) in their centring of individuals or communal construction processes, and (c) their reflexive recognition of the researcher's participation in construction processes.

5.2.2 Berger and Luckmann (1966): *the Social Construction of Reality*

The basic contention of Berger and Luckmann's (1966) argument is that reality is socially constructed and that the sociology of knowledge must analyse the process in which this occurs. They maintain that we should look at processes by which any body of 'knowledge' comes to be socially established as 'reality':

> As all human knowledge is developed, transmitted and maintained in social situations, the sociology of knowledge must seek to understand the processes by which this is done in such a way that a taken-for-granted reality congeals for the man in the street.

In essence Berger and Luckmann's (1966) analysis of the social construction of reality focuses on three processes: externalisation, objectivation, and internalisation. First, externalisation is about the creation of external features by human beings. The central premise of their argument is that a person's reality is constructed from experience and accumulated 'knowledge' about their general surroundings and their specific social context. The assumption is that an individual constructs 'knowledge' about themselves and others by labelling and categorising their thoughts, feelings and experience (Chell, 1997). The act of labelling, therefore, lies at the core of the process of externalisation, which is articulating those thoughts and feelings before other selves (Chell and Pittaway, 1998a). Berger and Luckmann (1966, p. 70) point out that all human activity is subject to habitualisation and any action that is repeated becomes cast into a pattern which precedes institutionalisation. For example, when people tell a story around the idea of the birth of a community, they externalise it by making the story accessible to others. This enters into the public realm where other people re-tell the story and the story begins to take on a life of its own (Burr, 1995, p. 10). Second, this externalised product of human activity becomes an object of people's consciousness in that society and Berger and Luckmann (1966) call this objectivation. This is the 'process by which the externalised products of human activity attain the character of objectivity'. Burr (1995, p. 10) argues that the story develops into 'a kind of factual existence or truth'; it, therefore, comes naturally to other generations, becoming institutionalised in a society. Berger and Luckmann (1966, p. 77), nevertheless, note that objectivity does not acquire an ontological status apart from the human activity that produced it. They emphasise the link between the reflexive nature of the relationship between the individual, the producer, and the social world, and his or her product:

> . . . man (not of course, in isolation but in his collectivities) and his social world interact with each other. The product acts back upon the producer. Externalisation and objectivation are moments in a continuing dialectical process.

Third, is the process of internalisation, by which the objectivated social world is retrojected into consciousness in the course of socialisation

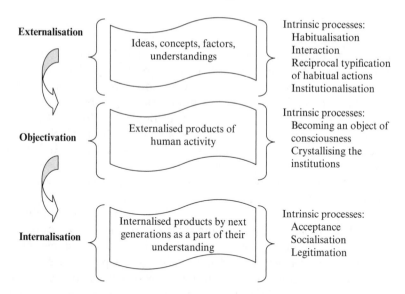

*Figure 5.2   An interpretation of Berger and Luckmann's social
construction process*

(Berger and Luckmann, 1966, p. 78). The configuration of the relationship
between these three dialectical processes is shown in the Figure 5.2. The
final aspect of internalisation involves the acceptance by the next generation of this story. Berger and Luckmann (1966, p. 77) draw attention to
the process of transmission to the new generation where the objectivity of
the institutionalised world thickens and hardens not only for the children,
but also for the parents as well, because the objectivity experienced by the
children would reflect back upon parents' own experience of this world.

Berger and Luckmann's (1966) exploration has shown how knowledge,
understandings and institutions are created through these social processes
of externalisation, objectivation and internalisation. Deriving from their
explanation, the individuals in the situation deal with it according to their
perception and interpretation of its elements, and their creation and construction of what it means to them. 'Reality is therefore subjective because
an individual's own experiences and social interactions will enable them to
use and develop a personal set of "labels" to give meaning to present and
future social situations' (Chell and Pittaway, 1998a, p. 5). It is also objective in so far as people use a common language to interpret and convey
the meanings of situations; they use certain ways and evidence in support
of their particular interpretation, which eventually becomes the accepted
or dominant interpretation – the reality (Chell, 2000, p. 68). Their notion

of objectivity is centred on the idea that social behaviours, actions and institutions tend to take on patterns and ways of doing reflexively, and they become routine over time. Thus, Berger and Luckmann (1966) in conceptualising reality by assuming that it is both subjective and objective, endeavour to bridge the subjective and objective features of social life. In Layder's (1994) opinion this bridge-building approach is a very constructive one. This draws a parallel with Bourdieu (1977, 1990, 1998) who developed such conceptual tools as *habitus* and field, which seek to transcend the dichotomy of subjectivism versus objectivism. His frameworks will be discussed later in the chapter.

From Holstein and Gubrium's (1994) perspective, Berger and Luckmann's (1966) version of social constructionism is primarily concerned with the cognitive principles governing the world of meaningful objects. The emphasis is put on the structure of the social world in a general sense, considering how that world is constituted as a stable entity, what comprises that world, and how meanings shape and are shaped by it. Therefore, Holstein and Gubrium (1994) argue that Berger and Luckmann's (1966, p. 233) focus is on the cognitive processes of 'universe maintenance'. Revisiting Burrell and Morgan's (1979) paradigmatic dimensions of objectivity vs. subjectivity and social change vs. regulation, Berger and Luckmann's social constructionist thesis is characterised by intrinsic processes of social construction. They include reflexive externalisation of individual psychology (thoughts, feelings, opinions and so on) through labelling and categorisation processes and the ensuing processes of objectivation through crystallising the labels, categories and institutions, and finally internalisation through acceptance, socialisation and legitimation to maintain social order.

5.2.3 Gergen's Social Constructionism

K.J. Gergen (1985) believes in a relational theory of social meaning or social order and, to him, it is the human interchange that should stand as the focus. 'Social constructionist inquiry is principally concerned with explicating the processes by which people come to describe, explain or otherwise account for the world (including themselves) in which they live' (K.J. Gergen, 1985, p. 266). Therefore, researchers are invited to play with the possibilities and practices that are made coherent by various forms of relations (Schwandt, 2000, p. 198). Adhering to social constructionism, then, points us not only to what is constructed, but also how it is constructed and the very question of what it means to say it is constructed (Patton, 2002, p. 102).

It is argued by some scholars (for example, Mather, 2002; Katzko,

2002) that K.J. Gergen's version of social constructionism is rooted in Hegelian philosophy (Hegel, 1874 cited in Mather, 2002), which is grounded in Weberian Verstehen sociology. According to Mather (2002), the affinities between Hegelian 'dialectical thinking' and K.J. Gergen's social constructionism are particularly evident in the edited publication entitled *Historical Social Psychology* (K.J. Gergen and M. Gergen, 1984). In essence, Hegelian dialectical thinking focuses on the reflexive relationship between human beings and their social environment. This is manifest in K.J. Gergen's interpretation of social constructionism throughout his writings, particularly when raising the problem of 'the external world'. For him, there is no transcendent reality from which to survey the connection between subject and object. In his own words 'in object related constitution a community essentially creates the objective world in terms of "what it is for us"' (K.J. Gergen, 2001, p. 422). Members of a society transform the 'subjective' into 'a tangible reality' that is a product of active perceptual constructions (Deetz, 1996; K.J. Gergen, 1999; Chell, 2000; Nicholson and Anderson, 2005).

Given this intellectual background to his version of social constructionism, it is an apposite moment to introduce K.J. Gergen's (1985) four key assumptions. Burr (1995) argues that we, the social science researchers, make one or more of these assumptions when working in a social constructionist genre. Burr's (1995) articulation of these assumptions is quite useful in relating the assumptions to methodological choices. The ensuing discussion incorporates her views:

Assumption 1.   A critical stance towards taken-for-granted knowledge (Burr, 1995):

What we take to be experience of the world does not in itself dictate the terms by which the world is understood. What we take to be knowledge of the world is not a product of induction, or of the building and testing of general hypotheses. (K.J. Gergen, 1985, p. 266)

This assumption highlights the need to take a critical stance towards taken-for-granted ways of understanding the world as opposed to positivism, where there is faith in the so-called objective, unbiased observation of the world. This does not necessarily mean that positivist researchers are uncritical or never test their assumptions. However, positivists are committed to a theory of 'truth' couched in a putative neutral observational language and the task of science is to enable the prediction and control of social and natural events (Johnson and Duberley, 2000, p. 26). This is a recurrent theme traceable back to Descartes (1960).

With the above statement of 'a critical stance towards taken-for-granted knowledge', K.J. Gergen's (1994, p. 4) main contention could be best summarised in his following question: 'How can theoretical categories map or reflect the world if each definition linking category and observation itself requires a definition?' In the social constructionist premise, 'the categories with which we apprehend the world do not necessarily refer to real divisions' (Burr, 1995, p. 3). It is how we know them, that is to say, how we grasp them in our minds and in society as such categories. Berger and Luckmann (1966) argue that formations of reality or knowledge are undertaken by the members of that society and they are 'real' or can be construed as 'knowledge' for those people. Social constructions of reality are couched in intersubjective experiences (Nicholson and Anderson, 2005). As suggested by Smith and Anderson (2004) everyone in society takes part in society's knowledge construction, even if not at the level of theorising by all members of the society. As mentioned in the preceding paragraphs, active perceptual constructions by the members of a society are critical in understanding underpinning processes of social construction of knowledge. Chell (2000) demonstrates how language guides our 'perceptual constructions' and sense-making processes by making inferences based on previous experiences and memories; by thinking forward; by filtering and framing and transforming the subjective into a more tangible and workable reality.

Assumption 2.   Historical and cultural specificity (Burr, 1995):
  The terms in which the world is understood are social artefacts, products of historically situated interchanges among people. (K.J. Gergen, 1985)

This assumption means that all ways of understanding are historically and culturally situated (Burr, 1995, p. 4). These particular forms of knowledge are viewed as the products of that culture and history. Berger and Luckmann's (1966) explanation of social construction deals with this aspect by claiming that externalised products of human activity, or the ways by which they are produced, can be understood in that society within their historical context. They present an exhaustive analysis of the processes of objectivation, institutionalisation and legitimation. However, the significance of the embeddedness of social construction processes in their cultural and historical context is not developed.

Assumption 3.   Knowledge is sustained by social processes (Burr, 1995, p. 4):
  The degree to which a given form of understanding prevails or is sustained across time is not directly dependent on the empirical validity of the perspective in question, but on the vicissitudes of social processes. (K.J. Gergen, 1985)

Social constructionism puts emphasis on human interaction. It is the daily interactions between people in the course of social life that are crucial to understand. K.J. Gergen (1985) explains the social processes by individuals' ability to remember a concept, share it with others and discuss it. So knowledge of the world is sustained by social processes through interaction in other words knowledge is what people do together (Burr, 1995, p. 6). The significance of social processes mainly stems from the ability to define the strength of an idea by its ability to pass through history, as could be inferred from K.J. Gergen. This is seen to be similar to, and different from, Berger and Luckmann's arguments. It is similar to their description of transmission of knowledge to internalise it. Therefore, the constant engagement of people in such interactions with each other forms the focal point in both versions of social constructionism. It is through this interaction and engagement that the meanings are 'generated by people as they collectively engage in descriptions and explanations in language' (K.J. Gergen and M. Gergen, 1991, p. 78). For K.J. Gergen, these relational processes are ongoing, more or less temporary and local constructions. However, Berger and Luckmann (1966, p. 117) tend to emphasise the creation of knowledge and social institutions in a sense that, once constructed, they are virtually self-maintaining in the absence of problems or challenges; institutions 'tend to persist unless they become problematic'. K.J. Gergen explains interactional practice and stresses how knowledge and social action go together and the processes of developing understandings and actions continually shape and reshape social actors' institutional realm, with context and activity being reflexively related. This theme, of course, resonates with Giddens' theory of structuration (Giddens, 1984, 1990).

This assumption is of particular import for the current research, as it forms the core idea in shaping the overall research aim, which is to explore the relational processes of entrepreneurial learning and managing as the underlying processes of venturing. The intention is to uncover such processes by which the nascent entrepreneurs relationally create meanings and understandings and develop their actions, as they form and run a venture. This calls for multiple levels of analysis.[1] It also relates to the notion of research, adopted in this study, as an ongoing relational process between the participants and researchers from a social constructionist standpoint.

Assumption 4. Knowledge and social action go together (Burr, 1995, p. 3):
Forms of negotiated understanding are of critical significance in social life, as they are integrally connected with many other activities in which people engage. (K.J. Gergen, 1985, p. 268)

K.J. Gergen takes the discussion one step further and discusses how people together sustain life in the continuous generation of meanings through social interaction. He asserts that generative discourse transforms social life (K.J. Gergen, 1999). Discourse is 'a connected set of statements, concepts, terms, expressions, which constitute a way of talking or writing about a particular issue thus framing the way people understand and act with respect to that issue' (Watson, 1994a, p. 113). This implies that discourse provides the means through which individuals achieve self-expression and realise ideas, visions and ambitions (Fletcher, 2003). The interconnectedness of developing understandings and actions through interaction and negotiation is a crucial element in K.J. Gergen's social constructionism.

This assumption has been influential in refining the research concern with entrepreneurial learning, and managing the processes through which business ideas are realised, negotiated and transformed into a viable business concept by forming a venture. This focuses attention on the intertwined nature of learning and managing experience during organisational emergence (that is new venture creation), because the key assumption is that developing meanings/understandings and actions are co-produced. This is also related to understanding what the nascent entrepreneur thinks she/he knows and what assumptions she/he makes about her/his reality.

At the heart of these processes lie communication processes. Following Hosking and Green (1999), the communication processes are relational ones and they refer to the realm of language and action. So their relational and action emphasis joins what is often separated – talk, action, things and events:

> Language (action) now is seen to include written and spoken words, non-verbal gestures, voice tone, artefacts of human activity such as a logo, a company uniform, interior layout and décor, music . . . Action is any word or artefact that might be co-ordinated with in some way, so constructing a communication (Hosking and Green, 1999, p. 2).

In summary, K.J. Gergen's first assumption is that the social world or knowledge of it is not viewed as a pre-existent domain. The social world is socially produced through human interaction and language. This process is characterised in Berger and Luckmann's understanding, by human interactions becoming externalised, objectified and then internalised. A further assumption is that our understanding of the social world is historically and culturally specific. It is more or less contingent upon time and context. Therefore, a social constructionist researcher seeks both temporal and contextual understanding. It is important to grasp the 'present' with reference to building on the 'past' and enacting the 'future'. This follows with the third assumption that social processes should be the focus of the researcher, who explores how these understandings and knowledge are generated and regenerated and, who should take account of the changing nature of the social world in so doing. The final assumption links our actions to our views, beliefs, understandings, and in a more encompassing sense, our narratives about ourselves and the world. In essence, how we view the social world will shape our response to it.

The individual, the 'human agent', her or his biography and life experience in forming these responses seem to be undermined by K.J. Gergen's ideas of social constructionism. As the study has developed, the idea of understanding the individual nascent entrepreneur's ways of thinking, her or his cognitive processes of entrepreneurial learning and then moving to the collective venture community level, has become more and more crucial. Martin and Sugarman's (1996) theory of bridging paradigms, that is bridging constructivism and constructionism, has been instrumental in refining the discussion pertaining to the social constructionist position taken in this research.

5.2.4   Martin and Sugarman's (1996) Theory of '*Bridging Paradigms*'

In their article titled 'Bridging Social Constructionism and Cognitive Constructivism: A Psychology of Human Possibilities and Constraint', Martin and Sugarman (1996) present an argument, which is mainly concerned with understanding the emergence and development of the psychological (mind, selfhood, intentionality, agency) from its socio-cultural origins. Therefore, their theory of the emergence of the psychological incorporates social constructionist thoughts, but still leaves room for human agency, self and creativity (Martin and Sugarman, 1996). The major premise of their theory is that the private-individual and the public-social domains conjointly mark our existence and development as individual and collective beings.

They distinguish between cognitive constructivism and social constructionism by signifying the different disciplinary roots of these approaches. Constructivism has its roots in the psychology of the individual and social constructionism in the sociology of the collective and the social world. Adopting Martin and Sugarman's (1996, p. 292) stance in research, which explored the interrelationship between the owner-manager and the first line manager, Chell and Rhodes (1999) argue that Martin and Sugarman's (1996) notion of the 'bridging paradigm' provides an enabling framework to understand how the private and the public worlds interrelate. Their bridging paradigm places the individual as agent in a socio-cultural frame.

The key arguments of their bridging paradigm rest on a number of premises: the starting point is that the individual is viewed as arising from the socio-cultural, but is not reducible to the social. In other words, the individual's experience is constrained by the socio-cultural, but not fully explained or caused by it. Individual psychology is grounded in, and enabled by, a shared sociality of conversational and inter-relational practice (Martin and Sugarman, 1996, p. 296). Thoughts are passed relationally through conversation and this implies both a sharing of ideas, influencing processes of interrelating in practice that, through reflexive processes, individual psychology is externalised (Chell and Rhodes, 1996, p. 172). At the heart of Martin and Sugarman's thesis lies the notion of agentic consciousness and yet the idea that individual understanding can transcend the collective social determination, because of human capacities of memory and imagination:

> Once again, our basic thesis is that our individual psychology arises from the social but is not wholly determined by it. The ways in which we learn to construct and interpret our experiences as human agents have their origins in our status as social entities, as persons in interaction with others. Forms for human psychological constructions are available in socio-cultural practices. Human constructivism is constrained, but not completely determined by these practices. This is so because the ways in which we become instantiations of what our cultures conceive to be persons are subject to our own unique experiences as individuals, and how we come to interpret and integrate these experiences as self-understanding agents. Human beings develop the capacity to exercise genuine reflexivity and some degree of self-determination . . . The personal theories we come to hold about ourselves, others and our circumstances are underdetermined by experiential data accumulated during our lifetimes. The transformative capacity in human psychology, and the mutability of individual human agents – our ability to learn, to change, and to innovate – are made possible by this underdetermination (Martin and Sugarman, 1996, p. 298).

Given these key assumptions, their theory can be encapsulated by three major features: an acceptance of the fundamental social constructionist premise of conversational and inter-relational practices, personal theories that people develop over time, and human capacities for imagining and remembering.

The first feature is the idea that the forms for organising thought and enabling meaningful cognitive constructions of our experiences, our selves, and others are embedded in conversational and inter-relational practices. 'Acting as a conduit through which public-social and private-cognitive domains can intermingle; they provide the possibility for the reflexive consciousness that is characteristic of individual psychology' (Martin and Sugarman, 1996, p. 299).

Building on the reflexive nature of individual consciousness, enabled as well as constrained by the socio-cultural, the second feature is that individuals accumulate various symbolic and relational tools through their appropriation of socio-cultural practices and conventions. These tools enable and constrain the personal theories individuals construct and hold about their experiences, themselves and others (Martin and Sugarman, 1996, p. 299). Each individual uses a theory of self or ideal personhood, to reference a unique experiential history and reflect on past, present, and future intentions, expectations and actions (Martin and Sugarman, 1996, p. 300).

This links us to the third feature highlighted in their theory, which is human capacities to remember and imagine: 'Only by remembering and imagining elements of the conversations in which we participate are we furnished with the symbolic and relational tools we require to consider past experiences and previous learning, and to entertain future possibilities' (Martin and Sugarman, 1996, p. 300). Thus, there is scope for human agency in this view. Human beings genuinely reflect on their experiences and while much of that experience may be routine, some experience is novel and has to be construed. New experiences entail the development of new ideas and theory to express one's reality (Chell and Rhodes, 1999) and that is why people develop personal theories to understand and manipulate their reality. We, human beings, develop and use these personal theories primarily in a way that is responsive to others around us. This is what Shotter (1993a, 1995) calls 'rhetorical-responsive social constructionism'. It is rhetorical as the responsive ways of talking and acting can have the power to move people into action. He sees individuals and managers in his particular study (Shotter, 1995, pp. 144–45) as reflexive, knowledgeable, and socially accountable agents, concerned to be the authors of their own socially constructed individuality or interests.

5.3 ONTOLOGY, EPISTEMOLOGY AND METHODOLOGY

Given the debate on research paradigms in general and social constructionist paradigms in particular, this section summarises the ontological and epistemological roots of the current study and the links between these and methodology. The assumptions that we make about the nature of reality form the ontological positioning in research. How do we know what we know, in other words, the general set of assumptions about the ways of inquiring into the nature of the world comprise the epistemological grounding. Epistemology comprises assumptions about what constitutes knowledge and how it relates to the current focus of the investigation (Burrell and Morgan, 1979, p. 66). Based on these assumptions, researchers develop an overall research strategy and devise a combination of techniques to study social phenomena (Easterby-Smith et al., 2002); this is called methodology. Therefore, ontology, epistemology and methodology are all interrelated. The following quote from Hosking and Green (1999, p. 2) locate this notion of interconnectedness in the context of a social inquiry in a powerful way:

> Social inquiry is an ongoing (re)construction in activities such as research, writing, teaching and consulting, and conference presentations. All social practices reproduce certain taken-for-grantedness about what exists: this is the question of ontology. So, for example, practitioners of the human sciences construct people (with personal characteristics such as motives, and cognitive maps), organisations (with structures, and a mission) and environments (complex, turbulent . . .). Such constructions of existence go together with notions of what can be known of these things (epistemology), and how such knowledge might be produced (methodology).

5.3.1 Ontology

The social constructionist paradigm challenges the idea that the world has a reality of its own as positivists believe. Reality is socially constructed, produced by the members of a society in the course of social interaction (Haar and Hosking, 2004). It does not have any existence apart from the human beings who form and reform it over time in particular contexts (K.J. Gergen, 1994; Burr, 1995). It is shaped according to context and time. Therefore, as Guba and Lincoln (1981, 1989) put it, the reality of the individual, compared with another individual or to the same individual at a different time, is not more or less true in the absolute sense, rather more or less informed or sophisticated.

The process through which reality is produced and its emerging nature is very much of concern in the social constructionist genre. It has been argued above that it is through social interaction that individuals make sense of situations and develop their realities. In so doing, individuals reflect on their own life experiences as reflexive human agents (Martin and Sugarman, 1966). Berger and Luckmann (1966, p. 69) claim that 'men together produce a human environment'. This production process does not only comprise sense-making but also enacting. Weick (1979) terms this process 'enactment'. The enactment includes a series of negotiations between the members of a community. These negotiations are seen by Hosking and Ramsey (2000) as a natural part of social process, as processes of co-ordination. They argue that a degree of practical consensus is achieved in ongoing ways of co-ordinating. Knowledge is contested and socially constructed. The way people construct their knowledge and how consensus is achieved in social life, particularly in organisational life, is taken up by Watson (1994a, 1994b, 2001b, 2002, 2003), who views the processes of enactment at the heart of strategic exchange activities in life.

Human beings continuously attempt to discern the significance of things, and to forge meanings and understandings pertinent to their particular existential purposes and projects (Martin and Sugarman, 1996, p. 301). Over the life course, as people change environments and social contacts, they develop the capacity to reconstruct their lives in ways that enhance their present situations, relationships and needs (M. Gergen, 1994).

So, realities are constructed, exchanged, negotiated, accepted and enacted in a society through language (Watson, 1994a, 1997; Haar and Hosking, 2004). By language, Hosking and Ramsey (2000) refer to the realm of action and of social processes – a social communicative process that people do together (K.J. Gergen and Thatchenkerry, 1996). The language provides us with shared categories for separating our experience and giving it meaning, so that our very selves become the product of language (Shotter, 1993a, 1993b; Burr, 1995, p. 44). What is intelligible to one individual is intelligible to a fellow individual who shares the same language (Berger and Luckmann, 1966). Hence, the symbolic and relational tools we come to possess through our participation in socio-cultural milieus enable us to interpret and integrate our experiences meaningfully and gain some understanding of our circumstances (see Chell and Pittaway, 1998a). However, it should be noted that our interpretations are generated 'from within the bounds of our unique individual histories, recollections of which provide much of the substance for our personal theories of self' (Martin and Sugarman, 1996, p. 301).

5.3.2 Epistemology

What can be known of the nature of these realities and how it can be known, in other words what 'the relationship between the knower and known' is (Lincoln and Guba, 1985, p. 37) comprises the epistemological debates of the research. Epistemology is about fixing a set of assumptions about better ways of inquiring into the nature of the world (Easterby-Smith, 2002). Social constructionism is one of the epistemologies of social sciences, which does not assume any pre-existing reality. The social constructionist paradigm provides us with 'a frame of reference' (Watson, 2003, p. 1321) with a set of assumptions about the nature of reality, the 'known' (ontology), the nature of the relationship of knower to known (epistemology) and some ways of designing a social research (methodology). Hence, a particular way of viewing these interrelated notions of ontology, epistemology and methodology is embedded in the social constructionist premise.

Lincoln and Guba (1985) describe their naturalist version of epistemology; in their understanding, the inquirer and the 'object' of inquiry influence each other and therefore knower and known cannot be divorced from each other. The explanation of this statement is two-fold: first, one should distinguish between the social sciences and natural sciences in terms of 'what the object of inquiry is' and 'what it means to the scientists'. For example, when the 1999 Kocaeli earthquake happened in Turkey, it was important for seismologists to amplify the recording of the movement of the ground from aftershocks so that they could get a sense of whether another main-shock or more numerous aftershocks would follow. For geodesists, 'the 1999 earthquake' meant further examination of the North Anatolian fault, which has produced a sequence of major earthquakes in Turkey over the years. Using a wide variety of techniques, geodesists and seismologists worked to map the earthquake rupture and its effects. The data they collected were used to better understand how the buildings failed in the earthquake. Therefore, one can argue that the scientist can distance herself/himself from 'the object of inquiry'. The magnitude of the after-shocks will not be affected by how the seismologist feels or thinks about it. Likewise, the length of the broken fault and related measurements will not be influenced by the geodesist's opinions about it. For a lay person or sociologist, 'the 1999 earthquake' meant the total destruction of a town, whose residents were dead in thousands. It resulted in major evacuations and migration towards larger cities, mainly Istanbul. Examining such impacts of the earthquake on human lives, a sociologist would influence the research process and research findings through their interpretation of the meaning of this catastrophe to the community and possibly wider world. Second, this notion that 'the inquirer' and 'the object of inquiry' are inseparable, is traceable back to differences between positivists' and non-positivists' views of the world and epistemological approaches to understand the world, as discussed above (see section 5.2).

In social constructionist writings, this is reflected, as research being an ongoing construction process between research participants and research-ers, who continually interact and shape each other's understandings and actions (Burr, 1995; K.J. Gergen, 1999; Hosking and Ramsey, 2000). The research participants influence the researcher's access to key resources throughout the research process; they reveal or hide certain accounts of their personal and organisational life; they extend or restrain opportuni-ties for further research, and so on. The researcher by contrast, as the research instrument (Marshall and Rossman, 1999), defines the focus of the research and scopes and re-scopes it, as she or he engages in conversa-tions with research participants at different stages of the research. She or he brings in her own values, world view, experience and a set of relation-ships into the research process.

Given this understanding of epistemology, it is worth mentioning

Bourdieu's (1999, p. 614) ideas about this relationship. In his well-known article entitled 'Understanding', he explores the particular interaction between the researcher and the researched in studying social phenomena. Recognising this interactionist nature of research, he focuses on our responsibilities as researchers. Consistent with this view, he posits that the researcher is an integral part of the research; further, he points to the importance of the notion of being attentive and responsive to the accounts provided by the participants. He draws attention to would-be-distortions in a research act. He sees our responsibility in terms of putting in every effort in order to comprehend as best we can participants' understandings and perspectives. Otherwise, the researcher is likely to distort those understandings. Bourdieu (1999) articulates such a responsive approach in his following words: '. . . The welcoming disposition, which leads one to make the respondent's problems one's own, the capacity to take that person and understand them just as they are in their distinctive necessity, is a sort of intellectual love'. Furthermore, this 'intellectual love' may result in interesting research material:

> By offering the respondent an absolutely exceptional situation for communication, freed from the usual constraints (particularly of time) that weigh on most everyday interchanges, and opening up alternatives which prompt or authorise the articulation of worries, needs or wishes discovered through this very articulation, the researcher helps create the conditions for an extra-ordinary discourse, which might have never been spoken, but which was already there, merely waiting the conditions for its actualisation (Bourdieu, 1999, p. 614).

The critique of Bourdieu's view on conducting research can be two-fold. Firstly, can a researcher ever really understand another person (that is a participant) even if one lifts the constraints as suggested by Bourdieu through an interview process? Secondly, in an interview act, research participants make their own assumptions as to what the interviewer is trying to gather and respond accordingly, even if the researcher makes none or few assumptions about her participants. Therefore, what Bourdieu is suggesting above can hardly be attainable particularly if the only research method used is an interview. What a researcher can strive for is egalitarian connectedness rather than control (Roulston, deMarrais and Lewis, 2003; Kvale, 2006) and being a non-judgemental and collaborative researcher. Participant observation is a method that enables a researcher to be a normal part of the culture and the life of the people under study (Blumer, 1966) and therefore a combination of interviews and participant observation helps researchers reach a fuller understanding of their participants' world and experiences. The use of these methods in the current research is discussed in the final section of this chapter where the research methods are explained.

Viewing the research as an ongoing construction between the researcher and the participants adds such additional demands on the part of the researcher as put by Bourdieu. Hosking and Ramsey (2001) join this discussion by arguing that notions of ontology and epistemology are joined rather than treated as if separate in social constructionism. They articulate their view through an argument on 'reflexivity' which involves reflexive recognition by the researcher of her or his self and acting as a part of the inquiry process and what is constructed. They, therefore, view constructions of self and other as relational, that is related to each other and to the discursive practices of particular local and historically related cultures (Hosking and Ramsey, 2001). Chapter 6 will present an in-depth discussion on reflexivity. The reflexive researcher lets the research take its shape in relation to her or his participants and this process of discovery is called methodology. Table 5.1 summarises the paradigmatic assumptions upon which this research rests.

5.4   BOURDIEU'S PHILOSOPHY AND CONCEPTUAL TOOLS

The primacy over social relational processes is embedded in the social constructionist genre. The conceptual tools that Bourdieu proposed to explain such processes and approximate social reality at different levels (individual, collective and society) form the central focus in this final section of the chapter. Taking Burrell and Morgan's (1979) framework (ontology, epistemology, human behaviour and methodology), Bourdieu's philosophy and his conceptual frameworks, as applied in this research, are presented in this final section of the chapter.

5.4.1   Analysis of Bourdieu's Philosophy: Ontological, Epistemological, Human Behaviour and Methodological Assumptions

Pierre Bourdieu (1930–2002) was a French sociologist and philosopher. Engaging in a rich discussion of Bourdieu's relational perspective that forms the core of his sociological vision, Wacquant (1992, p. 16) traces his approach back to the works of Piaget, Jakobson and Levi-Strauss. Nash (1999) argues that Bourdieu's philosophy is also strongly influenced by the phenomenology of Schutz (1967). Given these arguments, Bourdieu's academic endeavour can be located in the historical context of the social science field of late 1950s France, which was dominated by the 'objective structuralism' of Levi-Strauss and the 'subjective' existentialism of Sartre (Jennings, 1992; Özbilgin and Tatli, 2005). Bourdieu has defined

Table 5.1 Summary of paradigmatic assumptions using Burrell and
Morgan's four dimensions

Paradigmatic assumptions (PA)	Social constructionist paradigm	Source (s)
PA1: Ontology: What is the nature of reality?	Reality is socially constructed, that is produced and sustained by the members of a society in the course of social interaction. It is not fixed rather emergent and it is reproduced in certain relational processes not others. Human agents continuously attempt to discern significance of things, and to forge meanings and understandings drawing on their unique individual recollections of the past and pertinent to their particular present and future life projects.	Berger and Luckmann (1966), K.J. Gergen (1985), K.J. Gergen (1994), Burr (1995), Sarbin and Kitsuse (1995), Martin and Sugarman (1996), Chell (2000), Hosking and Ramsey (2000), Watson (2003).
PA2: Epistemology: What can be known of these realities and what is the relationship between knower and known?	Reality does not have any existence apart from human beings who form and reform it over time in particular context. So, the reality of the individual, compared with another individual or to the same individual at a different time is not more or less true in the absolute sense, rather more or less informed or sophisticated. Hence, knowledge of the social world is produced and sustained through social processes in certain cultural and historical contexts. Knowledge and social action go together and knower and known cannot be separated from each other.	Berger and Luckmann (1966), K.J. Gergen (1985), Rosen (1991), K.J. Gergen (1994), Chell and Pittaway (1998a).
PA3: Human behaviour: Determinism or freedom of choice? Scope for human agency?	Human agency is not determined by the socio-cultural but acts within it. In other words, individual experience is constrained by the socio-cultural but not reduced to it. Human beings apply their understanding of social events, conversations and interpret them in	Martin and Sugarman (1996), Chell and Rhodes (1999).

Table 5.1 (continued)

Paradigmatic assumptions (PA)	Social constructionist paradigm	Source (s)
	the light of their own experiences. While much of that experience is routine and understood, some experience is novel and has to be construed. People may use the familiar to construct an experience of the unfamiliar, but new experience triggers the need to develop new ideas, new theory to explain one's reality. Hence, people develop personal theories to organise, anticipate, understand and manipulate their reality.	
PA4: **Methodology:** How might such knowledge of human behaviour or the social world be produced?	The aim of social constructionist research is then to generate insights into how members of a social group, through their life experience and participation in social processes, enact particular realities and endow them with meaning which is integral to behaviour. Research is therefore viewed as an ongoing construction between the researcher and the participants with an objective to explain what is typical to those individuals being studied in a certain socio-cultural milieu. Therefore, the research design calls for a qualitative research approach, which is grounded in a natural setting, inductive and case-oriented, with associated methods of data collection and analysis.	Lincoln and Guba (1985), Rosen (1991), Chell and Pittaway (1998a), Hosking and Ramsey (2000) and Patton (2002).

the objective of his scientific work as seeking to overcome the binary opposition between objectivism and subjectivism through a 'structuralist constructivism or constructivist structuralism' (Bourdieu and Wacquant, 1992, p. 11) by locating 'relations' as pre-eminent in researching social phenomena. This is called 'methodological relationalism' by Wacquant (1992, p. 15) who explains it in the following way:

Against all forms of methodological monism that purport to assert the onto-logical priority of structure or agent, system or actor, the collective or the individual, Bourdieu affirms the primacy of relations. In his view such dualistic alternatives reflect a common sensual perception of social reality of which sociology must rid itself. This perception is embedded in the very language we use which is better suited to express things than relations, states than processes (Wacquant, 1992).

At the ontological and epistemological levels, Bourdieu's philosophy portrays reality as relational, which can help to explain occurrences of certain structures. His relational epistemology involves three concepts: social position, disposition and position taking. He suggests that all social actors are continually situated in a 'social position' of superordinate, identical, or subordinate status in relation to others (Pinnington, Morris and Pinnington, 2003, p. 15). Having the emphasis on the relational nature of this social positioning, Bourdieu argues that these socially positioned actors engage in practices, which cannot be understood other than as interwoven activities carried out in a specific domain of practice, or field. Based on the distinction of status and class, his concept of 'field' denotes the relations among the totality of individual and organisational actors, who are positioned according to the economic, social, cultural and symbolic capital they hold, in functionally differentiated parts of society. Anheier, Gerhards and Romo (1995) locate 'field' at the meso-level. However, it is operationalised at the macro-level in this research, building on the works of Özbilgin, Kusku and Erdogmus (2005), Özbilgin and Tatli (2005) and Özbilgin (2006) who developed such a layered approach based on Bourdieu's work and applied it to organisation studies. In this research on nascent entrepreneurship, the field pertains to the field of enterprise culture, its institutions in general and higher education institutions that provide enterprise education and training as well as business incubation programmes in particular.

Bourdieu's concept of *habitus* is applied at the meso-level. Activities in a field are produced by dispositions, which are acquired under the spe-cific conditions characterising this field, produce actions that perpetuate the practices and conditions found there (Schatzki, 1997, p. 287). This is his idea of *habitus* which is defined as the actor's embodied, practi-cal knowledge and comprehension of the world. The notion of *habitus* includes collective ways of thinking and acting, as well as unconscious and automatic dispositions that are continuously subject to revision during practice (Bourdieu, 2000, p. 142). One should examine the similarities and differences between the concepts of 'culture' and *habitus*. From a social constructionist standpoint, 'culture' is defined by Bloor and Dawson (1994), as a patterned system of perceptions, meanings and beliefs in a society, which facilitates sense-making and constructions among a group of people sharing common experiences and informs individual behaviour. The interplay of individual behaviour with the communal meanings and beliefs is emphasised by this definition, which resembles the notion of *habitus*. However, *habitus*, as a concept, takes account of 'the individual' to a greater extent and acknowledges the role of individual history and human agency as will be further discussed in section 5.4.2.

Bourdieu's concepts of dispositions and *habitus*, in connection with rules, link us to his portrayal of human behaviour issues. Bouveresse (1999) gives an account of regularity that *habitus* and its related notions bring to social life. Nash (1999) points to the idea that every cultural act is regulated by a distinct principle: how these principles are formed are explained by Bourdieu in terms of how human beings develop a 'feel for the game'[2] and are able to make choices within the limits of what is made possible by the *habitus*. It is the recognition that sociological explanations of events and processes require a concept of culture that allows the 'principle that regulates the act' to be abstracted as the generative mechanism of practice (Nash, 1999, p. 179). This is more or less similar to Berger and Luckmann's (1966) idea on social habits and habitualisation, as discussed earlier. Bourdieu's own answer to the question of why he revived Berger and Luckmann's notion is as follows:

> Why did I revive that old word? Because with the notion of habitus you can refer to something that is close to what is suggested by the idea of habit, while differing from it in one important respect. The habitus, as the word implies, is that which one has acquired, but which has become durably incorporated in the body in the form of permanent dispositions. So the term constantly reminds us that it refers to something historical, linked to individual history.

The way Bourdieu (1993) puts it above reflects 'individual' aspects of *habitus* in the sense that individuals internalise such habits, norms and principles and develop a 'feel for the game', as a part of their personal becoming, which is inextricably linked to their social becoming. Taking on board Nash's (1999) focus on regularity in the social realm, Shusterman (1999, p. 5) views *habitus* as behavioural expression and meanings through social relationships, but without the need to articulate them explicitly through rules or reasons. Bourdieu (1990, p. 81) puts it in the following way:

> The social game is regulated, it is the locus of certain regularities. Things happen in regular fashion in it: rich heirs regularly marry rich younger daughters. That does not mean that it is a rule saying that rich heirs must marry rich younger daughters, even if you may think marrying an heiress (even a rich one, and a fortiori, a poor younger daughter) is an error, or even in the parents' eyes for example a misdeed. I can say that all my thinking started from this point:

how can behaviour be regulated without being the product of obedience to set rules?. . . In order to construct a model of the game, which will not be the mere recording of explicit norms, nor a statement of regularities, one has to reflect on the different modes of existence of the principles of regulation and the regularity of different forms of practice; there is of course habitus, that regulated disposition to generate regulated and regular behaviour outside any reference rules; and in societies where the work of codification is not particularly advanced, the habitus is the principle of most modes of practice.

Human agents acquire mastery of their social world by way of durable immersion within it. Relating to his theory of practice, 'practical sense' operates at the pre-objective level, meaning it expresses this social sensitivity, which guides human beings prior to our positing objects as such (Wacquant, 1992). The analogy between a social actor and a ball player is an illuminating one:

> Practical sense constitutes the world meaningful by spontaneously anticipating its immanent tendencies in the manner of the ball player endowed with great 'field vision' who, caught in the heat of action, instantaneously intuits the moves of his opponents and team-mates, acts and reacts in an 'inspired' manner without the benefit of hindsight and calculative reason (Wacquant, 1992, p. 21).
>
> Each manoeuvre undertaken by the player modifies the character of the field and establishes new lines of force in which the action in turn unfolds and is accomplished, again altering the phenomenal field (Merleau-Ponty, 1963, p. 169 cited in Wacquant, 1992).

The notion of *habitus* is acknowledged by some scholars (Layder, 1994; Rizardo, 2004) as a conception that enables Bourdieu to transcend the dichotomy of objectivism and subjectivism in the sense that it provides people with a sense of the 'feel for the game'. In the context of organisations, Weick and Roberts (1993) employ the term 'collective mind', which is conceptualised as a pattern of heedful interrelations of actions in a social system. In their view, as heedful interrelating and mindful comprehension increases, a smoother organisational life is lived by its participants (Chell, 2008). This is useful in the context of studying nascent entrepreneurs during the process of new organisation creation as a part of a wider social system. It is important to understand how their sense-making and interrelating evolve during the venturing process and if and to what extent such heedful interrelating and mindful comprehension can be achieved.

Nash (1999) takes the argument forward and discusses how *habitus* enables individual trajectories to be studied, for *habitus* has a history and discloses the traces of its origins in practice. In this wider understanding, *habitus* thus unites the past and the present for, while being the product of early experience, it is subject to the transformations brought about by subsequent experiences. These transformations are achieved by the individuals, who operate within the *habitus*, and therefore are constrained by it, but not reduced to it. Those individuals, who develop a feel for the game during their lifetime, construct their realities and personal theories reflexively by reflecting on their individual experiences, understandings and interpretations of the world. That's why the *habitus* is a dynamic and emerging concept.

Methodologically, if human practices are strongly influenced by a certain *habitus* and therefore all practices give evidence of the structures of the *habitus* that constrain and enable them, the implication for a researcher studying social processes in particular contexts is to analyse social practices in such a way that the principles of the generative *habitus* are disclosed (Nash, 1999, p. 178). Bourdieu's notion of '*habitus*' came out of his early ethnographic studies in Algeria at the end of the 1950s. The stance that Bourdieu takes regarding research methodologies is rooted in his initial practical training as an anthropologist. The nub of his argument is his view of theory as practical and therefore his support for the fusion of theoretical construction and practical research operations. According to Bourdieu (1999), every act of research is simultaneously empirical and theoretical. A coding decision, a questionnaire construction or an interview schedule, all involve theoretical choices, conscious or unconscious (Özbilgin et al., 2005). For him, it is important to bear in mind that theory inheres not in discursive propositions, but in the generative dispositions of the *habitus* of social scientists (Wacquant, 1992, p. 35).

Through his concept of *habitus*, Bourdieu is criticised by some scholars (Mennell, 1994; Hodkinson, 1999) as being predominantly concerned with 'we identity', thus placing Bourdieu on the meso- and macro- level of the debate. In other words, undertheorisation of the 'self' and the 'individual' is problematic in Bourdieu's work. A thorough examination and integration of his other concepts (such as forms of capital and dispositions), to the ideas of *habitus* and field, can provide an enabling framework for analysis at different levels. It is the aim of the next section to clarify these conceptual tools in order to encapsulate their use in the current research.

5.4.2 Bourdieu's Conceptual Tools

Given the introductory discussion on Bourdieu's core concepts of 'capital', 'dispositions', '*habitus*' and 'field', in this section we will attempt to elucidate them and locate his theoretical constructs at various levels of analysis by combining them with Layder's (1993, 1994) idea of the interplay between individual (micro), situated activity (meso-relational) and context (macro). Bourdieu (1977, 1986, 1990, 1993, 1998, 2000) proposed the concepts of 'capital' and 'dispositions' at micro-level, *habitus* at meso-relational level and the 'field' at macro-level of analysis as stated in the previous section. Özbilgin and Tatli (2005) have developed a multi-layered analysis of his conceptual tools and offered a way forward for the scholars of organisation and management studies, which allows for a reading of the interplay between individual choices, capacity and strategies with the socio-cultural milieu, in a way that does justice to its relational and dynamic qualities. Özbilgin et al. (2005) have applied such a multi-level framework in researching the career choices, values and burnout of MBA students based on an empirical study undertaken in Britain, Turkey, Greece and Israel. The current research on nascent entrepreneurship, which explores the underlying processes of business venturing based on entrepreneurial learning and managing as experienced by nascent entrepreneurs, attempts to further this movement in entrepreneurship studies.

The first concept that lies at the micro-individual level of analysis is 'capital'. Bourdieu's (1986) concept of 'capital' is broader than the notion of capital in economics. It is used in a more encompassing sense to represent 'resource' that can assume monetary and non-monetary, as well as tangible and intangible forms (Anheier et al., 1995). Harker, Mahar and Wilkes (1990) in their book *An Introduction to the Work of Pierre Bourdieu* note the encompassing nature of 'capital' in Bourdieu's conceptualisation:

> The definition of capital is very wide for Bourdieu and includes material things which can have symbolic value as well as 'untouchable' but culturally significant attributes such as prestige, status and authority (referred to as symbolic capital), along with cultural capital (defined as culturally-valued taste and consumption patterns) . . . For Bourdieu capital acts as a social relation within a system of exchange, and the term is extended to all the goods, material, and symbolic, without distinction, that present themselves as rare and worthy of being sought after in a particular social formation.

Bourdieu (1986) distinguishes between four types of capital on which individuals draw in order to pursue their life projects: economic, cultural, social and symbolic. Economic capital refers to monetary income and other financial resources and assets. Existing in various forms, cultural capital includes long-standing dispositions and *habitus* acquired in the socialisation process (Anheier et al., 1995, p. 862). It involves formal educational qualifications and training. Social capital refers to the sum of the actual and potential resources that can be deployed through membership in social networks (Bourdieu, 1986). The last form of capital is symbolic capital, which refers to the capacity to define and legitimise cultural, moral and ethical values, standards and styles (Bourdieu, 1986; Anheier et al., 1995). Bourdieu (1998, p. 47) stresses symbolic capital as the amalgam, and the situated value, of all other forms of capital that individuals draw on:

> Symbolic capital is any property (any form of capital whether physical, economic, cultural or social) when it is perceived by social agents endowed with categories of perception which cause them to know it and to recognise it, to give it value. For example, the concept of honour in Mediterranean societies is a typical form of symbolic capital which exists only through repute, that is, through the representation that others have of it to the extent that they share a set of beliefs liable to cause them to perceive and appreciate certain patterns of conduct as honourable and dishonourable.

Three forms of capital (economic, cultural and social) become socially effective as resources, and their ownership is legitimised, through the mediation of symbolic capital. Bourdieu's concept of social capital places the emphasis on conflicts and power function, that is social relations that increase the ability of an actor to advance her or his interests (Siisiainen, 2000, p. 2). Compared with Putnam's (1993) conceptualisation of social capital that has three components, including moral obligations and norms, social values and social networks, the focus is on the social struggles of individuals in a field, from Bourdieu's perspective. In other words, social capital becomes a resource in the social and economic struggles that are carried out in different social arenas or fields (Siisiainen, 2000). Human agents make choices and develop themselves in the pursuit of capital attainment in their fields. Webb, Schirato and Danaker (2002, p. 3) make the point that they 'adjust their expectations with regard to the capital they are likely to attain in terms of the practical limitations imposed upon them by their place in the field, their educational background, social connections, class position and so forth'. This notion of social capital pertains to the current study in terms of nascent entrepreneurs' economic and social endeavours in the field of enterprise culture and creative industries.

The concept of dispositions is the second concept at the micro-individual level. The concept offers three layers of meaning: as an outcome of an organising action, as a way of being as inhabitual existence and action, and finally as a tendency, propensity or inclination (Bourdieu, 1985, 1986, 1990, 1998). Dispositions are wider and more inclusive than the concept of 'attitudes' as they embody both habitual (automatic) and cognitive elements (Özbilgin et al., 2005). Bourdieu's conception of 'dispositions' is useful in understanding nascent entrepreneur's choices, motivations, decision making as well as cognitive learning experiences during business venturing. Table 5.2 illustrates the translation of these concepts to the current research.

Dispositions cannot be isolated from perceived structures, because they are acquired under the specific conditions producing actions that

Table 5.2   Translation of Bourdieu's theoretical constructs to the current research

Bourdieu's conceptual tools	Translation to the current research
Micro-individual level	**Nascent entrepreneur**
Dispositions, capital, position-taking	Biographies, capitals, dispositions, entrepreneurial motivations.
Meso-relational level	**Venture community**
Habitus	Team or network of entrepreneurs. Mentors, clients, suppliers, bankers, venture capitalists, officials of industrial or regional development agencies etc.
Macro-contextual level	**Enterprise culture and higher education context**
Field	Enterprise culture discourses, institutions, frameworks, HEIs.

perpetuate the practices and conditions (Schatzki, 1997). This is the idea of *habitus* as the meso-level construct as explained in the preceding section in order to illuminate the 'human behaviour' dimension of Bourdieu's philosophy. Bourdieu (1990, p. 53) defines *habitus* as:

> A system of durable, transposable dispositions, structured structures, predisposed to function as structuring structures, that is, as principles which generate and organise practices and representations that can be objectively adapted to their outcomes without presupposing a conscious aiming at ends or an express mastery of the operations necessary in order to attain them.

One can think of 'professions' and 'professional environments' as an example. For instance, a nurse adheres to certain principles in undertaking his or her job, such as protecting patients' privacy, not disclosing any information about patients to a third party and following other ethical principles of his profession. Nurses have a view of their profession, which has developed through education and training in the medical field and enact their relationships with their patients, peers, with other professions with whom they interact.

There are three key points that Bourdieu signifies through the concept of *habitus* (Webb et al, 2002, p. 38). Firstly, knowledge (the way we understand the world, our beliefs and values) is always constructed through the *habitus*. Secondly, we are disposed towards certain attitudes, values or ways of behaving due to the influence exerted by our cultural trajectories and these dispositions are transposable across fields. Thirdly, the *habitus* is always constituted in moments of practice. In other words, it is always of the moment, when a set of dispositions meets a particular problem, choice or context. It is a 'feel for the game' that is everyday life (Bourdieu, 1990, p. 54). Some scholars (Webb et al., 2002) argue that there is almost an understanding of unconscious 'taking in' of rules, values and dispositions through the notion of *habitus*. However, Bourdieu (1998, p. 80) explains 'the feel for game' as the attainment of 'practical sense' by the human agents, something that is both conscious and unconscious:

> Having a feel for the game is . . . to master in a practical way the future of the game, is to have a sense of the history of the game. While the bad player is off tempo, always too early or too late, the good player is the one who anticipates, who is ahead of the game.

What Bourdieu is illustrating is knowing the game that is played out between human agents, which involves a knowledge of various rules, genres, discourses, forms of capital, values and imperatives that inform human agents' practices and that are continuously being transformed by those agents and their practices (Webb et al., 2002). A person acquires *habitus* which is made up of a number of ways of operating, and inclinations, values and rationales that are acquired from various formative contexts, such as the family or the education system. Practices and the negotiations, deliberations and option-takings that produce them, are simultaneously conscious and unconscious. Human beings think and act in strategic ways, and try to use the rules of the game to their advantage, but at the same time they are influenced by the values and expectations that they get from *habitus* (Webb et al., 2004, p. 58). Bourdieu (1998) qualifies his notion of *habitus* with the following example:

> Habitus are generative principles of distinct and distinctive practices – what the worker eats, and especially the way he eats it, the sport he practices and the way he practices it, his political opinions and the way he expresses them are systematically different from the industrial owner's corresponding activities. But habitus are also classificatory schemes, principles of classification, principles of vision and division, different tastes. They make distinctions between what is good and what is bad, between what is right and what is wrong, between what is distinguished and what is vulgar, and so forth. But, the distinctions are not identical. Thus, for instance, the same behaviour or even the same good can appear distinguished to one person, pretentious to someone else, or cheap or showy to yet another.

Returning to the discussion on the difference between *habitus* and 'culture', as presented in section 5.4.1, the notion of *habitus* acknowledges the 'distinctions' between individuals in making sense of, interpreting or constructing the world around them. As Martin and Sugarman (1996) have pointed out, human beings that operate within a socio-cultural milieu develop the capacity to exercise genuine reflexivity and some degree of self-determination over their life course. The differences in their choices, capacities, capitals that they attain and strategies that they employ can be attributed to such individual level engagements. 'Culture' focuses on the collective, whereas *habitus* transcends the dichotomy between 'collective' and 'individual' by allowing an examination of the interplay of individual and collective behaviour. Individuals possess some agency, even when following conventionally laid down paths shaped by *habitus*.

As highlighted by Özbilgin et al. (2005), the example of a worker that Bourdieu gives in the above quotation illuminates the context specificity of distinctions and the generative capacity of *habitus* as a meso-level construct, which accounts for the interplay of individual dispositions and capital with the context, which Bourdieu (1998) symbolises as the 'field'. Hence, the final concept 'field' lies at the macro-level of analysis. Bourdieu's conception of field is not used in the sense of domain, but rather as a 'field of forces', because it is important to see the field as dynamic, where human agents struggle to accumulate different capitals that will influence their positions within the field (Harker et al., 1990). These struggles are seen as transforming or maintaining the field of forces. 'Positions once attained can interact with *habitus* to produce different postures, which have an impact on the economics of "position-taking" within the field' (Harker et al., 1990, p. 8). Swartz (1997) delineates the 'field' as an important component of Bourdieu's relational methods:

> The concept of field at the macro-level of analysis is also instrumental in understanding Bourdieu's conception of relational methods. 'Fields denote arenas of production, circulation, and appropriation of goods, services, knowledge or status, and the competitive positions held by actors in their struggle to accumulate and monopolise these different kinds of capital. Fields may be thought of as structured spaces that are organised around specific types of capital or combinations of capital. For example, Bourdieu speaks of the intellectual field to designate that matrix of institutions, organisations, and markets in which symbolic producers, such as artists, writers, and academics, compete for symbolic capital. Even science itself – the self-proclaimed highest expression of objectivity – is produced within the framework of a field.

The implications of using the concept of field for methodology are discussed by Harker et al. (1990) and Barnard (1990). Harker et al. (1990) connect it with time and space issues, which are viewed as fundamentally significant in social constructionist research (Chell, 2000). The notion of field denotes 'social space' which refers to an overall conception of the social world comprising multiple fields that have some relationships to each other and points of contact. The social space of the individual is connected through time (life trajectory) to a series of fields, within which people struggle for various forms of capital (Harker et al., 1990, p. 9).

As pointed out by Barnard (1990), we, researchers, also occupy a position that is not outside the game when undertaking social science research. 'The objects of analysis within the field are the stakes in the game (capital), the strategies, the objectified histories of the agents (their positions and *habitus*) including, ineluctably, that of the sociologist' (Barnard, 1990, p. 78). The conceptual tools, that is dispositions, capital, position taking, *habitus* and field, constitute Bourdieu's (1998) generative formula in his relational method which entails the examination of the interplay between all these aspects of social life. 'This formula, which might seem abstract or obscure, states the first conditions for an adequate reading of the analysis of the relation between social positions (a relational concept), dispositions (or *habitus*), and position-takings (*prises de position*), that is, the "choices" made by the social agents in the most diverse domains of practice' (Bourdieu, 1998, p. 6).

Defining *habitus* as generative principles of context-specific practices, Bourdieu does not do justice to the inclusive nature of *habitus* in the above explanation by equating dispositions with *habitus*. As argued throughout sections 2.5.1 and 2.5.2, '*habitus*' is considered as a meso-level construct since it is a more encompassing concept that includes more than individual dispositions.

Drawing on these conceptual tools and combining these three levels of analysis (micro, meso-relational and macro), the reflexive relationship between nascent entrepreneurs and situations through which entrepreneurial motivations and intentions are realised by forming new ventures can be studied. Making sense of nascent entrepreneurs' business venturing experience and that of their entrepreneurial learning requires an examination of the interwoven nature of the relationship between their life histories, experiences, and capitals, in Bourdieu's sense, that they have accumulated so far and they are eager to accumulate in the future; positions that they endeavour to attain, and their *habitus* in terms of generative practices in a venture community and perceived opportunities and constraints within the regional and national domain of enterprise culture and higher education context which constitute the 'field'.

5.5   CONCLUSIONS TO THE CHAPTER

In this chapter, we have discussed the social constructionist paradigmatic stance taken in this research. Adopting Burrell and Morgan's (1979) dimensions in defining research paradigms, the paradigmatic assumptions (ontology, epistemology, human behaviour and methodology) have been amplified. 'Reality' as a social construct, that is to say, as produced and sustained by the members of a society who draw on their own labelling, remembering and imagining capacities in the light of their life experiences and projects, in the course of social interaction, is acknowledged at the ontological level. The emerging, relational and strategic construction of reality is emphasised. This paves the way for the scope of human agency in this construction process, which is often undermined by social constructionist writings.

Taking Martin and Sugarman's (1996) position, it has been argued that human agents continually attempt to discern the significance of things, situations and to forge meanings and understandings drawing on their unique individual recollections of the past and pertinent to their particular present and future life projects. What can be known of these realities, as the question pertaining to epistemology, finds answers in a relativistic and contextualised understanding of reality and knowledge: the reality of the individual compared with another individual, or to the same individual, at a different time and space, is not more or less true in an absolute sense, rather more or less informed or sophisticated. Knowledge of the social world is then produced, sustained and transformed through cognitive and social processes in a certain space over time. Individual experience is influenced by the social space – the socio-cultural – but not reduced to it. There is room for human agency in considering this reflexive nature of relationships. The methodological positioning concerns producing knowledge of human behaviour and relationships in a social constructionist way such that it would shed light on how nascent entrepreneurs as members of a venture community through their life experience and participation in social processes create and enact particular realities of business venturing and endow them with meaning. This implies the notion of research as an ongoing construction between the researcher and the participants with an objective of illuminating what is typical to those individuals being studied in a certain socio-cultural milieu.

Bourdieu's conceptual tools of dispositions, capital and position taking at the micro-individual level, *habitus* at the meso-relational level and field at the macro-level are viewed as enabling frameworks in this research. They allow for a layered analysis of the business venturing experience of nascent entrepreneurs with special attention paid to underlying processes of entrepreneurial learning and managing unfolding within a field characterised by enterprise culture, entrepreneurship education and support discourses. Given this methological foundation for the study, in the next chapter we turn to research design and the methods that were applied in conducting the fieldwork.

NOTES

1. The idea for multiple levels of analysis in organisation and management studies is advocated in the writings of Danserau, Yammarino and Kohles (1999), Drazin, Glynn and Kazanjian (1999) and Morgeson and Hofmann (1999) in a special issue of the *Academy of Management Review*. The need for multiple levels of analysis in entrepreneurship research is acknowledged by Davidsson and Wicklund (2001) and Davidsson (2004).
2. The metaphor of the game was introduced by Wittgenstein (1978) and was also referred to as the 'form of life' (see also Chell, 2008, p. 191).

6. Research design and methods

6.1 INTRODUCTION TO THE CHAPTER

This chapter presents the research design based on 'naturalistic inquiry' and an overview of social constructionist paradigmatic assumptions, research questions, associated methods of data collection and analysis, and criteria applied for establishing trustworthiness of this qualitative study. Defining research as a collaborative experience between the parties involved (the researcher, participants and users of research), the notion of reflexivity is crucial and is elaborated further in this chapter. Reflexivity calls for self-awareness of the reflexive screens that actors (researcher, participants and readers) have in a research act and that of the implications on constructing the research text. Reflexive screens are formed by a researcher's background, world-view and the scientific position taken.

6.2 SOCIAL CONSTRUCTIONIST PARADIGM LEADING TO RESEARCH DESIGN AND METHODS

The world can be understood only through human experience that is historically and culturally embedded (K.J. Gergen, 1985, 1994; Burr, 1995; Chell, 2008; Chell and Pittaway, 1998a). Revisiting the social constructionist assumptions as laid out in the previous chapter, knowledge and understanding of human experience are contextual and generated and sustained through social processes. K.J. Gergen (2001) asserts that social constructionism allows researchers to 'explore alternative understandings of "what is the case" and to locate meanings that enable us to go on in more adequate ways'. With a concern for holistic and detailed understandings of social processes embedded in certain settings, and a commitment to participants' interpretation of their experiences, we have adopted naturalistic inquiry as the overarching research design in this study. The associated research methods include observation, interviews, documentary analysis and research diaries. Table 6.1 shows the paradigmatic assumptions and

Table 6.1 Social constructionist paradigm leading to methods

	Research concern	Research questions	Themes/concepts	Research methods
Investigation of the social construction of the business venturing process	Social construction of business venturing process: Entrepreneurial activities Nascent entrepreneurs' commitment to the process and engagement with the activities	What is the nature of the business venturing process as experienced by nascent entrepreneurs? How do the selected nascent entrepreneurs view the process in terms of its salient characteristics? What are the processes of social construction involved?	Micro-level qualities: Nascent entrepreneurs' biographies, capitals, dispositions and cognitive frameworks Meso-relational level qualities: Business venturing process	In-depth interviews with nascent entrepreneurs Participant observation Making sense of business plans and other company documents such as memos and meeting notes
Investigation of the process of entrepreneurial learning	Underlying processes of business venturing: Entrepreneurial learning Entrepreneurial managing	How do nascent entrepreneurs develop meanings/ understandings/actions engaged in entrepreneurial activities of venturing? What are the important facets of their entrepreneurial learning experience?	Meso-relational level qualities: Process-relational characteristics of entrepreneurial learning and managing Generating a *habitus* by creating a venture community	Participant observation Interviews with nascent entrepreneurs Interviews with other key actors constituting venture community

Investigation of the relation of business venturing to enterprise culture and enterprise education	Enterprise culture and its associated institutions (universities in particular) and programmes (mainly education, training and incubation programmes)	How do the aforementioned processes (business venturing and entrepreneurial learning) relate to the enterprise culture in the UK, with its higher education institutions (providing a variety of forms of enterprise education or business support and development services)?	Macro-level qualities: Field of enterprise culture and its institutions – higher education institutions – and education/ business support programmes	Interviews with university incubator managers, enterprise educators and mentors

research questions leading to methods, conveying the sense of interrelationships between such key components of the research.

6.3   NATURALISTIC INQUIRY

Concurring with the social constructionist underpinnings, Lincoln and Guba's (1985, p. 228) naturalistic inquiry is made up of 14 axioms:

1.   Natural setting
2.   Human instrument
3.   Use of tacit knowledge
4.   Qualitative methods
5.   Purposive sampling
6.   Inductive data analysis
7.   Grounded theory
8.   Emergent design
9.   Negotiated outcomes
10. Case study reporting mode
11. Idiographic interpretation
12. Tentative application
13. Focus-determined boundaries
14. Special criteria for trustworthiness

Determining a focus for the inquiry is the starting point and as such focusing establishes the boundaries for a study. It defines the terrain and it should fit with the paradigm chosen. However, it cannot be overemphasised, 'those boundaries are not concrete; they can be altered and, in the typical naturalistic inquiry, will be' (Lincoln and Guba, 1985, p. 229). Similarly, the research design should emanate from the research itself, that is to say, the research design is emergent in order to allow for flexibility, once the fieldwork has begun. 'The naturalist expects such changes and anticipates that the emergent design will be coloured by them. Far from being destructive, they are constructive, for these changes signal movement to a more sophisticated and insightful level of inquiry' (Lincoln and Guba, 1985, p. 188).

The research takes the form of successive iterations of four elements: purposive sampling, inductive analysis of data obtained from the sample, development of grounded theory based on the inductive analysis, and projection of next steps in a constantly emerging design. 'The iterations are repeated as often as necessary until redundancy is achieved, the theory is stabilised and the emergent design fulfilled to the extent possible in view

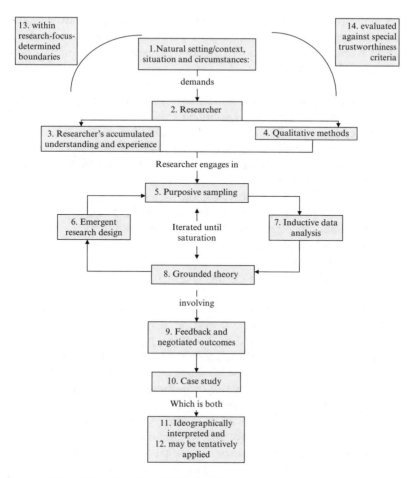

Source: Adapted from Lincoln and Guba (1985).

Figure 6.1 Naturalistic inquiry

of time and resource constraints. Throughout the inquiry, the data and interpretations are checked with participants and the accounts generated are repeated as case studies' (Lincoln and Guba, 1985). Therefore, the research is a collaborative experience, whereby findings are constructed in the course of the interaction with the participants and referred back to them. Special criteria are used for testing the worth of research as will be elucidated later. The diagrammatic illustration of the naturalistic inquiry is made in Figure 6.1, showing the interrelated nature of the 14 axioms and conveying the sense of progression through the research process itself.

A reinterpretation of naturalistic inquiry is provided by Patton (2002), who offers a more accessible, applicable and encompassing framework. He puts forward 11 characteristics of qualitative research based on naturalistic inquiry. These include:

1. Openness, responsiveness and flexibility through emergent designs
2. Focus through purposeful sampling
3. In-depth inquiry that generates rich qualitative empirical data
4. Richness and depth through personal engagement
5. Balancing the critical and creative through an empathic stance of understanding the case
6. Sensitivity to dynamic processes and systems
7. Appreciation of idiosyncrasies through a unique case orientation
8. Insight and understanding through inductive analysis
9. Contextual sensitivity
10. Holistic perspective
11. Trustworthiness through ownership of voice and perspective

These elements and their pertinence to the current research are explained in Table 6.2. These are strategic ideals that provide a direction and framework for developing a qualitative study. In practice, as noted by Patton (2002) and others (Guba, 1978; Lincoln and Guba, 1985), implementing naturalistic inquiry is always a matter of degree. Guba (1978) makes this point by depicting the practice of naturalistic inquiry as a wave on which the researcher moves from varying degrees of a 'discovery mode' to varying emphasis of 'verification mode'. As the fieldwork starts, the researcher takes an open stance and lets the data emerge, which reflects a discovery or inductive approach. As the patterns and major themes of interest are revealed, the researcher begins to focus on verifying and elucidating what appears to be emerging, which can be described as a more deductive approach to data collection and analysis (Patton, 2002).

This is, in fact, what lies at the heart of a 'grounded theory' approach as put forward by Glaser and Strauss (1967), who argued for the concepts of 'fit' and 'work'. What is discovered may be verified by going back to the study and examining the extent to which the emergent analysis 'fits' the phenomenon and 'works' to explain what has been observed. The term 'verification' has positivistic connotations. Therefore, instead of 'verification', the chosen term to describe this analytical process in this study is 'constant comparison', which serves the purpose of 'checking emergent patterns and interrelationships' throughout the concurrent processes of data analysis and writing-up. This will be further elucidated in section 6.6.

Table 6.2   Qualities of naturalistic inquiry based on Patton's framework (2002)

Qualities of naturalistic inquiry	Patton's description	Application in this research
Emergent research design and flexibility	Openness to adapting inquiry as understanding deepens; researcher pursues new paths of discovery as they emerge	Research design
Purposeful sampling	Cases for study are selected because they are 'information rich' and illuminative; they offer useful manifestations of the phenomenon under study. This may entail dropping certain cases in order to construct high-quality material	Selection of participants
Qualitative empirical data	Inquiry in depth, observations that yield detailed, 'thick' description; interviews that capture direct quotations about people's experiences and perspectives and careful review of texts	Participant observation In-depth interviews Analysis of documents Research diary
Researcher's understanding, knowledge, experience and engagement with the research participants	The researcher as the research instrument; direct contact with and gets close to, people, situations and phenomena of interest; the researcher's personal experiences and insights are an integral part of the inquiry	Reflexivity
Empathic and egalitarian neutrality and mindfulness	An empathic and egalitarian stance in interviewing seeks vicarious understanding without judgement by showing openness, sensitivity, respect, awareness and responsiveness; in observation it means being fully present (mindfulness)	Conduct of participant Observation and interviews
Dynamic and complex processes	Attention to process; assumes change as an ongoing process whether focus is on an individual, an organisation or a community; therefore mindful of, and attentive to, situation and context dynamics	Longitudinal participant observation Analysis of context dynamics

Table 6.2   (continued)

Qualities of naturalistic inquiry	Patton's description	Application in this research
Unique case orientation	Assumes each case is unique; the first level of analysis does justice to, and captures, the details of the individual cases under study; cross-case analysis follows from, and depends on, the quality of individual cases	Construction of case accounts
Inductive data analysis and creative synthesis	Immersion in the details and specifics of data to explore salient themes, patterns and interrelationships; begins by exploring, then comparing; guided by analytical principles rather than rules and ends with creative synthesis	Data analysis
Holistic and relational perspective	The whole phenomenon under study is understood as a complex system; focus on complex interrelationships and dynamics rather than cause-effect relationships	Case accounts
Context sensitivity and transferability to other contexts	Locates findings in a social, historical and temporal context; the possibility or meaningfulness of generalisations across time and space; emphasises instead careful comparative case analyses and extrapolating patterns for possible transferability and adaptation in new settings	Analysis of enterprise culture in the UK Case accounts
Trustworthiness through voice, perspective, credibility, reflexivity and transferability	The naturalistic qualitative inquirer owns, and is reflective about, her own voice and perspective; a credible voice conveys authenticity and trustworthiness; the researcher's task is to balance understanding and depicting the world in all its complexity, while being self-analytical and reflexive in consciousness	Research methodology

The nub of the argument is that it is important to recognise the nature of a qualitative inquiry in terms of discovery and verification of meaning, moving back and forth between induction and deduction, between experience and reflection on experience, and the practicalities of research that affect the extent to which a researcher can implement the aforementioned characteristics of a naturalistic inquiry. For example, closeness to, and involvement with, the people under study should be viewed as variable – varying according to the practicalities of fieldwork and yet moving back and forth between greater and lesser degrees of naturalistic investigation. Table 6.2 depicts Patton's framework with an emphasis on its application in this research. The type of the application is shown in the table. However, the degree to which these are applied will be revealed throughout case studies presented in Chapters 7 and 8.

6.4 REFLEXIVITY

Cunliffe (2003, p. 983) notes that 'reflexivity' is a notion, which has emerged within many disciplines, such as philosophy, linguistics, the natural sciences, sociology, psychology and recently in organisation and management studies (Watson, 1995; Calas and Smircich, 1999; Easterby-Smith and Malina 1999; Alvesson and Skoldberg, 2000; Johnson and Duberley, 2003; Cassell, 2005). In this section we explore what reflexivity means in the conceptualisation of research as a collaborative process between the researcher and the researched. Reflexivity is the process of critical awareness of the self as researcher, the human instrument (Guba and Lincoln, 1981) and therefore that of exploring the dynamics of the relationship between researcher and researched (Finlay, 2002). It is the scrutiny of 'how we personally engage with the inquiry', which forms the sixth question of any qualitative inquiry, as suggested by Patton (2002). See Chapter 1 for the discussion on the remaining five questions and their applications in the current research.

Reflexivity forces researchers 'to come to terms not only with our choice of research concern and those with whom we engage in the research process, but with ourselves and with the multiple identities that represent the fluid self' in the research setting (Alcoff and Potter, 1993 cited in Lincoln and Guba, 2000, p. 183). We all have many selves we bring with us to social situations, but, in the context of research, Reinharz (1997, p. 5) specifies these selves under three categories: research-based selves, brought selves and situationally created selves. Research-based selves are those we construct in a research act when we interact with our participants.[1] Brought selves are the selves that historically, socially and personally create our world-views, and perspectives. We bring these perspectives into specific research contexts, which, in turn, leads to construction of situationally created selves. Each of these selves comes into play in the research setting and consequently has a distinctive voice (Lincoln and

Guba, 2000). A somewhat similar argument can be presented by building on Bourdieu's (1977, 1990, 1993, 1998) ideas pertaining to the relational approach to qualitative studies. As explained in Chapter 5, Bourdieu uses a relational analysis for his explication of social phenomena, which situates individuals in their respective social positions based on both the volume and composition of their social capital. For Bourdieu (1977, 1993, 1999, 2003) reflexivity demands systematic reflection by the researcher aimed at revealing how her formative social location or habitat, to which there is a corresponding *habitus* or set of embodied dispositions and assumptions, influences the production of an analytically constructed account (Johnson and Duberley, 2003, p. 1289). Therefore, researchers should be aware of their own dispositions shaped by the norms, values and other regulatory forces of a particular scientific field. This is called 'epistemic reflexivity' by Bourdieu (1999, 2003) and the following is a powerful articulation of what it means in management and organisation research by Johnson and Duberley (2003, p. 1289):

> . . . management research cannot be carried out in some intellectual space which is autonomous from the researcher's own habitus. Indeed it would seem that epistemic reflexivity must relate to how a researcher's own social location affects the forms and outcomes of research as well as entailing acceptance of the conviction that there will always be more than one valid account of any research. Therefore, a key role of epistemic reflexivity is to negate the world as an objectively accessible social reality and denaturalise hegemonic accounts by exposing their modes of social organisation and reproduction.

As noted by a number of scholars (Hardy and Clegg, 1997; Holland, 1999; Johnson and Duberley, 2003) reflexivity entails some form of scrutiny of the presuppositions, which organisation researchers have internalised as members of particular research communities and will inevitably deploy in both constructing and disseminating research accounts to others in those communities. Further explication of the concept of reflexivity is provided by Johnson and Duberley (2003) who distinguish between various forms of reflexivity (such as methodological, deconstructive and epistemic reflexivity) underpinned by certain paradigmatic positions taken in research. Furthermore, Finlay (2002) discusses the multitude of ways in which reflexivity can be understood and exercised in conducting qualitative research. Our interpretation of these views to a research setting includes more than the revelation and reflection on our academic and philosophical underpinnings; rather it encompasses the awareness of the positions we hold as researchers in relation to our participants, to our data and, furthermore, to our audience.

A postmodern argument for reflexivity (see Chia, 1996a; Rhodes and

Brown, 2005) would go further and suggest that reflexivity demands that 'we interrogate each of our selves regarding the ways in which research efforts are shaped and staged around the binaries, contradictions, and paradoxes that form our own lives' (Lincoln and Guba, 2000, p. 183). Importance of self-awareness, political/cultural consciousness and ownership of one's perspective are all emphasised by the debates surrounding reflexivity in qualitative research (Patton, 2002). In MacBeth's (2001, p. 35) words:

> In the rush of interest in qualitative research in the past 15 years, few topics have developed as broad a consensus as the relevance of analytic 'reflexivity'. By most accounts, reflexivity is a deconstructive exercise for locating the intersections of author, other, text, and world, and for penetrating the representational exercise itself.

The form of reflexivity we expound in this research is guided by social constructionism, which unsettles representation of the world by suggesting that we are constantly constructing meaning and social realities as we interact with others and talk about our experiences. This view entails a relational approach leading to an explicit focus on the reflexive engagement with ourselves, the research participants, data and research audience – in other words, awareness of the importance and implications of myself as a researcher, my biography, critical standpoints and values on the research process, as well as awareness of the participants and that of the research audience, namely readers. Reflexivity is the ethical responsibility of a researcher. Payne (2000) provides a fuller discussion on reflexivity raised in terms of moral knowledge construction. Guillemin and Gillam (2004) portray a notion of reflexivity as a helpful way of understanding both the nature of ethics in qualitative research and how ethical practice in research can be achieved.

6.5   RESEARCH METHODS USED

From Czarniawska's (1997, p. 21) narrative standpoint, fieldwork is an expression of the curiosity of other, about people who construct their worlds differently from the way researchers construct theirs. The fieldwork was undertaken with an emphasis on understanding the world of nascent entrepreneurs from their perspectives, whilst they engage in the venturing activities. Hence, a number of qualitative methods were triangulated to generate rich accounts of these real-world situations, as they unfold naturally. The participant observation, in-depth interviewing and analysis of business documents were the main data generation methods, as illustrated in Table 6.3.

Table 6.3   Research questions, research cases and methods used to construct the case accounts

Research questions	Research cases	Methods
	KBrandArt	**Participant observation**
1) What is the nature of the business venturing process? What are the salient characteristics? Who are nascent entrepreneurs and how do they engage in venturing activities?	Participants: Nascent entrepreneurs: Denise, Adam, Luke, Charles, Paul and the account manager, Norman, they employed later	Attendance at the venture team meetings on every Monday (usually) for ten months Attendance at the INO meetings (three meetings) Attendance at the meetings where the nascent entrepreneurs were getting prepared for a pitch (four meetings)
2) How do nascent entrepreneurs develop meanings/ understandings/ actions while engaged in such entrepreneurial activities of new venture creation?	Key actors in the broader venture community: Participants through the Industrial Networking Organisation (INO) meetings: Martin (city council representative), Simon (another entrepreneur who set up a business in the creative industries (CI), Mike (another CI entrepreneur-copywriter), Peter (the solicitor who sets out the legal foundation) and Kelly (another nascent entrepreneur who is forming her business in the CI)	**Interviews** Interviews with the venture team members (nascent entrepreneurs – three interviews with Denise, the managing director) Interviews with the INO participants **Documentary analysis** Business plans for KBrandArt and INO Client presentation slides Internal memos Meeting notes (that fed into meetings) Press releases Website content
3) How do the above processes of business venturing and entrepreneurial learning relate to UK enterprise culture, with its particular education and business support programmes[1]?	**R-Games** Participants: Nascent entrepreneur: Rosie and her mentor Richard (who came and made an important interjection during the interview with Rosie)	**Participant observation** Observing the setting and her interaction with the mentor and clients over the phone **Interview** An in-depth interview that lasted for two hours **Documentary analysis** Operational documents on the wall (slides laying out the different aspects of business planning) and press releases

Note:
1. To address the third question, four interviews with university incubator managers and enterprise educators were carried out, in addition to the interviews that are used to construct the case studies. Two interviews were undertaken with the creative industries business officers of a local council and an RDA.

6.5.1 Participant Observation

As an important aspect of naturalistic inquiry, the notion of purposive sampling equally applies to selecting organisational sites, interviewing participants and observing situations. We have been interested in non-verbal elements of the research setting, interactions between the venture team members and other stakeholders in a wider community, and accounts and organisational discourse they were creating. Thus, observation had a particular value in this research. This quality of observation is highlighted by Spradley (1980), Marshall and Rossman (1999), and Mason (2002). We sought to discover complex interactions in natural social settings where people continuously negotiated the definition of social reality.

Steyaert and Bouwen (1997) argue that participant observation does not only shape the inquiry towards certain types of data collection but also facilitates it. Observing a meeting, for instance, allows the researcher to come in contact with the evolution of the different voices, as they develop and emerge in a living social context, expressing the construction of shared meaning (Gray, Bougon and Donnellon, 1985). Guba and Lincoln (1981) state:

> observation . . . allows the inquirer to see the world as his subjects see it, to live in their time frames, to capture the phenomenon in and on its own terms, and to grasp the culture in its own natural, ongoing environment (p. 193)

Observation can range from a highly structured notation of behaviour to more holistic descriptions of events (Marshall and Rossman, 1999; Angrosino and Perez, 2000). Observations, like interviews, are likely to take different forms at different stages of the inquiry (Lincoln and Guba, 1985, p. 275). Whatever the form is, it enables researchers to discover recurring patterns of relationships in the early stages of inquiry. After such patterns are identified and described through early analysis of field notes, checklists become more appropriate and context sensitive (Marshall and Rossman, 1999). Later, they may become more focused as insights grow.

Nevertheless, the method has certain disadvantages. First, it requires a great deal of the researcher. Second, ethical dilemmas, discomfort and even danger, and managing a relatively unobtrusive role make it highly difficult to accomplish (Marshall and Rossman, 1999; Silverman, 2005). Therefore, the question of 'which role a researcher is going to play' arises. These roles include observer as participant, participant as observer, 'complete' observer and 'complete' participant (Walsh, 2004, p. 229). The role of 'complete participant' entails complete covert research during which the observer, as a competently participating member of the social situation, is likely to generate a holistic knowledge of the situation on the one hand, but be hedged in by the expectations of the role she has adopted on the other hand (Marshall and Rossman, 1999; Walsh, 2004). The 'complete observer' simply observes people in ways that avoid social interaction with the observed. This reduces the possibilities of people reacting to be observed or of 'going native', but introduces another problem. The use of the term 'complete' is problematic in Walsh's classification of the roles of researchers. Degrees of immersion in the situation define the role of the researcher as participant or observer, observers being more distant and participants experiencing different degrees of knowledge and understanding.

The observer, by not interacting with the people under study, cannot reach a fuller understanding of their talk or actions (Junker, 1960 cited in Walsh, 2004; Bottorff, 2004). The 'participant as observer' role relies on a mutual understanding of a fieldwork relationship between the observer and the people being studied. This minimizes the problems of pretence. The final role, 'observer as participant', shifts the balance in favour of observation over participation, which prevents the researcher from going native but restricts understanding because limited participation in social activities heightens the possibilities of superficiality, so that important lines of inquiry may be missed (Walsh, 2004). One of the authors, who carried out the fieldwork, took a position of a 'participant as observer' at the outset of the fieldwork, where the nascent entrepreneurs and other pertinent social actors in the research setting were aware that the relationship was a field relationship, which relied on gaining access and establishing good working relations.[2] Walsh (2004, p. 230) notes that the 'participant as observer role' involves an emphasis on participation and social interaction in order to produce a relationship of rapport and trust. The problem, as Walsh (2004) and others (Gold, 1958; Bogdewic, 1999; Angrosino and Perez, 2000) have raised, is that it carries the danger of 'going native' through identification with the participants of the study. This problem was overcome by restraining the intimacy created in the social interaction, in order to maintain the role of the outsider on the part of the observer. To put it simply, establishing rapport and good relationships with the participants always involved putting up appropriate boundaries.

In Patton's (2002, p. 319) words, 'as the fieldwork progresses the intricate web of human relationships can entangle the participant observer in ways that will create tension between the desire to become more enmeshed in the field setting to learn more, and the need to preserve some distance and perspective'. This was a fine balance that needed to be observed during the fieldwork. For example, towards the end of the fieldwork, the team leader of the observed venture team, Denise,[3] introduced one of us at a meeting where external attendees were involved by using the following expression in a very convivial manner: 'This is Mine, from the University of Derby.[4] She is working with us'. This was such an important moment for us in the fieldwork, which proved to us that we had established rapport with the research participants. The expression 'working with us' also portrayed the venture team as 'larger', which helped the nascent entrepreneur in pursuing the act of 'legitimising the enterprise', as will be explored in Chapter 7, in which the analysis of the case account is presented.

The role of the researcher has its roots in the epistemological stance taken in the research. However, it provides an answer to the question of which roles are appropriate. The other question, which is frequently experienced by the researcher, is 'what roles are possible' (Marshall and Rossman, 1999). Fieldwork is permeated with the conflict between what is theoretically desirable on the one hand, and what is practically possible, on the other (Buchanan, Boddy and MacCalman, 1988). Therefore, fieldwork is constantly compromised by the practical realities, opportunities and constraints presented by the research on organisations in general and on newly founded organisations in particular.

The field researcher undertook the participant observation work mainly by attending the venture team's weekly meetings, which usually took place on Monday evenings, as well as attending some meetings where external parties, such as clients and other members of the sectoral networking organisation, were involved and work-shadowing. The field researcher took extensive field notes and identified recurring instances of activity and interaction in one meeting and extended this to several other meetings to examine a hunch. This was an inductive process. This process also involved some deductive elements such as seeking contrary or confirming evidence to test out these hunches. This is similar to 'grounded theory' approach as will be explained throughout the book. The research approach and training in respect of conducting participant observation work was heavily influenced by ethnographic approaches in general and Spradley's (1980) framework presented in his well-known work entitled *Participant Observation* in particular.

By means of participant observation, researchers observe the activities of people, the physical characteristics of the social situation and what it feels like to be part of the scene (Spradley, 1980). Participant observation allows the researcher not only to understand how this sense-making occurs and unfolds as nascent entrepreneurs engage in enterprise activity, but also to participate in the construction of the social world of these entrepreneurs. The researcher becomes the primary research instrument by accessing the field, establishing field relations, conducting observation and interviews, writing field notes, reading documents, recording and transcribing, and finally writing-up the research (Walsh, 2004, p. 228).

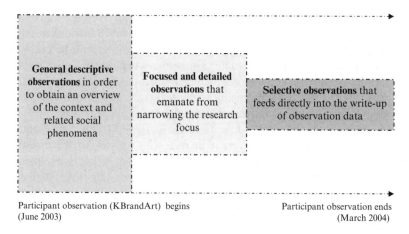

Figure 6.2   Phases in participant observation based on Spradley (1980)

The participant observer aims to understand the culture, setting and webs of relationships. People's constructions of the world and self are essential to the broader practices of culture-justifying, sustaining, and transforming various forms of conduct (K.J. Gergen, 2002, p. 183). This resonates with the notion of 'thick description' that the American anthropologist Clifford Geertz (1973) introduced. Thick description helps the researcher open up the participants' world (nascent entrepreneurs' world in this research) to the reader through rich and detailed descriptions of people, contexts and webs of social relationships that join people to one another (Denzin, 1989; Patton, 1990).[5]

During the course of the fieldwork the researcher begins by making broad 'descriptive observations', trying to get an overview of the social situation and what goes on there. These descriptive data are recorded and analysed and this leads to narrowing down the scope of the research and making 'focused observations'. Finally, after more analysis and repeated observations in the field, the researcher makes very 'selective observations'. These stages reflect changes in the scope of the observation as articulated by Spradley (1980, p. 34) in the Figure 6.2.

Conceiving of participant observation in three phases of observation and adopting the metaphor of a funnel, the broad rim of the funnel represents descriptive observations (Spradley, 1980). Every participant observation entails description of major features of all social situations – place, actor and activities. The level of breadth and depth vary at different phases of the observation (that is descriptive, focused and selective). However, three dimensions remain central. Expanding on this, Spradley (1980) offers a total of nine interrelated dimensions in every social situation as illustrated by Table 6.4. Once the descriptive qualities of the phenomenon under study are gathered, one can move to the focused observations, which call for narrowing down the scope of what is being sought. This requires investigating the flow of interactions and handling the business activities – depending on the roles – among the members of the venture team when observing the venture team meetings, and paying attention to the changes in the thinking and acting patterns in the subsequent meetings. Finally, selective observations represent the narrowest focus that involves identifying differences among the categories created in the previous phases. The idea of participant observation involving three stages, and the activities in each stage, supports the view that any naturalistic inquiry takes an overall inductive approach (a discovery approach), while 'grounded theory' elements of recognising supporting and contrasting data are an inherent part of such a study.

These broad dimensions allow the researcher to classify and record what is being observed in a structured manner. Croll (2004, p. 751) defines observation schedules as the means by which a researcher operationalises the aspects of the social world that are the focus of the study. It requires allocating the aforementioned dimensions to pre-determined categories. This idea of a pre-defined observation schedule lies within the positivistic tradition. In this research one of us carried out the fieldwork. The researcher, who carried out the fieldwork, therefore did not go into the field with such a pre-determined observation schedule. She took extensive notes of what she observed by paying attention to the setting, actors, activities, aims of the social situation (meetings in general), time period and interactions (mainly in the form of detailed notes of meeting talks) and letting any categories or patterns emerge themselves (Peskett, 1987). She did not tape-record the meetings. It was not permissible. The meeting talks provided enormously rich and useful data pertaining to the nascent entrepreneurs' construction of meanings, decision making and entrepreneurial learning over time. The researcher kept a fieldwork journal for each site whereby she noted all aspects of the social situation and the talks. Later she typed up some of her observation data that included extensive recording of meeting talks. It is important to note the role of memory and recall here. She completed the fieldwork notes in the fieldwork journal by noting any thoughts, hunches or observations immediately after the fieldwork visit.

6.5.2 In-depth Taped Interviews

If the observation allows us 'here-and-now experience in depth' (Lincoln and Guba, 1985, p. 273), interviews provide 'here-and-now constructions of people . . . reconstructions of such entities as experienced in the past;

Table 6.4   Nine dimensions of social situations to be observed (developed from Spradley, 1980)

Dimension	Application in this research
Space: the physical place or places	*Setting/context*: detailed information on the surroundings that will allow readers to put the study in a larger context. In the case of KBrandArt, an independent office decorated in a way that reflects the collective identity of the venture as well as the personality of each nascent entrepreneur; located in the city of Derby with close links with the other local creative businesses. In the case of R-Games, an office in the local university's incubator centre opposite the mentors' offices. And in the case of incubator managers or enterprise educators interviews, the offices in the incubator centres or universities that are committed to
Actor: the people involved	*Actors*: organisational actors that are the participants of the research. For KBrandArt: nascent entrepreneurs and other key actors at the meetings whereby the discussion of the formation of the sectoral networking organisation was discussed. For R-Games: a nascent entrepreneur and her mentor
Activity: a set of related acts people do	*Activities*: actions in a setting constituting significant elements of people's involvements. For example, enterprise activities which the venture team members are involved in, including daily activities of managing the venture as well as strategic activities of refining the business concept and shaping the direction of the business via different business opportunity routes
Object: the physical things that are present	*Participation*: nature and type of actors' involvement in such activities. For KBrandArt: venture team members' individual and collective construction of meanings pertaining to the activities engaged
Act: single actions that people do	*Process*: sequences of such activities, significant events, flow, transition and changes over time. For example the process of setting up the venture, process of managing the daily and strategic activities, process of change underpinned by the development of entrepreneurial learning and managing of nascent entrepreneurs
Event: a set of related activities that people carry out	*Relationships*: interrelationships among nascent entrepreneurs themselves (if a venture team), and those with other stake holders such as financiers, suppliers, customers, clients, mentors and enterprise educators

Table 6.4 (continued)

Dimension	Application in this research
Time: the sequencing that takes place over time	*Time period* involved
Goal: the things people are trying to accomplish	*Aims*: objectives underlying the decisions and subsequent actions pursued by nascent entrepreneurs
Feeling: the emotions felt and expressed	*Meanings and values*: the verbal production of participants' understandings of the situation(s) and philosophies behind such meanings/understandings that define and direct action

projections of such entities as they are expected to be experienced in the future' (Lincoln and Guba, 1985, p. 268). Qualitative interviews are often described as 'a conversation with purpose' (Lincoln and Guba, 1985, p. 100). The main purpose here is to understand the world of nascent entrepreneurs from their point of view, as Kvale (1996, p. 1) puts it, 'to uncover their lived world'. Interviewing is seen as a process of 'data generation' rather than collection because the researcher is co-producer of data as a result of an interaction between the researcher and the participants (Mason, 1996). In-depth interviewing was used and found useful as a research method mainly for accessing individual nascent entrepreneur's biographies, ambitions, values, involvement in the venturing process and future ideas or projects concerning the new venture – things that cannot necessarily be observed. Interviews enabled us to produce accounts of nascent entrepreneurs' perspectives on the entrepreneurial process in which they were engaged, and the views of enterprise educators or incubation managers, who were interviewed to address the third research question (that is the importance of enterprise education and business support) from a wider perspective. In-depth interviewing allows flexibility and the most compelling advantage, when achieved, is to reach a greater level of depth and complexity. In-depth interviewing enables the researcher to become attuned to subtleties in people's views, positions and perspectives and to respond accordingly, both at the time of interviewing and later in the subsequent analysis (McCracken, 1988; King, 1994). Interviews served the purpose of understanding the ways in which nascent entrepreneurs pursue their business ideas and construct their enterprise activities and social worlds. Similarly, interviews with the enterprise educators or incubation managers generated insights into the world of educators and business mentors, and their understanding and implementation of the principles of the enterprise culture in the UK, together with its institutions and funding opportunities.

In preparing for qualitative interviews, Lofland and Lofland (1995, p. 78) suggest asking the question 'just what about this thing is puzzling me?'. Bryman (2001, p. 317) argues that this can shape the questions to be asked but, on the other hand, one needs to be careful not to start with too many preconceptions. Using an interview guide enables a researcher to define areas of investigation broadly but not too specifically as an interview schedule would do. Making a useful distinction between descriptive, structural and contrast questions, Spradley (1979) emphasises the importance of the wording in a qualitative interview in developing rapport and eliciting information.

Referring to qualitative interviews as 'in-depth, loosely or semi-structured interviews' and as 'conversations with a purpose', we conducted in-depth interviews, which were loosely structured around themes such as the business venturing process, individual backgrounds (education and professional) and context. Therefore, we did not use 'interview schedules' where a formal schedule of questions are outlined and asked word-for-word in a set order during the interview. Instead, following King (1994, p. 19) and Patton (2002), we constructed an interview guide for each interview situation where we listed the topics to be covered in the course of the interview (see Appendix I for an example interview guide). An interview guide allows the researcher to be free to explore, probe, and ask questions that will elucidate and illuminate the subject (Patton, 2002). The topics were informed by our research questions and usually structured around broad categories from the theoretical frameworks used. Our personal knowledge of entrepreneurial process and learning, and informal discussions with people who have personal experience of the research area, were instrumental in developing probing questions in the course of an interview. These people included other colleagues and scholars as well as some practising entrepreneurs. In carrying out the interviews, other than the common opening question, as mentioned in the ensuing paragraph, the topics were not always addressed in the order in which they appeared in the interview guide. Some of them were raised by the participant or we introduced certain topics where they fit naturally into the course of the interview.

Having the interview guide at hand in the interviews, we usually started with an introductory question such as 'Can you tell me about your experience of starting up this business?' or 'Can you tell me about yourself and why you chose this route of setting up your own business?'. We then let the participant speak freely. We used probing questions such as 'Could you tell me more about the funding difficulties that you just mentioned?' and specifying questions such as 'What did you think then?'; 'How did you act in that situation?'; 'Would you act in the same way if you encountered a similar situation in the future?'; 'Would you elaborate on that?'; and 'That's helpful. I'd appreciate a bit more detail'. In the follow-up interviews with key participants, we furthered the conversations by attempting to explore their perspectives on 'what it means to be an entrepreneur' or 'what is learning associated with as an entrepreneur or small business owner' and 'the learning experience around a critical incident'. Learning is a difficult subject to study through interviews. However, critical incidents technique (Chell, 1998, 2004) proved to be helpful in eliciting the participants' account of what the incident means for them in relation to their learning experience in business venturing as discussed in the following section. We tape-recorded the interviews and then transcribed the audio-tapes.

Before moving on to the critical incidents technique, it is worth noting the importance of being a skilled interviewer in order to generate quality interview material. It is important to learn how to introduce the research project in a way that engages the participants' interest and makes them willing to accept their role in the interview (Fowler, 2004), that is talking about their experience openly. Equally, it is important to learn to manage the interview process effectively by phrasing the questions in an understandable and appropriate manner; being a good listener; being able to introduce probing questions as they fit; being able to deal with difficult interviewees, such as an uncommunicative interviewee; and ending the interview appropriately.[6]

Finally, as with participant observation there are ethical challenges in conducting qualitative interviewing. Interviews are interventions (Patton, 2002, p. 404) and the process of being taken through a directed, reflective process affects the interviewees and leaves them laying open thoughts or feelings about their own experience to themselves as well as the researcher. Adhering to the 'empathic neutrality' principle of naturalistic inquiry as laid out in Table 6.2, and observing the ethical standards of any research act (being respectful and showing openness to the participants' views without judgement) was followed as a principle in undertaking interviews.

6.5.2.1 Critical incident technique
The critical incident technique, as defined by Chell (1998, 2004, p. 218), is a qualitative interview procedure, which facilitates the investigation of significant occurrences (events, incidents, processes or issues) identified by the participant, the way they are managed, and the outcomes in terms of perceived impacts. The technique was originally developed by Flanaghan (1954) in psychology and rested upon positivistic assumptions. However, the ontological and epistemological roots of the critical incident technique,

as developed by Chell (1998), lie within interpretivist approaches, which assume that world is complex and can be understood through human experience – in other words a sense-making process undertaken by the researcher and the participants in the course of the research act, an interview process in this case.

The critical incident technique is a tool that allows for developing an understanding of dynamic processes within social interaction.[7] Critical incident technique has been applied in entrepreneurship research by a number of scholars (Chell and Pittaway, 1998b; Chell and Baines, 2000; Cope, 2000, 2003, 2005; Taylor and Thorpe, 2004). The latter studies (Cope; Taylor and Thorpe) are in the domain of entrepreneurial learning as discussed previously in Chapter 4.

We used the critical incident technique as a supplementary method in qualitative interviewing rather than a central one. After the initial introductory questions and generic probes as and when necessary, we asked the participants to identify one or two incidents that occurred over the period of the business venturing process. In the first two interviews, some participants were not able to comprehend what we meant by critical incidents. We overcame this problem by changing the phraseology and asked them to identify any 'significant occurrences'. This expression appealed more to the participants, connecting with their lived experience more easily, and they started citing some key events with people, issues and processes attached to them. In the subsequent interviews, we chose to explain the technique in more detail before posing the question. This worked better and generated interesting data. It is usually necessary to use non-technical language and provide an upfront explanation of the method before embarking on the interview. All participants in the research replied to the 'critical incidents' question by citing one, two or more incidents.

The most interesting aspect of using this technique in this research, which also marks the difference between this research and the previous studies that used the technique (Cope, 2001, 2003, 2005; Taylor and Thorpe, 2004) was the exploration of different meanings attached to the same incident by different venture team members in the case of KBrandArt (see Chapter 7). A final note on the use of the critical incident technique in this research is that the method served well for the purpose of addressing the first two research questions concurrently, facilitating the elicitation of the entrepreneurial learning experience around the key activities of the venturing process. The critical learning events were usually associated with the most crucial aspects of the venturing process such as securing funding, moving into an incubation unit, or setting up outside an incubator and employing a brand manager, who is the first sign of changing direction and growing the business. These will be discussed in detail throughout the book. What is worth underlining in conclusion is that the use of this technique has its roots in the social constructionist grounding of this research where the venturing process and related entrepreneurial learning experience are viewed as taking place within the exchange of relationships that nascent entrepreneurs are engaged in.

6.5.3   Documentary Analysis

Lincoln and Guba (1985) alert the researchers to the continuous triangulation of interview data with other sources. The sources included in this research were participant observation and analysis of documents. The documents were in various forms such as archival documents regarding the formation of the venture (mainly business plans), history of the organisation (in business plans and press releases), current documents about the strategies, planning and operations, meeting notes and even internal memos. These varied documentary records constitute a rich source of insights into organisational life, as they are one of the principal by-products of the interactions and communication of individuals and groups, at all levels, in organisations (Forster, 1994, p. 148) in their natural language. In studying organisational phenomena, if our task is to make sense of things, to get behind the surface and disclose the underlying significance (Kets de Vries and Miller, 1987), the organisational texts are very significant instruments as we can interpret the hidden meanings, consequences and motives behind acts and decisions. The text that is implicit in a specific strategic direction, or the underlying themes, the meanings behind the metaphors of managers and the reasons for selection of certain words can enable us to recognise the crucial assumptions underpinning organisational culture, strategy and structure (Kets de Vries and Miller, 1987; Forster, 1994; Atkinson and Coffey, 1997).

Researchers need to identify who the target audience is for a particular document. Business plans written at different times to suit different needs (a business plan for a SHELL Live Award compared to a business plan to attract funding, for example) and other documents such as meeting notes and internal memos or client presentation slides, all provided a rich source of case data to supplement observations and interviews. Patton (2002) notes how documents prove valuable not only because of what can be learnt directly from them but also as stimuli for paths of inquiry that can be pursued only through observation and interviewing. For example, in the KBrandArt case, the way they defined the business in the business plan was different to that in a client presentation slide. Therefore, we decided to explore this business definition issue at the following venture team meeting from each team member's perspective using the discussion to sharpen their product and service offerings and the business structure. The underlying issue shaping those conversations was the issue of how they define and redefine their business over time.

Documentary analysis has limitations: documents may be incomplete or difficult to access due to commercially sensitive information that is included. They may not make sense without the interviews or observations. Learning to study and understand documents and organisational texts as a source of data is a part of the repertoire of skills required for qualitative inquiry (Patton, p. 2002). More importantly, it is crucial to learn to combine these multiple sources (documents, observations and interviews) to provide a comprehensive account of the subject studied. Using a combination of data types increases the trustworthiness of the research.

6.5.4 Keeping a Research Diary

Finally, a research diary was used as a method through which we recorded any thoughts, ideas, occasionally some data, and analysis of data, from the very beginning of the research. We kept two diaries: a research diary where we noted any thoughts, ideas or hunches about our research, including the notes from literature and other secondary sources, and a fieldwork diary, which we called 'fieldwork journal for KBrandArt' and 'fieldwork journal for R-Games'. When we collected data in the form of tape-recordings of interviews or handwritten notes of meeting observations and talks in field settings, we also usually took notes of our thoughts or a significant phrase from the conversation in these fieldwork journals as the participants talked through their experience. This enabled us to add back some of the missing information by drawing some data from the fieldwork journals when converting them to write-ups. Another benefit of keeping such fieldwork journals was that after a field visit and the production of write-ups, we reflected on what we thought the main concepts, themes or issues were that we had gathered during the field contact, and reproduced them in the 'emerging themes' section that we created in these fieldwork journals. The research diary was very instrumental over the entire period of the research study as we were able to track the development of our own thinking of the research ideas and theoretical frameworks. It was enormously beneficial in conceptualising data during the iterative processes of data analysis and interpretation.

6.6   DATA ANALYSIS AND WRITING-UP

Naturalistic inquiry relies upon an emergent design, in which successive methodological steps are based upon the results of steps already taken;

they are not preordained (Lincoln and Guba, 1985). The emergent nature of the qualitative research entails the concurrent processes of data collection, analysis and writing-up. These tacit and iterative processes take place in the evolution of data gathering and analysis.

Operating within a social constructionist paradigm, data are not viewed as given by nature but as stemming from an interaction between the inquirer and the data sources. The data are 'the constructions offered by or in the sources' (Lincoln and Guba, 1985). What we are looking for as data are based on several assumptions. According to Ackroyd and Hughes (1992) they are rooted in the research questions: 'data, of whatever form, do not just appear or lie around waiting to be casually picked up by some passing social researcher but have to be given form and shape in order to qualify as data to a research problem . . . To be involved with data is to be involved within an inferential process, whereby the data, whatever their form and content can be created as "standing on behalf of" something else'. On a similar note, Lincoln and Guba (1985, p. 332) argue the following:

> Data are the product of a process of interpretation, and though there is some sense in which the materials for this process are 'given' it is only the product which has scientific status and function. In a word, data have meaning, and this word 'meaning' like its cognates 'significance' and 'import' includes a reference to values.

Data only become such when the researcher actively intervenes to attend to certain things to the exclusion of others (Wolcott, 1994, p. 3). This is in line with the following axioms of naturalistic inquiry as discussed in the preceding parts of this chapter: the human instrument, tacit knowledge and focus-determined boundaries. In the complex and multifaceted analytical integration of rigorous social science, creative artistry, and personal reflexivity, researchers transform interviews, observations, documents, and field notes into 'findings' (Patton, 2002, p. 432). The data collected are processed to create knowledge and made intelligible to the reader by the researcher's data construction process, relying on certain ontological and epistemological assumptions, addressing specific research questions and using methods of analysis that fit with the overall methodological choice and research questions.

Difficulties associated with analysing qualitative data are well-documented in the literature (Miles and Huberman, 1994; Patton, 2002; Silverman, 2005). Qualitative data analysis is labour-intensive. Time demands, sampling adequacy, credibility and data overload are the major difficulties (Miles and Huberman, 1994). The large unstructured volume of qualitative data is rather difficult to analyse and this makes data analysis the most challenging part of any qualitative research. This involves reducing the volume of raw information, sifting trivia from significance and constructing a framework for communicating the essence of what the data reveal (Patton, 2002, p. 432). Writing this up is an integral part of the analytical process. The researcher's decisions as to what to report, and how to report it, are all analytical choices.

In this research, we carried out inductive analysis, informed by a well-known research tradition, 'grounded theory'. Inductive analysis involves discovering patterns, themes and categories in the data generated. This can be achieved by becoming immersed in the data as advocated by Glaser and Strauss (1967) in their grounded theory approach: 'being grounded' means that embedded meanings and relationships can emerge from observation, interview or documentary data (Patton, 2002). The analytical focus stems partly from what the researcher has learned from the published literature and ongoing discussions with the scholars in the field. This forms part of the tacit knowledge as one of the axioms of naturalistic inquiry, referring back to Figure 6.1 in this chapter. Describing tacit knowledge characterised as personal, context-specific, deeply rooted in action (Ambrosini and Bowman, 2001) one can argue that it is constructed by the researchers' practical experience of undertaking social science research, including developing a sound understanding of the chosen discipline and research techniques. It is used in the research, cascading throughout the process (that is from purposive sampling to inductive data analysis and the iterative process of revisiting the emerging themes and literature until reaching the point of conceptual saturation).

Miles and Huberman (1994) list the common characteristics of analytical practices that are used across different qualitative research types. They constitute a set of analytic moves that can be arranged in a number of ways. Building on the naturalistic design and inductive approach taken, the way we have undertaken data analysis can be explained as follows:

- Producing interview transcripts and observation records (mainly reproduction of meeting talks and additional field notes)
- Assigning codes to a set of field material drawn from observations and interviews (see Appendix II for the list of codes used)
- Noting reflections and other remarks in the margins
- Sorting and sifting through the field materials to identify reoccurring explanations, phrases, regularities, relationships between themes and patterns, and differences
- Re-evaluating these patterns at the next field contact
- Gradually elaborating a small set of emerging themes discerned in the data collected.

This reflects a typical qualitative data analysis process. In the current research, early thoughts and ideas from the interviews or meeting talks were annotated on the transcripts. Key phrases, sentences or blocks of data were highlighted by using marker pens, colour-coded to unpack emerging themes. Some of these themes were deemed 'key' and 'important' based on our understanding of the subject area and initial research boundaries. More themes were added as other areas of interest and relevance emerged both from the interview and observation data. These were all a part of the process of refining the focus as explained above, reflecting the researcher's commitment to engage actively with the data, published literature and discussions with scholars in the field.

The interview summary tables (see Appendix III for an example) and observation data summary sheets (see Appendix IV for an example) were produced, conveying what was at that stage considered to be the most relevant and significant dimensions emerging from the interviews or observations. We used an 'index card system', as described in McCracken (1988) and Easterby-Smith et al. (2002), to transfer 'meaningful chunks' of data onto cards. The index cards were traceable back to interview transcripts and used to identify earlier patterns. Later, they formed 'departure points' in analysing the data through (NVivo).[8] These meaningful data units were re-marked in NVivo by applying nodes. This process is called 'unitising', using the language of grounded theory. The researcher deals with 'units of data' which are referred to as 'incidents' in the constant comparison method. Having located a unit, it should be entered onto an index card (and entered in NVivo), which should be coded in multiple ways that may be useful for the particular inquiry (see Lincoln and Guba, 1985; Miles and Huberman, 1994; Marshall and Rossman, 1999; Easterby-Smith et al., 2002). Categorising is the next step whereby unitised data are organised into categories that provide descriptive or inferential information about the context or setting from which the units were derived (Lincoln and Guba, 1985). Essentially, the method involves sorting units into provisional categories on the basis of 'look-alike' characteristics, which may initially be only tacitly understood in a naturalistic inquiry (Lincoln and Guba, 1985, p. 202). Coding becomes crucial in categorising data.

A coding system was set up based on Miles and Huberman (1994) and revised continually during the data collection and analysis processes. The codes were applied to individual cases (such as a nascent entrepreneur), observation materials (meeting talks) and documents collected. The codes were structured using Dawson's (1994, 1997, 2003) processual framework at a very early phase of the analysis. We should re-emphasise that even the most grounded approach depends on asking certain questions and forming an analytical focus deriving from some theoretical orientation. Embedded in the social constructionist paradigm, the theoretical frameworks of Dawson (Processual framework, 1994, 1997, 2003), Watson (Strategic exchange framework, 1994a, 2001a, 2001b, 2002, 2003), and our understanding of entrepreneurship (mainly new venture creation and the entrepreneurial learning process) brought focus to this study in its early phases. The shift from these frameworks to Bourdieu's conceptual tools at a later stage of the research (after the fieldwork was completed), was due to a better fit with the research aims as well as the social constructionist and process-relational nature of the research. This marked a significant point because it helped us undertake thematic analysis across cases by establishing multiple layers of analysis (micro-meso-macro) and finally construct a multi-layered framework of nascent entrepreneurship from the case accounts. How the principles of the grounded theory underpinned this process in the current research is the concern of the next section.

6.6.1 The Grounded Theory Approach

The grounded theory approach provides systematic inductive guidelines for analysing data to build theoretical frameworks that explain the collected data (Charmaz, 2000; Patton, 2002). Glaser and Strauss (1967) developed grounded theory, coming out of their research together that investigated the treatment of people dying in American hospitals. It emerged as a reaction to a positivist deductive approach that was prevailing in American social research of the time (Seale, 2004). In its original form developed by Glaser and Strauss (1967) there was an emphasis on the commitment to continual re-examination of data in light of developing arguments through the 'constant comparison method', which is a systematic tool for developing and refining theoretical categories (Seale, 2004). A grounded theorist becomes more and more grounded in the data and develops increasingly richer concepts and models of how the phenomenon being studied really works. A simplified model of grounded theory involves three stages (Silverman, 2005, p. 179), as shown in Table 6.5, which correspond to certain principles underlying the approach.

Strauss and Corbin (1990) provided a sourcebook for researchers on how to apply a well-established method by applying some distinctive, technical rules and procedures. The second edition of their book (Strauss and Corbin, 1998) formalised the procedure even more. They introduced three characteristic ways of coding data that include open coding, axial coding and selective coding (Seale, 2004). Open coding means making instances of data according to emerging analytic themes. Axial coding refers to exploring the interconnections of coding categories. Selective coding

Table 6.5   Elements of the grounded theory (from Silverman, 2005) and its application in the current research

Stages	Underlying principles	Application in the research
An initial attempt to develop categories which illuminate the data	Inductive approach	Inductive approach to data analysis
An attempt to saturate these categories with many appropriate cases in order to demonstrate their relevance	Conceptual saturation Constant comparison	Application of the constant comparison method in data analysis, leading to integration of data categories until reaching conceptual saturation in each case and across cases
Developing these categories into more general analytical frameworks with relevance outside the setting	Theory building	Writing the conceptual framework of 'multi-layered perspective to nascent entrepreneurship'

is the stage where core categories are identified. These are explained in great depth in their books. This is where Glaser (1992) disagrees with his earlier co-worker, Strauss, by criticising the over-technical, rule-following approach that Strauss and Corbin take in their text. Glaser (1992) places emphasis on the centrality of the idea of constant comparison as containing the simple central idea of 'grounded theorising' (Seale, 2004, p. 244). Douglas (2005), in his application of the grounded theory in examining the human complexities of entrepreneurial decision making, suggests that the process of iterative theory building, whilst grounded in a substantive inquiry, holds the capacity to generate further research questions and tentative explanations at broader levels.

A number of criticisms of the grounded theory approach have arisen over time. Some have criticised grounded theory for its failure to acknowledge implicit theories (such as preconceptions) that guide research projects at an early stage (Silverman, 2005). Other critiques have focused on its limitation to integrate theory verification to the process (Hammersley and Atkinson, 1995). Despite these critiques, the grounded theory approach, in its various interpretations, still works for some qualitative research and if applied with a certain level of rigour it enables the researcher to interact with data through self-awareness, self-criticism and openness to new ideas. In Seale's (2004, p. 247) terms:

> ... the spirit that lies behind the approach can be simply explained, and does not have to be attached to a naively realist epistemology, or indeed to an oppressive urge to force readers to regard its products true for all time. It demands a rigorous spirit of self-awareness and self-criticism, as well as openness to new ideas that is often a hallmark of research studies of good quality.

Juxtaposing objectivist and constructivist approaches to grounded theory, Charmaz (2000, p. 510) suggests that a constructivist approach to grounded theory reaffirms studying people in their natural settings and redirects qualitative research away from positivism. Her argument is threefold. First, grounded theory strategies need not be rigid or prescriptive. Second, a focus on 'meaning' while using grounded theory furthers rather than restrains interpretive understanding. Third, researchers can adopt grounded theory strategies without embracing the positivist leanings of earlier proponents of grounded theory. Following this advice, the grounded theory approach has been applied in this research to the extent to which the naturalistic characteristics of the research embedded in social constructionism have been retained. This has meant in practical terms identifying recurrent explanations, phrases, themes and patterns; assigning codes to these emerging categories manually on the interview transcripts or observation notes first with an additional mechanism of index-cards, and later developing codes as 'nodes' by using NVivo; integrating categories under subsets of themes and using these subsets of themes in constructing the case accounts; and writing the multi-layered framework of nascent entrepreneurship as will be presented in Chapter 9.

6.6.2   Writing-up the Research: Use of Wolcott's Framework Entitled 'Description, Analysis and Interpretation' in Constructing the Case Accounts

The fluid and emergent nature of naturalistic inquiry makes the distinction between data collection, analysis and reporting far less absolute (Patton, 2002, p. 436). The processed accounts are reported as case studies as the final products. Lincoln and Guba (1985) propose the case study as the reporting mode for naturalistic inquirers as it is the primary vehicle for 'emic' inquiry as opposed to 'etic' inquiry. Kenneth Pike (1954 cited in Patton, 2002) is the social scientist who coined the terms 'emic' and 'etic' in order to distinguish classification systems that anthropologists used in reporting their accounts based on the language and categories used by the people in the culture studied, an emic approach, as opposed to categories created by anthropologists based on their analysis of important cultural distinctions, an etic approach. The main challenge for us in conducting the current research was to understand the nascent entrepreneurs' world by combining participation, observation and immersion so as to become capable of understanding the setting as an 'insider-outsider' while describing it to and for outsiders. Case study reporting enabled us to provide thick descriptions first, which 'create thick interpretations in terms of the local theories that are structuring people's experiences' (Denzin, 1994, p. 506). It is the most responsive form to the axioms of a naturalistic inquiry. It provides an ideal vehicle for communicating with the reader as it provides them with a 'vicarious experience of the inquiry setting' (Lincoln and Guba, 1985, p. 214).

There is a debate on the case study in the literature as to whether the case study forms a research strategy or a final product. Yin (1994) takes the stance that it is an overall strategy with specific methods. Stake (1994, 1998, 2000) on the other hand, adopts the approach that case study is not a methodological choice but a choice of what is to be studied. Case is a 'specific, unique, bounded system' according to his approach (Stake, 2000, p. 436). In an eloquent way, Patton (2002) provides a discussion on cases as 'units of analysis' and the choice of cases is made during the design stage, which forms the basis of purposeful sampling, and revised later according to the richness of the data generated. The purpose of the process is to gather and present comprehensive and in-depth information about each case that results in a final product: the case study. The term 'case accounts' is used in this research to describe the cases constructed because the term 'account' conveys a stance taken with a view to presenting a rich and vicarious story of the participants.

Whether in the form of case study or not, the question of how to report qualitative data remains a central one. It finds some answers in Wolcott's (1994) book *Transforming Qualitative Data*. He draws a distinction between description, analysis and interpretation. Description deals with the question of 'what is going on here'; analysis addresses the identification of essential features and the systematic description of interrelationships among them, and interpretation engages with processual questions of meanings and contexts. His advice to novice researchers is to stay descriptive as long as possible:

> There is no best way to accomplish any of this. Doctoral students worriedly anticipating when and how to introduce their analytical or interpretive frameworks sometimes find the advice helpful to stay 'descriptive as long as possible'. This advice is biased in favour of the descriptive account while alerting students that there will come a point at which they will find it necessary to introduce something more than descriptive labels to keep the account moving forward in

a purposeful way. Should even that advice prove too 'writerly', how about this: Tell the story. Then tell how that happened to be the way you told it (Wolcott, 1994, p. 16).

It is significant to note an issue raised by Wolcott (1994) in moving from description to analysis as adopting frameworks which impose structure on the descriptive accounts. He argues that 'by having the framework in mind during the fieldwork, the researcher is assured that, when the various descriptive ingredients of the case are called for in an ensuing analysis, they will be at hand' (Wolcott, 1994, p. 20).

Based on this description, analysis and interpretation formula – he calls it D-A-I formula – Wolcott (1994) recommends three ways of organising and reporting data. One way is to stay close to the data as originally recorded. 'The final account may draw long excerpts from one's field notes, or repeat informants' words so that informants themselves seem to tell their stories' (Wolcott, 1994, p. 10). The underlying assumption is that the data 'speak for themselves' (Wolcott, 1994; Easterby-Smith et al., 2002). Building upon the first way (description), a second way of organising and reporting data is to expand and extend beyond a purely descriptive account with an analysis that proceeds in a methodical, systematic way to identify interrelationships between key issues. Following the second or springing from the first, he suggests the third way calls for interpretation. The researcher should pursue the aim of making sense of what is going on, to reach out for understanding or explanation beyond the limits of what can be explained with the analysis. Noting that description, analysis and interpretation are three primary ingredients of qualitative research, Wolcott (1994) emphasises the distinction, but also the overlap, between the three in transforming and presenting data. A balancing act between three components is required (Dexter, 2003).

Description, in the form of 'rich description' (Geertz, 1973) involves, in this study, telling the story of the nascent entrepreneurs who participated in the research, based on their own descriptions of the business venturing journey that they went through. Interpretation is the stage at which 'the researcher transcends data and cautious analyses and begins to probe into what is to be made of them' (Wolcott, 1994, p. 36). The interpretation is idiographic as it should be contextualised in the setting, and does not strive for, under naturalistic inquiry, generalisation. Interpretation is attained through a process of inference and inductive reasoning with reference to the analytical frameworks used, the literature reviewed, peer-group checks, member checks and the researcher's personal experience (Lincoln and Guba, 1985; Wolcott, 1994; Marshall and Rossman, 1999; Patton, 2002).

Interpreting data in constructing individual case accounts and making cross-case analysis, working towards building a conceptual framework and drawing conclusions constituted a very crucial process in this research. It is important to note that interpretation has several dimensions. The first dimension is the participants' interpretation of the research and their approach in responding to the questions asked at the interview or observation setting. The second dimension is the researcher's interpretation of the data as discussed throughout the chapter. The third one can be considered as the 'readers' interpretation of the research account. This does not negate the value of the interpretive research, but places the responsibility on the user of the research to retain awareness of the process, its implications, the nature of idiographic findings and the limitations of the uses of the research with regard to its potential application (Dexter, 2003, p. 144). Table 6.6 summarises the application of D-A-I framework in the current research with the objective if providing guidelines on how to read the case accounts in Chapters 7 and 8.

An important axiom of naturalistic inquiry is to establish the trustworthiness of the research, relying on the basic principle of research being a collaborative process between the researcher, participants and readers. In addition to fulfilling ethical obligations of sharing knowledge and procedural advantage of adding credibility to the findings, further data are usually generated as a result of activities such as member-checks or peer-audit (Marshall and Rossman, 1999; Patton, 2002; Dexter, 2003). The next section discusses the methods used in establishing the trustworthiness of this research.

6.7 ESTABLISHING THE 'TRUSTWORTHINESS' OF QUALITATIVE RESEARCH

Based on Lincoln and Guba's (1985) work, alternative criteria are provided by Patton (2002) for establishing the trustworthiness of qualitative research. Traditional positivistic criteria include internal validity, external validity, reliability and objectivity (Lincoln and Guba, 1985). The social constructionist paradigm, and naturalistic inquiry as the chosen research strategy, demand other criteria for judgement. Lincoln and Guba (1986) proposed 'credibility as an analog to internal validity, transferability as an analog to external validity, dependability as an analog to reliability, and confirmability as an analog to objectivity'. In combination, they suggest that these criteria address 'trustworthiness' (itself a parallel term to rigour) (Patton, 2002, p. 546).

Credibility refers to enhancing the credibility of findings through rigorous methods for conducting fieldwork and demonstrating the credibility

Table 6.6   Application of Description-Analysis-Interpretation (Wolcott, 1994) framework in this research

Components of D-A-I framework	What does it mean in this research?	How is it applied?
Description	Describing the story of nascent entrepreneurs' experiences of business venturing, with a focus on salient characteristics of each phase including conception, gestation, and fledgling new firm stages.	KBrandArt: describing the story of nascent entrepreneurs in terms of their aims in setting up the venture, motivations, current roles in the venture team and future aspirations; describing the story of their collective business venturing process embedded in a macro web of interrelationships with other stakeholders. R-Games: describing the story of the nascent entrepreneur with reference to her background to, and objectives in setting up the business, and the process she went through.
Analysis	Organising and reporting data to expand and extend beyond a descriptive account of the venturing process to provide a systematic account of interrelationships between key themes addressing the research questions.	KBrandArt and R-Games Analysing the research accounts inductively, looking at patterns of themes and interrelationships between themes concerning the research elements and questions (see Table 6.1), and constructing Chapters 7 and 8 in two major sections including the venturing process and underlying processes, with sub-sections in the case of KBrandArt and R-Games.
Interpretation	Inference and inductive reasoning with reference to analytic frameworks used (micro-meso-macro-levels), within a broader scheme of the grounded theory approach taken in the research. Description, analysis and interpretation are interwoven processes, and integral to the grounded theory approach.	KBrandArt and R-Games Interpreting the case accounts, by revisiting pertinent disciplinary debates covered in Chapters 2, 3 and 4; and with reference to the broader analytic framework constructed in Chapter 5 in relation to Bourdieu's work, embedded in a social constructionist paradigm. Constructing Chapters 7, 8, and 9 as a result of this process, which is integral to the grounded theory approach. * **The case studies should be read by taking into account the D-A-I framework, which underpinned their construction.**

of findings by having them approved by the constructors of the multiple realities being studied (Lincoln and Guba, 1985, p. 296; Patton, 2002, p. 552). In application, it meant prolonged engagement with the participants, persistent observation, member-checks, and triangulation of different sources (interviews, observation, documents and research diaries) and data coming out of these sources. The member-check, whereby data, analytic categories, interpretations and conclusions are tested with members of those stakeholders from whom the data were originally gathered, is the most crucial technique for credibility (Lincoln and Guba, 1985, p. 314). It may take the form of informal and formal checks, which are both valuable. The member check is congruent with the philosophical assumptions of the current research. If we believe that the inquiry is value bounded, the values of the respondent must be considered. Believing that the context is significant in attributing meaning to data, it is useful to carry that assigned meaning back into the context for verification (Lincoln and Guba, 1985). 'If the issue is whether the analyst has successfully produced a reconstruction of the respondents' constructions, the best way to determine that is to take the reconstruction back to the respondents for their examination and reaction' (Lincoln and Guba, 1985, p. 351). Table 6.7 summarises the strategies applied in order to meet these criteria in this research.

Transferability indicates application of research findings in other contexts. The findings of a qualitative research of this type usually illuminate a particular situation or small number of cases. As Patton (2002, p. 581) puts it, 'but what of utility beyond the limited case or cases studied?' This is the question that we are attempting to address by applying this criterion. Generalisability is not aimed for by this kind of research, relying on deeper philosophical and epistemological issues concerning generalisability as discussed in Chapter 5 of the book. What Cronbach (1975) offers is an alternative strategy that is believed to be excellent advice for the qualitative researcher by some scholars (Lincoln and Guba, 1985; Patton, 2002).

He puts forward the notion of 'working hypotheses' that are reached through describing and interpreting the effect anew in each locale and taking into considerations factors unique to that locale or series of events (Cronbach, 1975, p. 124). He adds 'when we give proper weight to local conditions, any generalisation is a working hypothesis, not a conclusion' (Cronbach, 1975). Concurring with the advice of Cronbach (1975, p. 125), Lincoln and Guba (1985, 1986) and Stake (2000), researchers should do justice to the specific cases through an appreciation of, and attention to, particularities of the context. In this way, one does a 'good job of particularisation' before looking for patterns across cases (Patton, 2002, p. 582). Lincoln and Guba (1985, p. 124) express this in the following way: 'The degree of transferability is a direct function of the similarity

Table 6.7   Establishing the trustworthiness of the research according to naturalistic inquiry tradition embedded in social constructionism

Criteria and strategies	Application in the current research
Credibility:	
a) Prolonged engagement	a) Understanding the culture and localities of the setting through prolonged engagement with the participants through participant observation; period of contact through return visits; and establishing rapport through interview style.
b) Persistent observation	b) Participant observation over a period of 18 months; multiple field visits to some sites; and immersion in data to identify salient patterns.
c) Triangulation	c) Use of multiple sources (interviews, observation and documents).
d) Member checks	d) Sharing interview transcripts, clarifying ambiguities and receiving comments; construction of a management report at the interim stage and later an informal discussion of the report with the venture team members; discussion of findings with the participants (in the KBrandArt case only) at the end of analysis.
e) Peer debriefing	e) Dissemination of research approach and findings at various stages of the research through academic conferences and discussions with the supervisors and colleagues in the researchers' social circuit.
f) Negative case analysis	f) Generating the case account of R-Games as the venturing case that took place differently (in a university incubator context) compared with the case of KBrandArt whose members set up the venture independently (outside an incubator).
Transferability	See Chapter 7 and 8 where the individual cases were presented with details of context and Chapter 9 where they are cross-examined by using dimensions of micro-meso-macro-levels. Findings only potentially transferable, not for generalisation.
Confirmability and dependability	See Chapter 5 (research paradigm) and Chapters 5 and 6 (methodology) constructed to illuminate and justify the research process. Retention of data for later checks. Rigour in the research process, including discussion with colleagues and supervisors.

between the two contexts, what we shall call "fittingness". Fittingness is defined as degree of congruence between sending and receiving contexts. If context A and context B are "sufficiently" congruent, then working hypotheses from the sending originating contexts may be applicable in the receiving contexts' (Lincoln and Guba, 1985). There is a caveat that the findings remain idiographically interpreted and yet can only be tentatively applied. The strategy for meeting this criterion of transferability includes providing thick description as much as possible. The question of what forms proper thick description remains unanswered. Lincoln and Guba (1985, p. 316) argue that it is not the researcher's task to provide an index of transferability but there is an onus on the researcher to provide the rich insights to the subject under study that make transferability possible on the part of potential appliers.

Confirmability and dependability refer to the characteristics of data that demonstrate confidence in process and outcome for internal coherence and external trust (Dexter, 2003) and they are attainable through audit trail and a reflexive journal (research diary).

6.8   CONCLUSIONS TO THE CHAPTER

This chapter discusses the progression from social constructionist paradigmatic assumptions and research questions to the research design, naturalistic inquiry, and associated research methods of data collection and analysis. Naturalistic inquiry is characterised by emergent design, which enables flexibility. Design flexibility stems from epistemological as well as pragmatic considerations. With an emphasis on in-depth understanding of the phenomenon under study, purposeful sampling is another characteristic of naturalistic inquiry, leading to rich cases. Qualitative data, which consists of quotations from interviews, observations and excerpts from documents, are generated in naturalistic inquiry as they capture and communicate nascent entrepreneurs' experience of the entrepreneurial processes in their own words. This entails personally engaging with, and getting close to the participants to the extent that the practicalities of the research permit.

As naturalistic inquiry involves fieldwork that puts the researcher in close contact with people and their world, the researcher's cognitive and emotional stance can be best described by Patton's (2002, p. 50) notion of 'empathic neutrality', which offers a middle ground between becoming too involved, which can cloud judgement, and remaining too distant, which can reduce understanding. By showing respect, openness, sensitivity, responsiveness mindfulness during the interviews and observations, we enacted our roles as researchers who sought honest, meaningful and credible findings.[9]

A dynamic and developmental perspective is another important aspect of naturalistic inquiry, which entails attention to process and assumes ongoing change: change in participants' views and behaviours as the study unfolds. Unique case orientation and inductive analysis are the other qualities of naturalistic inquiry. What lies at the heart of an inductive inquiry is to allow the important analytical dimensions to emerge from patterns found in the cases under study without being 'pigeon holed' into standardised categories (Patton, 2002, p. 56). In practice, as the fieldwork progresses and some patterns and themes emerge, later activities of data construction (observations and interviews) include both inductive (discovery) and deductive (constant comparison) approaches. An holistic perspective and context sensitivity are required in naturalistic inquiry, which manifested itself in a multi-layered perspective to studying nascent entrepreneur's venturing experience in this study, with an emphasis on the underlying processes of entrepreneurial learning and managing. The micro-individual, meso-relational and macro-contextual layers are examined, conveying a sense of the interplay at all three levels. Finally, trustworthiness should be ensured in naturalistic inquiry through reflexivity, which requires self-awareness of the reflexive screens and positions that all parties (researchers, participants and audience) hold and having an 'ongoing conversation about the [research] experience while simultaneously living in the moment' (Hertz, 1997). Critically reflexive practice embraces relational understandings of reality as a basis for thinking more critically about our assumptions, values and actions on others (Cunliffe, 2004). Such practice is important to entrepreneurship research and education because it helps us understand how we constitute our realities and identities in relational ways and how we can develop more collaborative and responsive ways of researching and educating nascent entrepreneurs.

Considering research as a process of organising our thoughts and findings to reach understanding, not an end in itself (Wolcott, 1994), this chapter has provided an account of data collection, analysis and writing-up processes. A research study offers an opportunity to pursue a topic that intrigues the researcher personally. However, narrowing down or slightly altering the topic may be required for mundane, practical reasons. Practicalities including the nature of the research (that is funded research) and the resources available shaped the study, as did the researchers, who have started with a scholarly interest and career aspirations and drawn upon their knowledge of the world, experiences and contacts. Chapters 7 and 8, present the case studies, which have been constructed by building on the data collected during this empirical investigation of the topic.

NOTES

1. See Chapter 5, section 5.4.2 for a related discussion that is based on Bourdieu's (1999) work.
2. This form of participant observation involved attending the venture team meetings; participating in the conversations when our opinions/thoughts were asked; and actively contributing to some of the 'brainstorming sessions' where the team of entrepreneurs discussed their ideas for a pitch to win the marketing campaign of the local university that one of us worked for.
3. Denise is not the actual name of the research participant. A pseudonym is used to conceal actual identities of research participants and their ventures including the location of ventures as explained in Chapter 7.
4. We originated this piece of research when one of the researchers was based in the University of Derby, who moved to Southampton later on and completed the fieldwork and the write-up.
5. See Denzin (2001) for a detailed discussion on thick description.
6. See King, 1994: 21–24, for a detailed discussion on practical issues in carrying out qualitative interviews.
7. See Chell (1998) for an expanded discussion on the critical incident technique, which combines a detailed account of how to undertake an interview using the technique with some examples.
8. NVivo is a qualitative data analysis software, which helps researchers organise and analyse large volumes of unstructured qualitative data by classifying the data under categories and establishing relationships in the data.
9. See Schwandt (2000) and Patton (2002) for a related discussion on the 'Verstehen' premise and Max Weber, who brought the term 'empathy' into social science to highlight the importance of comprehending the motives and feelings of people in a social-cultural context.

7. Case study I: KBrandArt – a story of the venturing process

7.1 INTRODUCTION

KBrandArt is the pseudonym we use to represent this case venture. The case account is about the emergence and further development of a young creative venture in Aurora by a team of five nascent entrepreneurs, who have shared different experiences but similar ambitions in life. In order to conceal the actual names of the people involved the pseudonyms Denise, Charles, Paul, Adam and Luke were used. A pseudonym was also used for the location of their venture as 'Aurora'. The venture team grew to six people during the course of the fieldwork as they employed a brand manager, Norman, whom they met through networking.

The venture team members, Denise, Charles, Paul, Adam and Luke, set up KBrandArt in the city of Aurora in 2001, as a multimedia design and production company, independent from an incubator context. They were all students at the local university, studying different subjects in art and design, such as video, graphic design, and music. KBrandArt was an extracurricular activity that existed separately from their coursework. Their aim was to expand on their already existing activity and develop a real business through a fully-fledged venture, synergising the skills and competencies that each team member had. After just ten months in business, they won the 'Shell Livewire Entrepreneur of the Year Award for Aurora and Aurorashire' and were also recognised for their team development by winning the Workforce Development Award. Their team roles arose naturally, in the sense that each played to his strengths, and no one's position was contested. Denise has taken on the responsibility of being the managing director. Sales and marketing is Luke's responsibility. He is assisted by Paul, Adam and Charles who deal with development and research. The creative production tasks are allocated as follows: Charles leads the interactive studio; Paul leads the music production department; Adam leads the design and imaging studios; and Luke leads the video production department.

The company initially offered a comprehensive multimedia design and production service to businesses and organisations, such as marketing and promotional firms or departments, trainers and educators, and other creative businesses. Their client base is focused on the leisure and culture industries, working with a specialist clientele providing bespoke, creative imaging and presentation solutions. This client base has paved the way for an expansion of the company portfolio into corporate and local government sectors. As the business started to expand, the nascent entrepreneurs felt the need to move out of their first offices in a business centre where a number of SMEs were located. They moved to their new premises in March 2003.

The researcher met the venture team in their new offices in May 2003. She discussed the aims of the research by means of a research protocol and asked for permission to be a participant observer in their organisation for a period of time. Denise, as the managing director, agreed that she could attend their Monday board meetings, where the five discussed all issues and activities pertaining to the development of their business. A 'Friday afternoon' meeting that focuses on creative issues had just been introduced. The idea was to form a session where all projects and work-in-progress were laid out on the table to outline new ideas to the rest of the team or to present creative solutions to technical problems, and seek the team's help in resolving them.

The venture team was observed at its Monday meetings for ten months (June 2003–March 2004) by attending 18 meetings in total. The researcher went to their offices on Monday afternoons; stayed for 3–4 hours before the evening meetings started; and observed their interactions while dealing with the daily aspects of the business. The researcher also joined three Friday afternoon meetings and attended three Industrial Networking Organisation (INO) meetings, where a mix of creative companies and RDA officers participated. The INO was founded by KBrandArt in July 2003, having identified the need to develop a supportive, industry-led network for the creative industries community in the region.

From the above sources, the KBrandArt case account was generated, drawing on fieldwork that included participant observation, interviews with the nascent entrepreneurs and two other members of the INO, so that we could gain a deeper understanding of the views of the broader venture community. This was clearly complex because it necessitated understanding the creative industries context, and the position of the firm in that context. The latter was gleaned from analysis of documentary evidence such as the business plans of KBrandArt and INO, a consultancy report for INO, meeting notes and some internal memoranda.

KBrandArt was explored early in the process of becoming a fully fledged business, when the venture team members chose deliberately not to go down the route of starting in an incubator organisation – the common practice for nascent entrepreneurship in the region particularly in the creative industries – but developing the venture independently and initiating what became a leading sectoral networking organisation – the INO – for regional creative industries. Their story is presented in two sections in this chapter. The venturing process is described in the first section with a view to highlighting the dynamic and emerging nature, which is linked inextricably to the emergence of the nascent entrepreneurs involved. Key events, decisions and developments in different phases of the venturing process are discussed in this section, aligning with the stages and activities captured by Aldrich (1999) in his book *Organisations Evolving*, discussed earlier. The second section delineates the underlying processes, which are entrepreneurial learning and managing.

7.2 VENTURING PROCESS: EARLY CONCEPTION AND GENERATION (2001–2003)

KBrandArt was developed as an independent venture while the nascent entrepreneurs were still university students. Interpreting the national and regional context of the creative industries in a different way than their counterparts, the members of KBrandArt followed a route of setting up the venture outside the incubator run by the local university.

> As soon as we looked at the incubators, such as NH and BM, we decided consciously not to go down that route. Even though you are creating your own venture through incubation, your client basis wants to see you as an individual. You need to be seen as an independent entity. You know, incubators have this 'cotton-wool type' of label. . . . From an outside perspective, we consequently might have that stigma because we are graduates of the university and developed the company while we were in the university . . . so developing the team outside is probably messier than developing it inside an incubator. You have to go to the deep end. Most of the time it is a search of what is going on, what and how we should go about conducting this business. We had to deal with an awful lot of details when we left the university but it was a conscious decision. Probably it motivated us to target forward in terms of how we can develop the company, how we can organise it to a quicker start [Managing Director: Denise].

This was a challenging route for starting a business as there was little planning. A team of art and design graduates, with a shared interest and complementary expertise, came together to set up a nascent enterprise with a view to develop a larger and more structured operation – a fully fledged venture. Theoretically, the phases of development are separate, but at KBrandArt 'conception' and 'gestation' periods are interwoven.

Ideation (that is the idea of starting a business out of their activities at the university) and mobilisation of resources appear to be complex processes. As noted above,[1] the activities during this process of nascent entrepreneurship are said to involve giving serious thought to business, looking for equipment and software, investing their own money in the business, seeking financial support, looking for premises to rent, receiving money from early sales (such as nightclub events, social events that they organised together as students), creating a new legal entity and organising the start-up team. Indeed this list of steps taken arguably straddle the initial evaluation of an idea – judging whether it is indeed an opportunity – and the actions required to set in motion the development of the opportunity as a nascent enterprise (Chell, 2008, 2009). Certain decisions had to be taken and implemented quickly. This involved prioritising, multi-tasking and coping with uncertainty, most of the time to the detriment of the team members' personal lives, during these two frenetic phases of business venturing. Talking through their experience, Denise reflected further on the complex and emerging nature of venture creation as follows:

> There were many issues we needed to discuss – financial, technological and other commercial issues. So it was a lot of hard work. You are committing yourself to something wholeheartedly, you are talking about personal investment, networking and long nights to work things out . . . We needed to prioritise things. The question of what is urgent becomes fundamentally important.

Referring back to the conception phase, the venture developed from their experiences and ambitions during their time together as students at the local university (1999–2001). KBrandArt was an extracurricular activity that existed separately from the projects that they were producing for their degrees. They were organising night events for companies and undertaking group exhibitions. As they were coming towards the end of their studies, they realised that what they were doing was commercially viable and they started to contemplate various ways of taking it forward:

> We realised that what we were doing did have commercial viability and it was more experimental . . . We were attracting people genuinely interested in what we were doing. So, we sort of thought that this could well be something seriously we need to consider when we finish our degrees as a full-time venture. We had already created the name and we experimented with it for three years.

In 2001 they had already formalised the business and hired an office in a business centre, which provides office-space for SMEs at affordable rates. They spent nine months there carrying out early activities of business formation. According to one of the nascent entrepreneurs, the situation in these early days did not represent the best way of doing things and this gave a spur to move forward. The decision to relocate was made in a similar way to the decision to start the business outside an incubator organisation. It was made collectively and agreed unanimously, after a series of discussions amongst the start-up team members. The researcher's observations did not reveal any tensions during this decision-making process, which appeared to be driven by the perceived need to become independent and portray an image of a dynamic, cutting-edge, young and creative company to the market. In Luke's words:

> There was a company that was interested in us, in this venture. They wanted to help us set up KBrandArt as a limited company by providing an office space and marketing and sales services, in the sense that we could provide them and they could sell our services . . . When we left the university, we went straight into an office that these guys helped us find in the same business centre that they were operating in . . . In nine months time we realised that what they were looking for and what we wanted did not quite match. It was a dead end where they were trying to take us. We wanted to set up KBrandArt because we wanted to work for ourselves and be autonomous. We took control back and moved out after nine months.

When they started the business, it comprised five 'owner/managers who are all directors' according to the business plan that they wrote in 2001 to participate in the ShellLive Award Competition.

> We all act as managers responsible for the daily running of the business, and as production staff for creating and producing the company's revenue earning output (KBrandArt, Business Plan, 2001).

Denise, who had demonstrated business acumen to the venture team, became the managing director. Adam's title was 'business development officer'. The titles of the others (Paul, Luke and Charles) were stated as 'directors' in the business plan. The management responsibilities were shared: the daily operation of the business is Denise's responsibility as the managing director; sales and marketing activities are managed by Luke, assisted by Paul, Adam and Charles, who deal with development and research. In addition to the managerial domain of strategic development and day-to-day running of the business, the entrepreneurial team has shared responsibilities over creative departments in the firm (that is areas of production). Building on their respective expertise and skills, Luke heads the video production department; Charles leads the interactive studio; Paul is responsible for music production; Adam leads the design and imaging studios including print and published material; and Denise heads the account management and customer care.

When their first recruit, Norman, was employed as a brand manager in 2004, he was assigned to work closely with Denise in managing client accounts in their portfolio, attracting new clients and further strategising for the business. These decisions concerning their responsibilities, based on recognition of each other's competencies, were taken in the gestation period (2001–2003), during which they were putting together the start-up team. As with many other new ventures, these functional divisions between the members of the entrepreneurial team have not been strictly observed. The functional boundaries have been nebulous. Furthermore, the management structure has evolved over time as the business has grown and they employed other people.

While celebrating the second year of their business venturing process, the researcher witnessed the nascent entrepreneurs reflecting on their ambitions to create not only an individual space for themselves, but also a 'collective voice', working together as a team, working with clients and other players in the field. Evidently, people construct organisations to accomplish things they cannot perform on their own (Aldrich, 1999). The elements of individual experience, knowledge of each other and that of the art and design world, and their constructions about each other's motivations and skills, are all at play in the decisions and strategies they make. Indeed, those very decisions and strategies are embedded in the entrepreneurs' own personal beliefs and life philosophy, social milieu and position within it, their experiences and the narratives that they create in making sense of them (Lindh de Montoya, 2004). Relying on their individual knowledge and experiences as artists and designers in the creative industries field as well as their collective experience of starting the business in a business centre and getting assistance from another venture, the nascent entrepreneurs decided to form the business outside an incubator or an environment of the 'managed workspace' kind. Sharing a common interest in 'making KBrandArt work', they employed several strategies, such as entering the Shell Live Award competition, and having a marketing strategy edge to their creative business, with a focus on branding in order to differentiate themselves from the competitor multi-media businesses. Keeping the production in house was another strategy for differentiation from other players, such as advertising or marketing agencies, which usually draw on outsourced production of the advertising and marketing material.

Their projections of the future, which are linked to the motivational factors for start-up, are worth examining. The nascent entrepreneurs used 'metaphors' (Morgan, 1997) to convey their ideas and perception for the future of the venture. Recently, Smith and Anderson (2004, pp. 137–39) have provided a comprehensive account of academic work in entrepreneurship exploring the role of metaphor. The authors suggest that metaphors, as a part of the entrepreneurial narrative, often communicate moralistic messages. They are used to echo the underpinning role of moral actions within entrepreneurship, perpetuating the importance and strength of the use of metaphors in a wider societal context. Here, the nascent entrepreneurs were asked to make sense of their future through an image or a picture. The purpose of the questioning of this kind was two-fold. Firstly, we wanted to facilitate their narrative construction about themselves because, having worked with the art and design students studying entrepreneurship, we came to understand that art and design graduates tend to convey their ideas and messages through objects, symbols or pictures more effectively. Secondly, we were aware of the powerful use of metaphors in organisational analysis (Morgan, 1980, 1997; Smircich, 1983; Chia, 1996b; Weick, 1998; Inns, 2002; Haslam, Posmen, Ellemers, 2003) and just recently in entrepreneurship research (Anderson, 2003, 2005; Thorpe, Gold, Holt et al., 2006). Thus, it was timely to test out any metaphorical language adopted in this case.

Denise's narrative, which includes the motives for setting up KBrandArt, its present state and involvement in the regional creative industries sector, and its future, reflects a remarkable clarity of her self-awareness and understanding that the entrepreneurial process is a collective and emergent process with certain objectives that she believes should be relentlessly pursued. Denise described the future with a 'tall building with many floors and the KBrandArt team celebrating the success together with joy and laughter on the top floor'. This can be attributed to her dedication to the success of the enterprise as a collective entity. The many floors suggest the stages that the team has undergone and are still undergoing, reinforcing the developmental and phased nature of the entrepreneurial process. An entrepreneur constructs one floor after another. As she or he moves on, building the layers of the work, the entrepreneurial dream of reaching the top becomes closer. The construction of this 'success image' by Denise also reflects the way in which she personifies herself with the business as a high-performer and high-achiever. Denise's individual role in the venture can be best described as a strong leader, who adopts a participatory and transformational approach in her leadership. Considering the informal (their relationship as five friends) and formal organisation (the enterprise: KBrandArt) that are created and managed, she relies on 'entrepreneurial leadership qualities' (Kirby, 2002) in making the team work fluidly and oriented towards the achievement of both short and long-term business objectives during the business venturing process. The transformational aspects of her leadership pertain to 'boundary-spanning activity', which she is constantly engaged in; creating the opportunity, for example, for the sectoral networking group, leading to a formal organisation, and exploiting the corporate market with refined and sharpened product and service offerings. Taking a process-relational stance (see Chapter 3), these activities exemplify the notion of 'entrepreneurship as a process of creating', leading to a state of 'economic creativeness' (Anderson, 2005, p. 591).

Charles' view of the future is linked to his construction of the venture from a relational perspective, and he communicates his projection of the future through an image of 'a peacefully working team of strong individuals who rely on each other for mutual support, have a strong sense of what is essential for success and lead productive lives – but not necessarily working in straight lines'. Through this statement, he acknowledges the importance of working relationships between team members and entrepreneurial awareness of working in a dedicated and focused manner with an objective to attainment of success. The 'brain' metaphor (op.cit.) provides a useful analogy, in which the focus is on complex interrelationships between parts leading to a whole in an authoritative and productive way. Charles' remarks also reveal his mental models and drivers to get involved in setting up this business. A drive for independence, expressed as 'independence as opposed to ownership' in his interview, and creativity are the underlying factors, recognising that creative minds do not often follow linear paths. According to Charles, creativity should be at the centre of his work. Drawing an analogy between his girlfriend's job – a bank teller working in a small bank branch – his views can be explained by the use of a metaphor, the bank as a machine, contrasted with a creative venture, like KBrandArt, which is an organic extension of the nascent entrepreneurs' self as art and design graduates. Based on observations of his actions during the meetings and daily conduct of the business, Charles had a calming influence; he showed that he was able to facilitate the process of reaching a shared understanding of particular situations, creatively framing the tensions between the nascent entrepreneurs over contested decisions. This might be characterised as the role of a peace-maker. On balance, he portrays more of a manager-type vision in the team, using Chell et al.'s (1991) typology.

Paul's construction of the future involves his passion for an international business: 'an international business out front with us and with enough resources to develop all my brilliant creative ideas for further wealth creation'. His future aspirations involve a comfortable life that is secured by an income stream and wealth through assets that he has built up. The current stage in which the team are operating can be best encapsulated in Denise's words: 'we have moved out from the comfort zone by embarking on this start-up activity'. However, Paul, usually taking on the role of the implementer in the team, has an ultimate objective of 'building assets' over the years that would warrant reliable and constant economic capital. Belbin's (1981) resource investigator team role applies to Paul, as a nascent entrepreneur who is constantly seeking and gathering resources, usually in the form of information and contacts. The entrepreneurial activity, in which Paul has been involved, has helped him develop entrepreneurial knowledge, understandings and actions. It is worth drawing an analogy here: the way he describes the start-up process as experimental and self-taught underscores his heuristic learning style.[2] This learning element of the venturing process will be elaborated further in section 7.4.

Adam, leading the graphic design and print-based operations of the business, has always played a key role in envisioning the future of the business and formulating strategies alongside Denise. Rather than being a freelance and trying to wait for jobs to come along, he thought that it was better to be proactive and start his own business. He describes his meeting with the other members of KBrandArt as a turning point in his life, because it paved the way for this synergistic team-work, enabling them to commercialise their artistic practice by building on each other's competences. His view of the future of the business is paradoxically mechanical: 'a clock that is intricate in its parts; carefully and neatly put together and perfectly functioning in application'. There exists a strong emphasis on the 'whole' (the venture) that includes various parts (such as business lines and associated departments such as video, interactive design, graphic design, as well as business functions such as marketing, finance operations and personnel management), which were carefully engineered over the years. It is paradoxical because he recognises the dynamics of their business in the creative industries in terms of each client and each project being different and that a customised approach and niche marketing are the very essence of their business activities. Despite the emerging nature of the business activity, he portrays a structured approach to conducting business, conveying an image of everything and everyone ticking along like clock-work. This is linked to how he enacts his role in the process of nascent entrepreneurship, leading to forming and growing KBrandArt. By taking part in the steering group meetings of INO and reaching a wider pool of social contacts, and accessing key information and people, he enacts a role of an assembler. Similar to Charles, he portrays more managerial rather than entrepreneurial characteristics in the team compared with Denise, Paul and Luke. His vision is rather mechanistic and conveys an image of a well-oiled machine in describing the new venture.

Finally, Luke, relying on his creative faculties and interpersonal skills in his undertakings as part of the team, conveys a less ambitious, but more energetic image, talking through the drivers that drew and involved him in the business venturing process: 'when we were faced with leaving university, it was just the obvious; none of us had had the time to look into what careers we could actually follow because we had been doing university; and so it was like right I can't wait to finish university so we can concentrate on KBrandArt'. He constructs the future in the form of himself as an entrepreneur: 'flying from one place to another pursuing new business opportunities; enjoying working with people I like; and providing products and services that satisfies them and myself'. The metaphor of a butterfly can be used to delineate Luke's construction of his entrepreneurial self. He brings positive energy and dynamism to the venture creation; he talks and acts whilst keeping an open mind to new ideas; and, portraying different images of possible futures to the other venture team members, constantly questions the present leading to the future. His individual role is very much of a questioner, challenger, reflecting on the participant observation work that we carried out. His ego-centred vision has created tensions with the others at times. However, they seem to find ways to move forward at the venture team meetings that were observed.

The central argument here is that discourses about the future are related to the nascent entrepreneurs' past experiences, individual and collective construction of realities pertaining to the current and future state of the business, and the volume of capital that they draw on and aspire to attain. As argued in Chapter 5, Anderson (2005, p. 596) suggests that entrepreneurship is about tomorrow, possible future states of being: '. . . each "event" may be new and idiosyncratic, but it needs to have some basis in our existing meaning systems' and 'all action exists in continuity with the past, which supplies the means of its initiation' (Cassell, 1993 cited in Anderson, 2005). This, we suggest resonates with our interpretation of Bourdieu's conceptual tools, applied to entrepreneurship: in particular the notion of developing a dialogue between an established *habitus* and emergent *habitus*. The social constructionist approach taken in this research[3] has supported the emergence of these insights.

7.2.1 Transforming the Business Idea to a 'Business Opportunity'

Whilst the team was still at university, the commercial viability of the group exhibitions and other activities that they carried out, such as event organisations sparked off a business idea for a full-time venture. With different expertise and similar mindsets, they experimented with their group work for a while and identified that they could synergise their skills to embark on a more serious joint project – setting up a creative media business with in-house production. The process of venturing is characterised as emergent, creative and iterative, with a low level of planning involved (especially if compared to the other two cases of the research project). This

meant the exploitation of contingencies rather than pre-existing knowledge about every aspect of the business development.

> We knew that the development of the company was not going to be plain
> sailing; it was going to challenge us and it still does. We are going to come up
> with things round the corner that we are not going to be aware of – that is quite
> exciting! (Denise).

> I think in those early days, when it was all new – and it still is new in the sense
> that the company is developing and new projects are taken on – when we first
> started, even understanding how a business was run, that was really challeng-
> ing, which was on one hand quite stressful, but at the same time you got quite
> a buzz from it when you manage to get over the challenge. I think once you get
> that feeling inside you that gets you over little challenges as you are building up,
> there is quite buzz attached to it, the real sense of pride, not really pride but a
> sense of achievement you get from it (Denise).

> . . . when we were faced with leaving university, it was just the obvious; none of
> us had had the time to look into what careers we could actually follow because
> we had been doing university and KBrandArt and so it was like right I can't
> wait to finish university so we can concentrate on KBrandArt (Luke).

The energy reflecting content of the words that most of them used during
the interviews revealed their excitement and enthusiasm for the venture
idea. Their belief in teamwork, coupled with exposure to the relevant
industry knowledge and contacts, generated an active learning and can-do
attitude. Although they did not follow a formal business incubation programme, the incubation period that lasted for almost three years was very
important in transforming the business idea into a viable business opportunity and to the development of their entrepreneurial competencies.

The business plan, which was written to attract funding, articulates their
start-up activity as a collective process:

> We have been operating KBrandArt for 22 months. The business developed
> from our experiences and our shared ambitions during our time together as stu-
> dents at the university. KBrandArt was an extra-curricular activity that existed
> separately from the coursework that we were producing for our degrees . . .
> Looking over the past, present and future of the business the passion has con-
> tinued to grow for what KBrandArt is and what it is becoming. The dedication
> and hard work is transparent in both the work that KBrandArt produces and
> how the business has developed and grown . . . . The sustainable development
> of the business has been primarily through its people, community and profits in
> order to take the business forward. (KBrandArt Business Plan, 2003).

The business plan won the Shell Live Award 2002 in the region and was
recognised for its team development. This was their description of the
business in the business plan:

We offer a comprehensive multimedia design and production service to businesses and organisations that make it their business to communicate, such as marketing and promotional firms or departments, trainers and educators, and other creative businesses. Initially our client base was focused in the leisure and culture industries, working with a specialist clientele providing bespoke, creative imaging and presentation solutions. This base has opened up to include other markets, and we have now secured business in the corporate and local government sectors. In addition we service the multimedia and e-media industry as content providers, supplying photography, design, music, video, graphic design and illustration either on commission or as an agency for other 'creatives'. We set our mission statement as follows: 'KBrandArt offers a unique combination of cutting edge creativity and vision, with a comprehensive multimedia audio/visual presentation and production service to the increasing design-conscious commercial world.

This statement is interesting because it goes beyond a simple view of developing a multimedia business. The team pride themselves in having a unique combination of skills, that is, creative artistic talents and marketing communications skills, which enables them to provide a combination of creative multimedia production and marketing strategy business. They underwent the process of sharpening their business and associated restructuring of the enterprise. As they have always been alert to, and seeking, opportunities in the marketplace to strengthen their market positioning, they refined the business concept as a 'brand communications agency with in-house production'. This will be elaborated in the next section and interwoven with a discussion of the social construction processes involved.

7.2.2 Social Construction Processes Involved

For KBrandArt, defining and redefining the business was observed to be a crucial part of the venturing process. At the team meetings, the processes of sense-making and developing understandings of the market, the needs/views of stakeholders (that is, customers, suppliers, employees, the local community and government), and their own needs/rewards and future objectives as entrepreneurs, facilitated the process of refining the business idea. As such, the following narrative illustrates the social construction process among these nascent entrepreneurs that form the venture team. In other words, it points out how a small team of nascent entrepreneurs construct, deconstruct and reconstruct meaning in relation to developing a venture through a generative dialogic process. The 'generative dialogue' underlying venture creation is one of the emergent themes that concurs with the notion of 'generative characteristics of conversations' developed by Steyaert, Bouwen and Looy (1996).

Denise (D) opens the meeting by mentioning that Norman (N) has some agenda regarding brand positioning. Norman is the new addition to the team who has been brought in to help them frame the emerging business; Luke (L), Adam (A) and Paul (P) are also present:

N: (introduces and explains the goal) Well, I have some form of internal document which sets out how we should talk about ourselves. What we do. How we do. Just looking at the process, KBrandArt Production's proposition is much clearer and clearly based in production in video whereas KBrandArt Studios' is basically in media. I see a number of issues here that you need to clarify. It is challenging but we should decide . . . I started to say 'We' now . . . Going down that route, you should tell me 'hang on we are not confident' and we should find the way you feel most comfortable (talking to everybody).

L: That's why you are here to push us.

N: Yeah (soft laugh) First of all, I'm not sure what KBrandArt Studios does or KBrandArt generically. We are going out there and what do you stand for. We have got to be consistent in that respect. Consistency in how we present ourselves to the market offerings is a must. Then creating value strategically and creatively is the key issue in brand positioning. Production arm is very important and it is based in certain areas and it does underline your expertise. So, we can say we do these . . . all this brand communication stuff. But we have got the production arm as well.

Denise gives an example from one of the projects with a client. She reinforces Norman's view that the business should focus on the unique combination of creative marketing and production. She talks about how they can realise that by providing the technical side as well.

Norman asks a question around the name 'Studios' to everybody:

N: What about Studios? Are you all comfortable with the name KBrandArt Studios?

A: Well, not really and we discussed this before but it is about the website, isn't it?

D: You can still have the domain name.

N: I wouldn't be worried about the domain name. What we are, what we are offering through what is the key issue to clarify.

L: KBrandArt becomes the solution to the creative consultancy and the production [process] is the technical side of it.

N: Where does the 'studios' fit then? I'm inclined to have KBrandArt and KBrandArt Productions.

A: KBrandArt does employ a range of activities.

D: But it doesn't cover the strategic studio.

N: It doesn't exclude it. At the moment, it doesn't imply it. When I am going to a meeting, I'm saying I'm from KBrandArt Studios because it is longer – better than saying just KBrandArt. Then the implication is I'm from a media company or what?

D: The trouble for me, is KBrandArt clearer?

N: Adam is right. The name 'KBrandArt Studios' poses problem in people's minds. Something more strategic I'm after. I'm just thinking if it could work against us.

D: The whole future is very much on the people who we have. I mean the clients. . . [She does not appear to be sure of what she is saying . . . looking at the piece of paper in front of her.]

N: Well, future seems to me lies in agency type of consultancy rather than studios. I don't think Studios implies that.

A: Lots of things happened in the Studios. So I don't want to ditch Studios but it might mean that it is mainly around the production. What about; is the strategy production and creation underneath? (Adam directs his question to Norman).

N: That's one of the things that I am coming to. We are not going to solve it here and then.

D: I've got to think in my head about how it communicates better.

She seems to be confused and worried. She turns to Adam and carries on talking:

D: We should have 'KBrandArt' as the main name, Brands Communications Agency. Everything you produce is brand communications, a website or a video.

A: Not exclusively. Everything we do is brand oriented.

N: I think it is the issue of whether the name poses obstacles. Yes, everything we do is brand oriented but. . . [Interruption by Paul]:

Paul (P) joins in the conversation. He is usually quiet and does not talk much at the meetings unless he is spoken to or he feels his interjection is necessary.

P: The question is should the name have to be explicit in that respect? (He is asking of Norman).

N: OK! If you take the name issue away for the moment, the thing is how much equity does it have? Are we going to use anything? Can we inject something into it? Does the word 'Studios' pose obstacles to where we want to be seen. (Pause) The next issue is it all about brand communication?

L: Well. Let's stick to the issue. What is brand? (Asking of Norman)

N: There is a wide interpretation of what a brand is. So, I would describe us as a brand communication agency . . .

Luke is not convinced and repeats his question:

L: From what you're saying I don't get what your definition of brand is . . .

Denise seems to be bored with all this 'conceptual talk' as she puts it at times when we have informal talks with her. She asks Luke:

D: How do you define it then?

L: I don't know . . . Brand is about everything that touches the consumer . . .

Talking to everybody but looking at Denise mostly, Adam argues:

A: Your corporate identity in a way. Clients want us to produce campaigns of the highest creative standard to achieve their brand positioning or strengthening . . . whatever . . .

N: [replying in a reaffirming way] Yeah but the other thing is to deliver what you suggest. I mean the issue is to meld the production side with the strategy side. So, rather than talking about disciplines like video, website, motion graphics or print design we need to also talk about marketing activities: advertising, PR, live events, digital marketing . . . Talking about those things support the fact that you guys are actually delivering the strategy side. We need to start talking about those things. Because what people want to see is that you are competent in this area. Two elements here: first, how we describe ourselves is the main issue . . . [Interrupted by Denise]:
D: It is about selling a package that people can relate to.

Denise reminds that they had this discussion almost a year ago but at that stage they weren't sure about what they were – an advertising agency or a brands agency or a creative production company? Norman continues:

N: Why we need to be talking about advertising and direct marketing as well is because we are moving to the brand communications side. We are more than a creative production firm . . .
L: Are we? [Asking everybody] I am not quite sure.
D [responding to L]: We should be . . .When Freddie talked about the emphasis on the brands agency, I thought we might lose some of our advertising customers but we need to consider from whom we can get proper projects. Production side will continue . . .
N: Absolutely . . . It doesn't deny it at all.

This dialogue exemplifies the view of entrepreneurship as a process of becoming. It is a transitive process that may be characterised as enacting a possible future. Post ideation, the identification and evaluation of the perceived business opportunity, follows from entrepreneurial activities of refining the business concept, strategising for future and mobilising resources, to actualise new possibilities that arise through active engagement amongst the team and other stakeholders in the business community at large. Clearly, intending to make sense of the venture community members' ongoing constructions of the development of the venture, their thoughts are shaped by, and shape, their conversations in ways that allow them to proceed with the venturing process. This occurs for example when engaging in the strategic matters of the business, such as steering the business towards a certain direction, as the above meeting talk conveys. Gergen and Thatchenkerry's (1996) conceptualisation of generative dialogue has the potential to be applied to this case study. They describe it as a meaningful interaction between parties as part of a transformative process. The generative dialogue enables the participants, working collaboratively, 'to formulate models of understanding or action that incorporate multiple inputs' (ibid, p. 368).

Focus on social construction processes, and continual strategic exchanges between the nascent entrepreneurs were apparent at the meetings we attended. This does not necessarily indicate that the members of the venture team reached a shared understanding by the end of the meetings. On the contrary, there were a lot of woolly conversations! However, they managed to find ways to develop enough confidence to improvise and enact the business as a team. Certain team members (mainly Denise and Adam) were attempting to frame the process of creative thinking and conversing by steering the agenda towards accomplishing important tasks and thinking ahead. However, this collective enacting part of the process cannot be separated from generative conversing. The actors involved in starting and developing the venture, attempted to find ways to work together through exchanging views, interacting and constructing understandings about various issues of a venture. Paul, for example, stated:

> Venture creation is such an iterative process that enormous effort has to be put in to ensure that whatever you are setting out is achievable. I mean the enterprise you're creating is going to meet the realities of the world, demands of your customers, your investors, your suppliers and even your staff. You're continually reflecting on what you are providing to them and how you are doing this as well. Sometimes you have lengthy discussions about a problem or routine action between team members. But we get to some point eventually and move on. In this way, the decision you make or the way you act in one situation may be different than the previous one. To me, this is where you are putting your learning into motion and managing your business.

This reinforces the theme that the venturing process is characterised by 'generative conversing and collective enacting', through which practical meanings and actions occur between the venture community members spontaneously in their responses to each other. Shotter and Cunliffe (2003) describe this in organisational settings as 'the particular way in which we voice our utterances, shape and intone them in responsive accord with our circumstances that gives our utterances their unique, one-occurrent meanings . . . Put simply, meanings are created in the spontaneously coordinated interplay of people's responsive relations to each other'.

In an entrepreneurial context it is also associated with the idea of entrepreneurial managing. Further, when the members of the venture community discuss their jobs or opportunities as two of the sub-headings of their meeting agenda, they are able to use their responses or the responsive instructions in the conversations, to guide the organisation and assembly of the bits and pieces of information available to them. Thus, they heed each other carefully (Weick and Roberts, 1993). For example, they come to certain understandings about their relationships with each other, with their customers or regional bodies, and try to identify different business opportunities. Moreover, they are on a quest for networking opportunities to enhance their business. As such the nascent entrepreneurs, as we shall see in the next section, have joined wider communities.

7.2.3　Becoming a Venture Community: Formation of a Regional Networking Organisation

Having different roles, complementary contributions or overlapping skills, the nascent entrepreneurs sustain dense relations of mutual engagement and they become participants in other communities of practice, through their further involvement in, for example, self improvement tasks with relevant parties. It therefore appears that the term 'venture community' is plausible to describe such a group of people, including the nascent entrepreneurial team and their stakeholders. They perform their roles by joining wider communities at times and stage their performances in ways that make sense to others. The questions of how they join other communities and how they deploy their social capital in order to obtain resources, ideas and raise the profile of their business in the larger business community, find some answers in their networking approach.

The strength of networking activity lies in the possibility of individuals reaching actively and purposively outside their immediate social circle and drawing upon information, advice, and assistance from a large diverse pool (Chell and Baines, 2000). When the members of KBrandArt actively engage in such relational activities of networking through fellow entrepreneurs, friendships, regional and national business support agencies or customers, they see this as a fundamental part of both their personal change and that of the business. This is in tune with Johannisson et al.'s (2002) suggestion that collective innovativeness, flexibility and capacity is created through relationships between different agents in entrepreneurial settings. When reflecting on their involvement in initiating an industrial network named the INO in this study, we had the following conversation with Denise:

> Denise: . . . there is a whole world outside. You have to seek out opportunities. Creating a business is about filling a gap in this industry. Creating INO is similar to creating KBrandArt – filling a gap that exists because people do not know each other. So we have seen the need to have a network within the region which could bring people together. 60–75 per cent of businesses in the CI do not have office bases. That's a major thing in taking an active role in INO. If you are a copywriter or photographer or architect who works with your equipment and mobile phone, how do other people know about you? . . . The network is about who knows who, so that who can help who? (*She starts drawing a figure on a piece of paper.*) It is actually a big thing that you have got main figures, actors. Then you have other people around the central figure. In the network, it has got everybody tied into it. You have got to make sure that all these circles are connected and then building this person here and there who knows that person and that person . . ..
> Mine: A sort of a relationship building?
> Denise: Yes, exactly. It is basically a process . . . a process of creating something new. It is learning to do as well. And learning from those people who are more

experienced, who have been in this business for a lot longer than we have; or, learning from each other when you come together by sharing different ideas, knowledge simply through chatting.

The INO has developed from the efforts of Denise and Adam, who strongly believed that they should give a shape to their networking activity, which should serve more than the purpose of forming strategic alliances. They initiated the network and put enormous time and effort into bringing together the key players in the region. The steering group included representatives from the city council, local university, and the regional development agency and other nascent and experienced entrepreneurs in the creative industries. Denise and Adam represented KBrandArt.

The INO is a good example of how KBrandArt team members are deliberately networked and trying to build this process of forming the INO as a part of their own venturing process. In this way, they open up new business opportunities and give a structure to the networking activity in the creative industries by taking ownership of the emerging nebulous organisation. This has evolved through a series of networking steps. First was the organic formation of the venture through the coming together of five people while they were at the university. That was a networking activity. And, second, there were looser connections to people outside that small group of fellow students. They learned quite quickly of the need for networking with these other skills and expertise. Forming strategic alliances appears to be the key activity throughout their business venturing process. Third, these nascent entrepreneurs engaged in networking activity beyond the process of becoming a part of the network. They lead the sectoral network organisation with a strong sense of ownership in order to raise the profile of the new venture. In an entrepreneurial sense, there was a higher order question involved: the question of 'whom do we need to ally in order to be able to take this business further'. This was coupled with 'how can we create a tighter network out of looser connections between people in the creative industries so that we will not only benefit from the networking activity, but also be able to influence future developments by taking the ownership of the initiative?'

The social organisation of the enterprise relies on strategic exchanges with a number of stakeholders. When Denise and Adam discussed the need for, and the possibility of such a networking organisation to bring the regional creative sector together, the business owners, freelances, representatives of the local government authorities (the city council and Business Link) and those of the RDA, were ambivalent: they expressed their reservations and support at the same time. Taking the initiative in May 2003, KBrandArt took the first tentative steps by organising various meetings, forming the steering group and commissioning a consultancy project in order to better understand the realities of the creative industries and new business development.

The following is an excerpt from our field notes reflecting on an INO meeting where the network members were discussing the possible ways of establishing the network and organising the first public event in order to endorse it:

Denise starts with apologies from Kelly (K), a small arts business owner, and then turns to Peter (P), a solicitor, who sits next to her and says:

D: It is your turn now.
P: Is it? Denise, if you want to.

Then he looks at Mike Kent (MK), who is sitting opposite Peter, to make a start. Mike, with a confused look, asks 'Should I start?'

MK: Right. OK! I don't want to go through the minutes but it is important to mention a couple of things.

They have a one page A4 sheet in front of them. It lays down the agenda for the meeting with the people's names attached to each point/task. So they are following the meeting agenda as set by Denise and sent to each of them in the morning. At the beginning of the meeting, Peter made a comment about receiving it this morning. Denise responded by saying 'Yes, as always I am very organised'. The other document that they have is some parts of an INO consultancy report. Apparently, they have to decide on certain issues, which have been raised in the consultancy document regarding the structure of the new organisation, its legal status, the financial matters, etc. MK continues:

MK: I copied the relevant pages this time rather than the whole thing. Simon, can you share it with Adam? I don't know why I have failed to have enough copies this time.
S: Fine.

Adam nods. They start discussing the page entitled INO: Organisational Structure – Board of Directors. MK mentions the meeting he had last week with GOVEM (Government Unit of East Midlands). From that meeting, he brings in some regulatory aspects such as changes to legal requirements, for example. Then he talks about organisational structure in terms of some amendments to the report. (As I understand they are going through the specific parts of the INO consultancy report to come up with a final document which will set the foundations of the new organisation and Mike was assigned to do this in a detailed manner at the earlier meeting). They look through the definition of the board of directors, which reads too broad according to Adam:

A: Do we need to be more specific about this? (Asking everybody)
P: Yeah, probably . . . And I think we should make the decision now as to what the definition should be.

MK: Right . . .

D: What does advocacy role involve? (Asking Mike)

MK: Denise, basically it is more than giving some advice . . . (He quotes from page 18)

P: Is that what you mean?

MK: No, I've changed it. Two things really; what I was trying to do was to realise the responsibility of the chair really and add the advocacy role.

Martin (MR) seems to be uninterested in the conversation going on and he probes his opinion on discussing these details:

MR: In terms of funders, the specifics are not that important, are they? (Asking to everybody in tone, but looking at MK)

D: But things like remunerations . . . [MK interrupts Denise]

MK: I'll come back to that Denise.

D: OK! Cool.

P: How does paragraph 4 and 6 reconcile?

MK: I ponder that as well. I don't know how we will sort that out.

Now they all start paying extra attention to those paragraphs, reading them through. Denise makes a joke about the writing style of the consultant. MK says:

MK: Paul tends to repeat himself, doesn't he? He has an ability of telling the same thing in three or four different ways. [Martin joins in the conversation]

MR: Yeah, 20p for each word.

All laugh. They move on to the other appendix of the report which is the INO financial plan. To Denise, it is important to know how much time they need to dedicate to INO when it starts operating:

D: I think there is a lack of grasp of how much time we need when this thing is up and running.

MK: yeah.

D: We are all professionals. One of the problems of these sorts of boards, people lack commitment because they do prioritise things. It is important to know whether the money is going to individuals or organisations . . .

They discuss this in relatively great detail. And this discussion leads to the legal status of the emerging organisation. As the discussion goes on and on Adam interjects:

A: Can we decide that at this stage we're not really interested in charity status?

S: I thought we are.

D: No, I don't think we are necessarily.

They move on to discussing the specifics, regulations and implications of being a charity. They take the discussion forward and talk about the audit of INO accounts:

MK: I thought we are willing to open our accounts as a very nature of the organisation.

D: Yes, we are. We would like to be transparent and open.

They all agree. Then they shift the conversation to the wording of the financial plan. One decision they come up with is to replace the expenses with costs. They carry on with Appendix 6.2, funding costs. Martin identifies one point which is taken positively by the rest and they agree on the amendment as he suggests. They resolve the issue quickly on this matter:

D: Claps to Martin . . .

All laugh. Denise has been very positive and making jokes so far. Denise and Peter prompted the same question at the same time. Martin makes a comment stating that they are sharing the same brain. Peter responds ironically:

P: Which is a bit worrying really because I think D has got a bigger one.

Martin, Peter and Denise laugh at this comment while the rest read the document. They keep on talking. Martin has been picking on things which are slightest details such as 'mostly unlikely' should be 'most unlikely'. They alter it accordingly. Then they move on to Table 8 of the business plan and Mike reminds them that they discussed this last time, so his part of the meeting agenda is coming to an end but one final point remains: consultant role? Denise instantly joins after Mike's final words: consultant? Who and how? She starts informing them what she has done regarding her action point as set at the previous meeting and which constitutes the second item on today's meeting agenda.

D: After the discussion with EM Media, they are happy to dedicate one person as consultant. They also said they are happy to help us to apply for extra funding. They will be able to give the money because they know the project from the beginning, they've worked with us. They know the report and they know that we know what we are doing and where we are going.
MR: This is one person, one day a week?
D: Yes.
MK: Do we need to specify in this document that EM Media is going to provide this person?
D: I think so.

MR and P nodded. Agreeing with them MK says this is all he can think of at this stage and closes his session, fulfilling his task as point number one on the meeting agenda. They all appreciate Mike's contribution and thank to him. So what they have discussed so far is the first point of the agenda that Denise emailed to them this morning.

The other important issue is recruiting members to INO. This discussion is likely to take a while. They consent that delivering some tangible benefits will attract people to the website and subscribe to the network. Martin is very keen on this tangible benefits business. He goes on and on in terms of the implications of such things. The others remain quiet. Adam and Simon appear to be unconvinced with the ways Martin is suggesting to achieve this aim. Then Peter interposes and

*says 'let's leave it for now'. Denise says 'a clap to Peter. It was a bit chairing!'
Slight laughter follows. They go on talking the third item on the agenda: The
main concern is private-public sector divide and the appointment of directors
accordingly.*

P: We did discuss last time the board being an interim board, didn't we?
MK: For 12 months.
P: Yes, maybe we should say in this document that directors will be appointed
for 12 months. In short to medium term, INO will benefit having Martin as the
director . . .
S: I am not sure. I just don't like the idea of Aurora City Council (ACC) having
a seat on the board which derives from a private sector-driven initiative . . . It is
not about you personally Martin . . .

*Seeming to be very keen on the post of director, Martin tries to explain that he
doesn't represent the ACC. Adam asks 'are you not an employee of the ACC?'.
Martin replies yes and no. Currently being the employee of ACC and holding this
post, he says, doesn't mean that he will be looking at issues from ACC's perspective. Being the most convinced, Peter adds:*

P: We obviously can say that, hang on Martin, this view represents ACC, and
also we should be able to sack our directors, shouldn't we?

*Adam puts his earlier question in a different way and asks whether Martin will still
be an employee of the ACC when he comes and works one day with them on INO.
Martin says yes and no and goes on and on about it.*

P: We are not painting the devil on the wall here, are we?
D: No. (Playing the role of a mediator) On this matter it is important to get
everybody's opinion and to reach some sort of agreement.

*They cannot reach a consensus in the end and move on to discussing the trading
name, as Denise puts it, of the organisation. Martin says it is almost pointless to
come up with an idea now. We should keep it as broad as possible. Denise makes
a point about registering the company. Mike responds asking what is going to be
the address of the company.*

MK: I know we've got time for these things but they are linked to the registration issue.

*Mike puts emphasis on the reciprocal nature of this organisation. This discussion
is followed by the one on the venue for the next meeting. Denise talks about the
nature of the event. She says she wants a broader appeal so inviting people across
sectors and so on. Peter is focusing more on endorsing the INO as the main aim
of the launch.*

*Final point on the meeting agenda was the minor amendments to the website.
Adam takes over the conversation and elucidates some necessary changes. Finally,*

Denise mentions the organisation called NESTA (the British Design Initiative) and she says she has been searching some alternative organisations and has come up with this. She gives brief information about it and says it could be something to further explore for future collaborations. Simon makes a final point and describes the changing nature of the CI working group, and subgroups in ACC. How the subgroup is divided into two as workspace group and strategy group is the main issue. They all agree that it is such an unnecessary move.

D: Increasing bureaucracy nothing else.
S: Well, I think I've made my reservations about ACC clear by now, haven't I?

They agree that the date for next meeting is 2 March. They all appear to be happy about the time management of the meeting. Denise mentions:

D: Well, we've done well. Haven't we? Well done Peter as the chairman.

They all laugh and leave the office one by one. Martin stays a bit longer and discusses something with Denise by looking at a website.

Field work of this kind provides an opportunity to understand the emerging contexts in which strategic exchanges between stakeholders, take place. As such, the analysis of the INO steering group meetings are shaped by context, actors, activities, participation, process, relationships, time period involved, objectives, meanings and values. The contextual base (the values and objectives behind KBrandArt; the other stakeholders involved having an open and synergistic approach, while at the same time reinforcing the ownership of the INO) is especially significant in developing understanding in an emerging business, where organisational members have shared histories and implicitly shared futures (O'Connor, 1997). The main actors, Denise and Adam, as the members of KBrandArt venture team, have shared a history together since their university years and they share a certain objective and a constructed view for the future of their business and partnership. The other members of the INO involved in the steering group meetings have their own agenda and expectations from this networking activity; however, they gather around the table with a mutual objective and mission under the new organisational structure being created.

The efforts of the nascent entrepreneurs of the case, particularly those of Denise, and those of some participants such as Mike Kent, freelance copywriter, can be described as 'legitimacy building' through dialogue. As interactions occur and especially as legitimacy claims were deemed to have failed, 'legitimacy-seeking' behaviour was observed. For example, Martin's desire to be appointed director of the newly created network organisation was not welcomed by some members of the group, such as

Simon – a nascent entrepreneur in the creative sector of the region – and triggered a debate concerning the public-private sector divide. The formation of the INO is characterised by a bottom-up approach where the needs of the creative industries businesses in the region have been identified by the creative business founders themselves, who pushed their agenda through governmental and non-governmental organisations. In the eyes of those who participated in the conversation by arguing against the idea of having Martin as the director, the appointment of somebody from the city council contradicts the nature of the enterprise and undermines its legitimacy as a private-sector-driven initiative. For Denise, Adam, Peter and Mike, it is important to make sure that a consensus of some sort will be reached about several aspects of the enterprise, in particular its legal status, registration of its members, appointment of directors, and marketing events. These exemplify 'legitimacy building' actions, as they unfold during the venturing process.

In the subsequent steering group meetings the nascent entrepreneurs were seen to modify their claims in order to legitimise what they wanted to build, the INO, as the network organisation driven by KBrandArt. The conversations about developing the network organisation, INO, shaping its direction and shaping their company narrative, KBrandArt, changed significantly over a period of several months.[4] As with O'Connor's (2004) study, this research supports Gartner et al.'s (1992) conceptualisation of the emerging nature of entrepreneurial behaviour embedded in situations of ongoing change, ambiguity and equivocalness. As discussed in Chapter 6, this may be viewed as 'entrepreneurial managing' by changing the equivocalness of interactions among a number of stakeholders into the non-equivocal interactions of an organisation (Gartner et al., 1992, p. 23). It involves legitimacy building, the negotiation of meanings, enacting, promoting and sustaining co-ordinated effort by creating structures and systems of operating. It is also linked to performing certain actions and discourses while omitting certain others. The way in which Denise and Adam pursued the initiation of the networking activity under the new organisation, INO, and secured the funding from the local governmental agencies for the consultancy project in collaboration with others, entailed certain performances characterised by power relationships as a part of the intervention programmes of the enterprise culture. In Steyaert's (2004, p. 20) terms, 'every performance is conversational in a broader sense, as its intertextuality introduces and omits certain discourses and power relationships, implying societal scripts of which some are hard to change while others can be resisted'. The conversations of the above kind reflect these performative dimensions of nascent entrepreneurship, which also implies a dynamic and agentic capacity of nascent entrepreneurs. The performative dimension is a function of the volume of capital under their disposition, the form of legitimised actions in relation to a *habitus* and field (Tatli and Özbilgin, 2006).

So, how do nascent entrepreneurs generate different forms of capital? What strategies do they employ to transform, allocate and distribute their volume of capital between different forms? These questions find some answers in the following section.

7.2.4   Capitals and Transformation Between Different Forms of Capitals

Bourdieu's (1986, 1990; Bourdieu and Wacquant, 1992) conception of capital is comprehensive; it represents more than resource, which individuals draw on in order to pursue their life projects; rather capital has both facilitating and constraining characteristics. As discussed in Chapter 5, Bourdieu (1986) proposes four forms of capital: *economic* that constitutes monetary income and other financial resources and assets; *symbolic* capital that refers to attributes, such as prestige, status and authority; *cultural* capital that indicates factors such as education and forms of language; and *social* capital that refers to institutionalised networks of relationships based on recognition (Özbilgin and Tatli, 2005). Further, Bourdieu (1986, p. 248) proposes that social capital is 'the aggregate of the actual or potential resources which are linked to possession of a durable network of more or less institutionalised relationships of mutual acquaintance and recognition'.

The social capital that KBrandArt venture members attained, during the conception and gestation periods of the business start-up process and through the creation of the INO, is a fundamental aspect that emanates through the business venturing process. This corroborates the Anderson and Jack's (2002) view of entrepreneurial network formation as an activity which provides the opportunity to observe the creation and use of social capital. They explain how individual entrepreneurs, whom they studied, used the networking process as a means of generating information sources, for developing resources, and as a mechanism for acquiring business potential. They argue that networks operate like a series of bridges that link numerous individuals with different sets of resources. The experience of KBrandArt team members concurs with their argument. They are the main participants in the process – the creators of social capital (Anderson and Jack, 2002).

This view suggests that social capital through the networking process creates the conditions for the effective exchange of information and resources. However, what Denise stresses in the above extract, and also what was apparent in the steering group meetings of the INO, goes beyond Anderson and Jack's (2002) argument. They argue that building a social capital bridge concerns linking individuals to, as it were, produce a robust social capital bridge that will enable its members to have better access to a richer range of resources and information. This applies to the networking activity of KBrandArt in the sense that they used people, other resources and information, but the networking activity has also formed a significant part of their entrepreneurial identity and business construction. The social capital generated has both facilitating and constraining facets. They have shaped and reshaped their identities and their business through their engagement with other people who are parts of the network. These engagements have facilitated new routes to, for example, recruit a brand manager and restructure the emerging organisation; and also constrained some activities, such as conducting their relationships with local public sector organisations, including the local government, RDA and university.

Entrepreneurial identity construction in relation to the construction of the business can manifest itself in different ways depending upon the context and situations being dealt with. In the case in point, initiating the idea for a networking organisation such as the INO and taking the lead in making the idea happen adds to our understanding of entrepreneurial motives for power and ownership. Ownership does not just mean ownership in the legal or financial sense, but the 'total identification with its success or failure' (Gibb, 1987, p. 24). The motivation and commitment that nascent entrepreneurs have to pursue the project of new venture creation from its early conception to its successful development define the notion of ownership. It is linked to their entrepreneurial emergence as individuals because they commit themselves to a project wholeheartedly by taking certain risks. They develop a sense of their own identity as entrepreneurs, including understanding what strengths and weaknesses they have, in order to start-up, operate, sustain and grow this venture. The transitional points, for example, developing the common university project to a fully-fledged business, refining the business concept by structuring the business areas and recruiting people to take it one step further, and forming strategic alliances, are key processes for exploring changes in the nascent entrepreneurs' construction of self. The transitional points that entrepreneurs go through reflect how they cope with challenges and overcome problems (Foss, 2004). How the nascent entrepreneurs in the KBrandArt case relate their artistic and creative side of themselves and their business to a social context; how they interpret these experiences of interacting with various stakeholders and drawing information and resources; how they cope with changes; how they develop the ability to make more informed decisions for the future; these are all fundamental questions in understanding entrepreneurs' identity construction.

This entails building different types of capital throughout the process and transformation amongst types of capital. For example, the cultural capital that they built in their respective art and design areas enabled them to start part-time production and develop a business opportunity by taking the work to larger scale as a full-time venture. The social capital that was created during the university years spans the development of various partnerships, particularly in the early days of venture formation. Establishing their own business and ensuring its sustainability and growth are viewed as a measure of success based on which they effectively generate symbolic capital in the form of power, ownership, independence and effecting change in their lives and the regional creative industries community.

The interplay between entrepreneurial identity and business constructions may be viewed as the processes facilitated by the transformation of the social and cultural capital to symbolic and economic capital. The transformation to 'symbolic capital' is the ultimate goal because it shapes their own personae as entrepreneurs and, at this point, certain symbolic qualities of independence, power and ownership are made manifest. However, there is also the transformation to 'economic capital' because both cultural capital (their artistic and design background) and social capital (networks, strategic alliances) are deployed to further develop the enterprise with an economic objective to generate wealth and profit. Symbolic capital of entrepreneurial knowing, has two aspects that are 'opportunity recognition' and 'coping with the liabilities of newness'. It is also transformed to 'economic capital', that is pursuing business opportunities and generating wealth (Politis, 2005).

The time dimension of the processes of capital creation and transformation is worth noting. Anderson and Jack (2002) suggest that the production of social capital represents a useful investment as social capital endures beyond the transaction and beyond the lifetime of the firm. Although the members of KBrandArt, who have put considerable time and effort in initiating and developing the INO network, seem to be uncertain about its short-term returns, they agree on its benefits in the long run. This is also linked to the issue of developing different network mixes according to the development phase of the venture, with reference to Lechner and Dowling (2003), who suggest that firms need to build the necessary relations at different stages proactively. Figure 7.1 summarises the transformation between different forms of capital, presenting 'economic capital' at the centre of the model in the context of nascent entrepreneurship.

The entrepreneurial actions described here are driven by the economic motives. As such, we revisit the perspectives of Chell (1997, 2000) and Steyaert (1998, 2003) on the economic aspects of the venturing process, and note that the personal and social becoming (Chell and Baines, 2000) of the venture team members are steered by their intentions to generate wealth. They are very concerned with the expanding client portfolio as

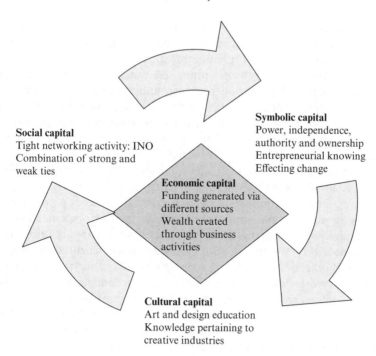

Symbolic capital
Power, independence,
authority and ownership
Entrepreneurial knowing
Effecting change

Social capital
Tight networking activity: INO
Combination of strong and
weak ties

Economic capital
Funding generated via
different sources
Wealth created
through business
activities

Cultural capital
Art and design education
Knowledge pertaining to
creative industries

Figure 7.1   Transformation between different forms of capital

well as generating revenue streams. Fletcher and Watson's (2003) incorporation of making a living, which can be linked to small business ownership, to the definition of entrepreneurship gains a different dimension in this study: the individual and collective becoming of entrepreneurs is intertwined in their economic becoming, characterised by their intention to accumulate wealth and by their risk-taking to enact the emerging business with the ambition to grow it. Therefore, the drive behind the entrepreneurial process is beyond making a living, which is mostly associated with so-called life style entrepreneurship or small business ownership, using Chell et al.'s (1991) typology in a slightly modified way.

7.3   UNDERLYING PROCESSES: ENTREPRENEURIAL LEARNING AND MANAGING

Our position on the process-relational view of entrepreneurship broadly concurs with Fletcher and Tansley's (2003) view on entrepreneurial emergence described as 'a relational process – always occurring in relation to something else'. Such relational practices are used by the venture community members to coordinate strategic and everyday activities of the enterprise. Moreover, it is from within these ways of relating to each other that people can make sense of their surroundings and come to know the world around them (Holman and Thorpe, 2003). From a social constructionist standpoint, Hosking and Fineman (1990) support this argument by suggesting that the way in which we come to know, and what we know, is based within these wider relational activities.

Encapsulating the emerging themes, business venturing as a process of entrepreneurial becoming, through constructing and reconstructing the meanings, situations, problems and actions of the nascent entrepreneurs, enables us to view the whole experience as a developmental process. Understanding their strengths and weaknesses and changing roles within the business as the venture develops indicates entrepreneurial learning. In relation to others, the nascent entrepreneurs of KBrandArt have come to know what works for them by encountering short and long-term strategic aspects, and everyday realities, issues and problems of the business. In Shotter's (1995) and Shotter and Cunliffe's (2003) terms, they develop their own practical theories and become practical authors who create a unique sense of their shared circumstances that enables them to act in ways that are intelligible to each other.[5] Rae (2004b) discusses 'practical theory' as a resource in entrepreneurial learning, highlighting its implicit, intuitive, tacit and situated characteristics. Thus, the process of developing practical theories constitutes an essential part of nascent entrepreneurs' learning, which involves a change in their thinking and in their subsequent actions. Therefore, practical theory becomes a component of their cultural capital – the development of their knowledge and belief structure about the practical workings of creative industries – and which offers a more appropriate concept – than resources to illuminate entrepreneurial learning.

Most of the nascent entrepreneurs in the case study emphasised the role of learning by doing in their venturing experience. What is immediately striking about considering this dimension of their entrepreneurial learning is that the metaphor of a maze (Learned, 1992) becomes pertinent in explaining the new venture creation process that nascent entrepreneurs go through. The nascent entrepreneurs in the case find their way by navigating through an intricate and usually uncertain and confusing network of interconnecting pathways. They have learnt to choose the most suitable pathway, which works for the situation in a particular context at a particular time, to exit the maze and proceed with the venturing process. The entrepreneurial managing side of this heuristic process is connected to finding ways to take the venture forward by enacting what they are learning. This is done by changing the equivocal interactions with stake-holders to non-equivocal ones and therefore adapting and modifying these practices.

In addition to the themes cited in the entrepreneurial learning litera-ture, such as learning to explore business ideas and create a viable busi-ness opportunity, learning how to garner resources, learning to manage yourself and others as the venture grows, learning inter-related functions of the business (such as marketing, finance and operations), this research has revealed that the entrepreneurial process is more complex and can be understood from a multi-level perspective that links micro-level learn-ing (personal learning of nascent entrepreneur) to meso- and macro-dimensions and, moreover, that the behaviours and actions at each of these levels are intimately interlinked. In this case study, the entrepreneurial learning process involves learning to legitimise the business (KBrandArt) and other related enterprise activity (such as the creation of the sectoral network organisation, INO); learning to perform certain discourses (for example, constructing a business plan for the Shell Live Award competi-tion or restructuring the departments of the business and communicating the business concept to clients via redesigning the website); changing the unexpected to their favour and tapping into the strategic alliances that they form in a context of creative industries and enterprise culture. These activities reflect the interwoven nature of the entrepreneurial learning process at micro-, meso- and macro-levels as depicted in Table 7.1.

7.3.1 The Role of 'Critical Incidents' and 'Learning Episodes'

There is a growing body of literature acknowledging that significant events or episodes impact on entrepreneurial learning (Chell, 1998; Cope, 2001, 2003, 2005; Rae and Carswell, 2000). As discussed in Chapter 6, nascent entrepreneurs develop certain understandings while responding to mean-ingful opportunities and problems. Their entrepreneurial learning is emer-gent arising from such formative experiences (Chell, 1998; Cope, 2005). In their study, Rae and Carswell (2000) demonstrate the importance of wider learning episodes where entrepreneurs provide evidence of seminal periods of learning that has influenced them.

The use of critical incidents technique is delineated in Chapter 6, with particular reference to techniques developed in entrepreneurship by Chell (1998, 2001) and Chell and Tracey (2005). The nascent entrepreneurs were asked to identify critical incidents or significant occurrences over the period of the business venturing process. In the current research, it was interesting to explore what criticality meant in their eyes and which occurrences they chose. Equally, the examination of different meanings

*Table 7.1   Entrepreneurial learning process showing micro-meso-macro-
            level aspects*

Aspects	Micro-level	Meso-level	Macro-level
Learning to identify business opportunities	✓	✓	✓
Learning to garner resources	✓	✓	✓
Learning to manage yourself	✓	✓	
Learning to manage different functions of the business	✓	✓	
Learning to legitimise the business (as a part of learning to cope with the liabilities of newness)		✓	✓
Learning to form strategic alliances (strategic networking capacity)		✓	✓
Learning to change equivocal interactions to non-equivocal ones		✓	
Learning to perform certain discourses while omitting others (performative capacity)	✓	✓	✓
Learning to get lessons from failures and successes	✓	✓	
Learning to use and exert influence (developing agentic capacity)	✓	✓	

attached to the same incident by different venture team members shed important light on the socially constructed nature of the entrepreneurial learning process. Table 7.2 shows the critical incidents reported by the nascent entrepreneurs in the KBrandArt case.

These incidents exemplify key moments or movements during the business venturing process. Winning the Shell Live award in 2002 marks a turning point for the team; perceived as getting recognition and raising the profile of the enterprise activity that they were engaged for some time. This is related to the importance of the team's efforts to legitimise the start-up, including various activities from creating a legal entity, developing prototypes of products and services, to developing higher-level, credible and trusting relationships with stakeholders in the region (c.f. Davidsson, 2006, p. 73). The small volume of economic capital combined with the larger volume of social capital generated helped the venture team build confidence in what they were doing and expand the entrepreneurial activities that they had started.

A more recent and mutually acknowledged incident was recruiting

Table 7.2   Examples to critical incidents reported by the nascent entrepreneurs

Nascent entrepreneur	Critical incident reported
Denise	Winning the Shell Live award
	Getting the Princess Trust Fund
	Creating the INO
	Recruiting Norman as the brand manager
Charles	Creation of the interactive department of the business
	Winning the Shell Live award
Paul	Recruiting Norman as the brand manager
	Moving to new premises
	Creating the INO
Adam	Creating the INO
	Recruiting Norman as the brand manager
Luke	Moving out of the business centre
	Recruiting Norman as the brand manager

Norman as the brand manager in September 2003. The meanings that they attached to this incident are worth exploring. Denise, as the managing director, attributed its criticality to keeping the business fresh and dynamic, supporting team management of the venture, creating an additional skill base, and providing practical advice to help build the company and growth:

> Denise: After the first few years in the business, you might feel that you are in a little comfort zone but you have to wake yourself up and think: stop it and get on the ball; keep pressing forward. I think it is easy for people to slip into comfort zones, I think you have to be mentally self-driven to make sure you don't slip into it. When you are managing a company, there is nobody looking over your shoulder so much; it is very lonely at the top, shall we say, but it has changed because we brought in Norman . . . I can bounce ideas off Norman and it is an interesting dynamic bringing in new people!
> Mine: Can you expand on this please, Denise?
> Denise: Bringing in Norman was a good moment, it was refreshing! It was something we had been waiting for. We had been talking about needing someone to increase the sales, bring an extra skill base to the business to help develop the company; and kind of be a someone who has been in the industry for a while and could act as an outside perspective looking in and could help build the company . . . all the advice we had had in the past had been very textbookish and then Norman came in and gets the guts of the company and sees what is actually going on and sees different potential and opportunities. We had worked with Norman on a three-month kind of basis, just on projects that came in on a contractual basis and then we thought if we bring him in on this and started working full time just think what we could manage with just having an

extra person in, so by bringing him in full time it definitely made a difference, a real difference!. . . Bringing an extra person – you are bringing in extra hands that could potentially double your turnover if there is only two of you selling and bringing the company in different directions.

Mine: Exactly! You have just started to grow the business.

Denise: I think that really, it is something that I was not really more supported. I am not asking Business Link to give me support. I think it's understanding that once a company gets into its third year there is a lot of dynamics at play and to grow that company in the right way that suits that company is really important; I think it is more crucial than the start-up phase, in a sense.

Mine: Why?

Denise: Because the growing bit can really be different to a company in its turnover and it can change it from mainly sitting in that comfort zone area to really making an impact on the economy and just give a new breath of life. I suppose at the growth stage, and depending on how they grow because there is a lot of advice on how to start a business, I think all that is fine and taken care of virtually. I think when you are growing you need somebody who can come in and observe things closer, and be able to give practical and outside perspective, that they understand not just generic stuff. Because when you are growing, it is important to ask the question of which way do you grow first? At the moment we are quite fortunate we can grow by the video department, from getting freelances in and employ that way . . . I think every company must go through this, this stage, you either change for the better or you stand still or you go down. There are three really obvious things you are going to do; but I think by making change it is only going to have positive effects really – even if you make a mistake . . . because you learn from it really.

Mine: I was going to ask how you relate this to learning really . . . entrepreneurial learning particularly.

Denise: Learn by doing.

The above conversation with Denise, which is a part of the follow-up interview with her, highlights not only the meanings that she attributed to the key moment and movement of bringing in Norman as the brand manager during their business venturing journey, but also hints at the key learning episodes around it. She views Norman as somebody who can help them to grow the business in revenue terms, but also provide a vision for the future of the business. Therefore, the criticality of this incident is two-fold: it is a short-term tactical move as well as a long-term strategic move made by the venture team. As discussed in Chapter 4, nascent entre-preneurship is imbued with three modes of organising, which are vision, strategic organising and tactical organising (Lichtenstein et al., 2006). This critical incident of recruiting a brand manager and the meanings attached to the incident by the team can be cited as an example of such modes of organising. Wickham (2004, p. 268) argues that entrepreneurial vision is a picture of a new world that entrepreneurs conceptualise and use to interpolate their understanding of why people will be better off with it, the source of new value that will be created, and relationships that will exist.

'It specifies a destination rather than a route to get there' (Wickham, 2004, p. 268). In this case account, Norman, the new recruit to the company, is considered by Denise as an important catalyst towards such an organisational change, which is characterised by refining the business concept, by guiding the venture team along the tough journey of growing the business, and by attracting other people to the venture.

The way in which Adam views Norman's recruitment to the venture as a critical incident is linked with this strategic planning process. His emphasis is on mundane and daily aspects of conducting the business, such as improving their capacity to appeal to different types of clients, getting recognition from the market, as well as shaping the direction of the business:

Adam: Taking Norman on board was a decision that would come up in meetings every month or so that we felt we didn't have; when we, for example, are tendering for work we know our way of doing it, but we don't know if it is an acceptable way of doing it. As far as our peers or the industry is concerned, that is not the issue, but it is what clients are used to seeing; that is the issue. And obviously we can't go to our competitors and say 'how do you pitch for work?' And so we were looking for an older, wiser head to get involved in our business in some way. Somebody with experience from industry who could tell us the way we were operating: if it was fine as it was or whether there were serious points lacking. One idea was to get some kind of non-executive chairman who would be sitting on board meetings once a month and just look at the way our business was going and use his experience from the industry for the last 30 years . . . Norman has not exactly come in that capacity. He has come in a lot more full time, a lot more hands-on, but he has still got experience from industry, which admittedly we have now got our own experience but it is very much the experience we have made ourselves not received knowledge in a sense. So it has been quite important to throw that into the mix . . . So it has been a big dramatic change, but it wasn't a hard decision to make. It was something we knew we wanted. The hard part was finding the person to provide that . . . It is one of the reasons we set up INO: to get that kind of mutual knowledge sharing. Creating INO was critical. We thought we might find potential employees as well but we knew it would take time.

Adam connects one critical incident, employing Norman, with another one, creating the networking organisation, INO:

Mine: Can you elaborate on the development of the INO?
Adam: Things are moving on, but slowly. We have got the consultancy report; I mean the business plan for INO. Now we have handed our comments back to them. They are just tidying up, but we are hoping that it is going to be signed off in the next couple of weeks. We can move on and actually start to implement it . . . At the moment INO is a loose consortium of interested individuals and companies and turn it into something a lot more formal with a membership roster, a website portal that people can actually find out more information about and get services from in some way and be quite strict with plans, a series

of events and seminars over the next year or so. In a kind of real world sense we trust to gain any benefit out of that. The whole thing does need to be formalised a lot more and so that we are having to work less and other people are involved in doing the work. And we can grow the network and grow it more organically; actually get some real committed members, not necessarily at the steering group level, but people who come to the events regularly and can see the benefits of getting mutual business from each other. We can find, as I said earlier, more potential employees or just freelances or people we can use; because we are going to need to grow again in about six months to a year. We are going to want to take on freelances that we can trust and that we know; and we are struggling to find them at the moment for the projects. We could do with more programmers to help with the website. I could do with more just basic art workers to implement my ideas and start to make them happen, but we don't know many people. INO is a fairly big network, but we are still struggling to find people we would trust to do work for us . . . It is in our interest if INO keeps going and grows . . . By its nature it is collaborative. Everybody has always needed to buy in skills or look to collaborate through mutual grounds . . . So finding that quite a few companies work that way in partnership for various things and it gives us greater flexibility because different companies might offer different specialisms.

Adam sees the development of the INO as a beneficial movement for their business and for the region, considering the dynamics of the creative industries. Knowledge sharing, finding a more qualified and trustworthy workforce, and developing collaborations between people by venturing on mutually interesting and rewarding projects form the core themes in the above extract from his interview. His learning experience surrounding the development of the INO is characterised by developing an enhanced understanding of the importance of the social capital that a nascent entrepreneur in the creative industries should generate and tap into; having a more flexible and collaborative outlook in the way they pursue their business; creating more opportunities and thinking through possibilities, not certainties.

The entire experience of creating the INO has been a steep learning curve according to Denise, whose storyline was located within the macro-field dynamics of enterprise culture. For example, how nascent entrepreneurs perceive government programmes and their approach to funding such initiatives and finding a way to work through the politics and bureaucracy involved:

Denise: What we did with the INO is we started something, the really interesting thing – it is a great opportunity and we laid down the opportunity for the government to make an opportunity of, by helping to get it off the ground. I think I have learned quite a bit to do with the politics involved with government and councils and everything and I have met very interesting good people . . . I have got good insight into the public sector, positive and negative, and I am probably more sceptical of it, but once it gets off the ground we can show you what the potential is in respect of the network. I am very impatient! I would like to get it off the ground quicker because I would like it to happen.

Making things happen is an expression that Denise used firmly on another occasion, when they held the first social event, bringing people together to endorse the new INO. Denise, as the director general of the INO as it appeared on the PowerPoint slides that she used, opened her talk, which lasted for not more than a minute, with the importance of the INO for them and the region and concluded with the capacity that she believes she has as a person, who creates and makes things happen:

> INO is very important for us to get together and create a synergy. I was here three years ago and when I proposed this idea, people were sceptical about it. Here I am today! We are formalising INO as a company soon. So people who know me know that I will do what I promise to do. I make things happen. Thanks.

Denise's entrepreneurial qualities of self-efficacy (Bandura, 1995) and determination surface in her talk and in various other conversations that we had during the course of the fieldwork. The meanings that she attributes to this critical movement of developing the INO pertain to learning more about the macro-field dynamics, including governmental programmes and institutions, as well as raising the profile of KBrandArt in the regional context of the creative industries. From a social constructionist standpoint, creating an organisation of these multiple relational possibilities produces power dynamics. As Hosking and Hjort (2004, p. 260) point out, '. . . talk of the entrepreneur is very obviously (though implicitly) talk about power. It seems that one can form this (entrepreneurial) life by constructing power over others'.

Creating the INO in the region, organising a social event to endorse it and making an announcement of this nature (the quote presented above) can be described as 'multiple, simultaneous, and inter-related inter-acts' (Hosking and Hjort, 2004, p. 261), which involve multiple contexts and multiple actors. Examples include the discourse of the new venture, KBrandArt, leading a regional networking initiative, that of the RDA supporting nascent entrepreneurs in the creative industries, and that of the local university's initiatives to establish better links with the nascent entrepreneurs and small business community, as a part of their remit through the newly founded Centre for Entrepreneurial Management.

Paul, another nascent entrepreneur of the team, has similar views that pertain to the creation of the INO; he associates it with the meso- and macro-qualities of the business venturing process, including raising the profile of their enterprise, creating further business lines, regional trading, and communicating the right message with the people of the creative industries in the region.

The launch of the INO occurred in January 2004; it was a social event where one of the authors participated in the talks, networking activities and knowledge sharing. The INO's aim was conveyed in the publishing material for the event that formed a fieldwork text in this research as follows: 'The aim is to create a sustainable network for independent creative businesses in the greater Aurora area that encourages growth through collaboration and creates a collective voice for the industry'.

The discussions held with people who were running or working for creative businesses in general, and discussions with the KBrandArt team members, shed significant light on how business-led networks, such as the INO, were perceived to have the potential to unlock creativity and enterprise and to influence the creation of an entrepreneurial culture by fostering partnerships, collaboration and the exchange of ideas. These are considered as defining market forces in the creative industries. It is important to shape the attitudes and perceptions of people who work in the creative industries, towards being more enterprising and entrepreneurial; create new markets; expand production chains; encourage diversity and deliver business support, and even financial assistance.

The nascent entrepreneurs in this case demonstrate some entrepreneurial qualities responding to the dynamics of the macro-field in which their business venturing process is embedded. They do shape such dynamics and they are shaped by them. For example, critical incidents, namely recruiting a brand manager to help shape the direction of the business or creating an industrial networking organisation, reflect how they develop their vision and communicate it among themselves and to the outside world.

This notion of internal relationships and the ability to envision the development of the business opportunity over time resonates with other studies (Filion, 1991). In their study of relationships between owner managers and first line managers, Chell and Tracey (2005) developed a model, which includes five components: competency, role, style, vision and an emotional bond comprising trust and mutual respect. Vision is defined as the ability of an individual to conceptualise their plans in vivid mental pictures (Chell and Tracey, 2005, p. 585). In sharing their vision for the venture, the nascent entrepreneurs used different metaphors as discussed in section 7.2 of this chapter. Their vision of the future of the business varies from 'a tall building with many floors constructed with timber and glass' to 'a clock that is intricate in its parts; carefully and neatly put together and perfectly functioning in application', synchronising with their individual roles in the business and also their emerging entrepreneurial and organisational identities. As demonstrated by Chell and Tracey (2005), vision is contingent upon a number of factors, including a tacit knowledge of the market, leadership style and personal aspirations of the entrepreneurs involved. The way in which the research participants communicate their vision, through metaphors and such mental pictures of how they see the future of their business, is a powerful indication of their entrepreneurial biographies, ambitions and how these ambitions should be fulfilled in their lives.

7.4 CONCLUDING REMARKS

This chapter has presented the business venturing experience of five nascent entrepreneurs, progressing from their informal organisation during their university years to the formal organisation of the venture, anonymously called KBrandArt. Their business venturing process is defined by heedful interrelating (Weick and Roberts, 1993) of micro-individual nascent entrepreneur's biography and capitals, infused by the meso-level relationships with the broader venture community and associated actors, and their creation of a *habitus*; and further complicated by the macro-level dynamics of the regional enterprise culture and creative industries.

This case is the principal case account of this study of nascent entrepreneurs, drawing on a prolonged and intense engagement with the team through participant observation, in-depth interviews and documentary analysis. The next chapter presents the second case, Rosie's venturing story in creating R-Games in the context of a university incubator. The case account reads differently to the KBrandArt case, mainly due to the main data collection method being a lengthy in-depth interview. The following case account should be read in conjunction with Tables 6.3 and 6.6, outlining the research methods and writing-up framework underpinning the construction of the case study.

NOTES

1. See Chapter 4 for a discussion of Aldrich's work pertaining to nascent entrepreneurship.
2. See Chapter 4 for the discussion of entrepreneurial learning.
3. See Chapter 5 in relation to the works of Berger and Luckmann, 1966; Martin and Sugarman, 1996; K.J. Gergen, 1985, 1994, 1999; Chell, 2000, 2008; Nicholson and Anderson, 2005.
4. This resonates with O'Connor (2004) who demonstrates how legitimacy building emerges in conversations that entrepreneurs have among themselves, their audiences and their environments.
5. To recap the debates concerning 'practical theory', the idea was developed by Argyris and Schön (1975) in their work entitled *Theory in Practice* in organisation studies. Key aspects of Bourdieu's (1977, 1990) work on theory of practice have been discussed in Chapter 2 (pp. 50–54). In entrepreneurship literature, Rae's (2004b) work can be given as an example of an application of the idea.

8. Case study II: setting up R-Games – Rosie's venturing story

8.1   INTRODUCTION TO THE CHAPTER

This case account concerns the business venturing process undertaken by a nascent entrepreneur based in a regional university's incubator centre.[1] As in the previous case study, her name, the name of the venture and that of the city were anonymised; and the pseudonyms Rosie, R-Games and the city of Gold Coast used respectively. She was a law and business student who was a self-employed taxi-driver during her spare time. The enterprise activity at the university changed her life dramatically and contributed to making her entrepreneurial dream of creating a game business happen. Her venturing story is characterised by relentless pursuit of a business opportunity with a strongly communicated objective of being rich and important. The process that she went through concurs with the emergent approach to the entrepreneurial process, and, paradoxically, with the planned approach, as will be explained. From the outset, her law and business background and training through the business mentoring and support programme in the incubation centre helped her develop her entrepreneurial awareness and commitment for a successful start-up.

The case study is structured in three parts: the first part delineates the business venturing process. This is followed by a discussion of underlying processes of entrepreneurial learning and managing in the second part. The learning process is characterised by developing entrepreneurial competencies as well as learning how to generate and transform different forms of capital that can be recycled within the process of start-up. The chapter concludes in the third part with a summary of the key arguments and lessons from her case account.

8.2   VENTURING PROCESS

Rosie was earning her living as a taxi-driver before she began her degree course at the university. Her business experience was limited to the extent to which she had worked for an advertising firm, which was jointly owned by her partner and brother. The decision to go back into education and study for a university degree was ignited by her frustration with the jobs she did, and her enthusiasm and willingness to develop herself and fulfil a sense of achievement:

> I was left with no jobs or qualifications when my brother and my partner fell out and decided to end the business. I then worked as a taxi-driver for so many years just for living but it was very frustrating because I am intelligent and I have got a brain. I cannot hold a job that doesn't give the stimulation that I need to keep going. Then I had a second daughter and for a long time I felt like all I was doing was just being a full-time mother. I couldn't live like that any longer and that's how I took the courage to take a step to come back to education and do a degree.

Rosie's story exemplifies the motivations of self-realisation, financial success, personal satisfaction and independence. Such motives highlight the cultural and social capital that she developed as a result of her formal education, previous work experience and enterprise training in the incubator environment. A combination of these factors (Davidsson and Honig, 2003) helped the nascent entrepreneur, Rosie, deal with the complexities and human interactivities of the venturing process, advancing through the start-up process and moving rapidly towards the infancy and adolescence phases.

During the years that she was taxi-driving, she came up with the idea for her board-game. The game would feature taxis as pieces and the players would have to make their way around a board featuring tourist attractions, trying to pick up as many fares as possible. It was a simple but original idea for a game. When she approached some game companies to sell the idea, she did not receive any support and she encountered so many obstacles:

> What I had done with my taxi-driving was to come up with the idea for this board-game. I envisaged a Gold Coast board and the taxi firm that I worked for as the playing instrument and I thought the tourist attractions in Gold Coast would be the destinations on the board. I did a bit of research and I contacted some game companies but I always got the doors closed on me. They all sign-posted me to agents and at the moment you get to an agent, they want to see a finished production line or sample. So you just can't go with an idea!

It was not until the time she spotted posters for the Enterprise Challenge competition run by the university that she gave serious thought to actualise her business idea and took the first step to turn it into an opportunity:

> When I enrolled on my law degree, in my first semester, I saw the advert for Enterprise Challenge 2003 with a £15000 prize. I didn't think they would accept an idea for a game and I almost did not enter. HD, who organised the

challenge, really encouraged me and finally persuaded me to enter. On the day of the deadline I bumped into her in the Union and at that point Louise, my daughter, had been really ill and I hadn't completed the application forms. However, she gave me some additional time . . . Stage 1 of the Enterprise Challenge is an entry form. It is an excellent way of doing it because what the form asks you: What is your idea? Who are your competitors? Who are your customers? How would you market or advertise it? Where do you see yourself/ your business in five years time? That was the first time that I had ever actually sat down and written something about my game. I wrote my goal down and it really got me thinking and I won the first prize. I won a £1000!

Rosie spent the £1000 on securing her intellectual property rights and getting a prototype made. At the same time, she was refining her game concept. She decided to design a game board featuring London streets and tourist attractions and she named her game 'Destination'. This was an important decision she made, upon which we will reflect later in this section. She entered stage two of the Enterprise Challenge:

It took me a few months to get the game concept right and also to write my business plan for the Enterprise Challenge, stage two. Stage two of the competition is where your business plan and a prototype are presented. I won £2000 at stage two and I used that money to set up my game company, R-Games, to pay the legal costs and get in the incubation unit, get technical service, get my business card printed and so on.

It was a steep learning curve that she was going through: developing the game concept (that is the product), dealing with legal issues (such as intellectual property rights) and constructing a business plan, which entailed an in-depth consideration and analysis of the market, resourcing the venture (finance, people and knowledge) and operational issues. As discussed in Chapter 4, these activities constitute important entrepreneurial endeavours in the conception and gestation phases of nascent entrepreneurship (Aldrich, 1999), moving towards the infancy stage. The boundaries between these stages are hazy. At the time of the interview (August 2004), Rosie was moving towards the infancy stage as she produced the fledgling new venture, R-Games. Developing her understanding on how to start a business, she made a few mistakes along the way:

I wasn't informed about the intellectual property rights . . . So really the money that I paid on patenting the product was wasted and I am not going to use the patent. I registered the trademark and the design and the copyright was granted to protect my game.

After moving to the incubation unit, the venturing process gained momentum mainly due to the mentor support and networks that were available.

Through a constant process of negotiations and exchanges (Watson, 2001b, 2003; Rae, 2002, 2003) with people in her social circle, her business started to emerge. This could be attributed to the consequences of the interplay of the variety of interests, understandings and initiatives of the parties involved. Her main interest was getting the business to take off and move towards the ultimate aim of growing a successful venture. The mentors in the incubator centre were interested in helping her develop her new venture, which would add to their repertoire of success stories in the university, and took certain initiatives such as organising the Enterprise Challenge competition and providing guidance to the nascent entrepreneur for her entry to the competition. These interactivities between all actors involved represent the meso-relational dynamics of the venturing process. The nature of this activity concurs with Fletcher's (2003) arguments pertaining to the constructive aspects of new business venturing, embracing the dynamic processes of organisational emergence and identity formation as nascent entrepreneurs make sense of the world through interactions within their *habitus* and field.[2]

Rosie decided to take a year out of her degree in order to get R-Games off the ground. The search for sponsorship to cover the cost of initial production and sorting out the usual administration required for setting up a business were amongst the activities that she engaged in. In carrying out such start-up activities, she marks the importance of support networks, which indicates that even solo nascent entrepreneurship is a collective activity:

> I got enormous support from my two mentors in the incubation centre and from the university in general . . . It was proven that I had the idea for the game years ago when I was working as the taxi-driver. I tried to look into ways to get my product into the market. I kept coming up against brick-walls because I was on my own. Since I came to the university, every door has been opened. Coming to the university, taking steps to do what I do now is the best thing that I've ever done.

Taking lessons along the way as to how and with whom to deal, she found the person to do the illustrations; he created the board and the box for the game. Through him she got the contacts for the factory in India (where games such as Monopoly are also produced), to manufacture her game at low cost and high quality. Hence, networking does appear to have a significant bearing on the intensity of the entrepreneurial activity she engaged in:

> Through networking I got the contacts for the factory in India. This was through the guy who did the illustrations for me. This is to illustrate how

effective networking is . . . This factory in India is jointly owned by X and Y and it is the highest quality but ultimately the lowest price . . . With the cost of production coming down, I no longer needed that £35 000. In actual fact, all I needed per edition would be £6000 plus the VAT. So you are looking for £12 000. Obviously it is just for the production, and promotion or advertising are not included. At least I knew that I could get my product manufactured, to get me to the stage that where I have got to finish the production of samples, to give them to distributors, who were trying to get orders. So I then had to decide: having failed with the earlier sponsorship attempts I was back to square one. How can I raise the money to do it? This was the main question!

Finding funding proved to be the most difficult part of the venturing process. She was faced with the inflexibility and rigidity of the banking system in general and the small business loan schemes in particular:

> I went to the bank and I wanted to get a loan and it was declined because I am a student and I don't have a regular income . . . I then tried to go through my bank for this small firms loan guarantee scheme but they said that because at that moment I didn't have any confirmed orders, even though it is a fantastic idea in their eyes, it was still speculative. They wanted to see enough purchase orders to cover the entire production of the game. But to get the purchase orders I needed to get the samples. To get to the samples, I needed the funding.

Her reading of this situation (that is a lack of financial support from financial institutions) brought about significant decisions. Having made strenuous efforts to secure funding from such financiers, she was left with the sponsorship option. However, she was able to turn this situation, which was perceived to be negative, to a favourable one by making the decision to develop the first edition of the game at the same time as the London edition because she could attract sponsorship for the first edition relatively easily and use the money for the initial costs of both editions. This is again a good illustration of the entrepreneurial decision-making process (Chell, 2001), which embodies characteristics such as turning a problem into an opportunity, speediness, flexibility and adaptability, and closeness to the market:

> There has never been a Gold Coast game and at that point I had already decided that I wanted to do the London edition first because I could get it ordered by Hamleys and then have a good grounding for further editions. I wanted to do the Gold Coast edition but why wait for next year to do it? Why not do the Gold Coast edition at the same time with London and raise enough money through sponsorship for both? Because it was covered by the local press that I had been to the university, I had won this competition and I'd organised a launch at Hamleys. I could now go to people at Gold Coast who knew about what I was doing.

She configured her sponsorship relationships creatively in order to secure sufficient and long-term financial resources. She approached a large local organisation, who had sponsored the Enterprise Challenge, and secured an initial £2000 of funding. Using her weak ties (Granovetter, 1973, 1983; Jack and Anderson, 2002) effectively, she generated further sponsorship opportunities:

> I am glad that I hadn't stated that I wanted £500 from the first sponsor. I am just glad that I asked for an offer. They provided £2000 and the lowest I got was £1000. From that point onwards the minimum I got was £1000. I then got sponsorship from Marriott Hotel, Cascade Shopping Centre, the City Football Club, the news, the local radio and lots of others. I have established strong relationships and raised enough money from the first edition to cover both London and Gold Coast. So, that's all for sponsorship.

A series of important decisions followed this one, such as to launch the London edition in Hamleys in the week beginning 25 October, which was half-term week and well in advance of Christmas. The point was to raise the profile of the business with press coverage, to launch the Gold Coast edition in mid-November, to catch the Christmas sales, and to price the product appropriately at £18.99. These decisions involved understanding and evaluating what the customers are looking for, pitching the product at a price customers would be willing to pay, developing creative insights into customers' buying habits and understanding the norms or conventions in the market place. From an entrepreneurial standpoint, the decision-making process that Rosie went through can be cited as an example of how strategic choices carry an implicit entrepreneurial outlook, deriving from the specific individual characteristics and experience (micro-level qualities); the specific relationships with, for example, business mentors, sponsors, and customer groups, involved in setting up R-Games (meso-level qualities); and the specific market sector and creative industries, (macro-level qualities) towards which those strategic choices are addressed (Karataş-Özkan, 2006). These constitute significant aspects of the venturing process, just as constantly seeking to create further business opportunities and tapping on the resources and knowledge of people in your social circle do:

> . . . To get to where I have got to now, everything to me has been a networking exercise . . . Even with the computer game version. Again Nick P put me in contact with the person who does computer games for Virgin. The Pro-Vice Chancellor of the university got in contact with the Department of Creative Technology and they cherry-picked a masters student to develop a prototype for me for the computer game version. He is going to develop it as a part of his final project, which means he will work hard on it. And then I will have a pretty

working prototype to show Richard Branson and offer this: every Virgin flight that comes to the UK, they all have little computer screens on the back of the seats. I believe that they actually have something called 'Destination' on that. It fits perfectly because my game is called 'Destinations-London'. So it is a matter of how I can sell my game as a computer game to a company like Virgin!

Relentlessly and consistently dedicating her time, effort and resources to developing her new venture, Rosie redefined the business concept as a souvenir game rather than a family-fun game, as she got a better understanding of the business, market and industry, and was provided with support and direction from her mentors in the incubation centre. She explains how she elaborated the business concept as follows:

> I was promoting this as a family-fun game. That could be distributed in mainstream stores nationwide but has the extended market of tourism because it features all the attractions in London and Gold Coast. Through my mentors' advice and help what I have been really realising is actually my niche market. My niche market is the award-winning souvenir game . . . There are lots of board-games but there isn't another award-winning souvenir game. It is award-winning because I won the award for the Challenge . . . So the award-winning souvenir game can be adapted to any capital city of any country and be sold as a souvenir, but also has an extended market of being sold as a family-fun game distributed in mainstream stores.

The use of the new concept of award-winning souvenir game is three-fold. First, she emphasises her unique selling point by differentiating her business venture, particularly when presenting it to potential investors. Second, she considers this a good way of rectifying the problem of seasonality of the business. Third, she creates further business opportunities (by developing editions of the game for other capital cities and licensing them out), which is at the heart of the entrepreneurial process:

> Through refinement of the business concept my answer to the potential investor's question of 'How are you going to compete with all these other games?' is that I am not competing with all these games. My niche market is the souvenir. I am targeting tourists who want to buy souvenirs but I can also sell it as family-fun game. Because 70–80 per cent of games are sold every Christmas period, it is seasonal. However, souvenir games can be sold throughout the year because people travel the world. They get souvenirs from airports or Regent Street because it is an attraction itself, Hamleys is. I could also do a New York edition, Rome, Paris, San Francisco, Sydney, anywhere in the world! I may possibly license out other editions.

The opportunities are endless according to Rosie. It is a matter of having the drive, determination and belief to succeed. In her own words:

If you have got enthusiasm and the drive and determination to make something happen, then it will happen. Something I have learned to accept is that failure is a lesson to get for future success . . . I made the contacts, used all of them to generate further resources. I got the sponsorship. I found the perfect illustrator. I made the optimum manufacturing deal. This is all success. Every little thing, every hurdle you get over is a success itself.

In an interview for the university's local magazine she cites her passion and deployment of social networks as the key for the venturing process: 'I've had so much support, sometimes even from complete strangers. I think people are always willing to help if your passion for something really shines through. I always bring the conversation round to the game when I meet someone because you never know who you are talking to and what opportunities could come up' (Fieldwork document, R1: 14). In the same magazine she reiterates the entrepreneurial qualities that she holds when answering the question concerning the future: 'Once the business is up and running, I'll get straight back into my law and business degree. Doing a law degree was always an ambition of mine, but I never dreamt I'd end up forming my own business along the way. After I graduate I hope to specialise in intellectual property rights, and if anyone dares to infringe one of my copyrights, trademarks or patents, then I will pay myself to sue them!'

On a final note, she was featured in *Times Higher Education* where she described the entire journey of creating R-Games as a learning experience: 'The launch and the sales are work-based learning' (in *Times Higher Education*, 2004, p. 1). Entrepreneurial learning and managing, which underpinned the nascent business venturing process that she went through, is the concern of next section.

8.3 UNDERLYING PROCESSES: ENTREPRENEURIAL LEARNING AND MANAGING

Revisiting Deakins (1996, p. 21), entrepreneurship involves a learning process, an ability to cope with problems and learn from them. It is important to identify key issues in the learning and development process of entrepreneurship. One of Rosie's mentors, who came to visit while I was interviewing her, stated the following, which encapsulates her entrepreneurial learning experience:

If you asked me what her unique qualities are, I would say her dedication, hard work and self-belief in her capabilities. She learnt over this period of start-up that 'mistakes are acceptable' and we learn better by failing at times. 'Success breeds success' has been her motto throughout and her passionate and ambitious nature has brought about her relentless pursuit of the business idea and looking backward and forward when acting upon circumstances.

This statement reveals a number of important and interrelated aspects of entrepreneurial learning. The first aspect is the notion of entrepreneurial commitment and awareness facilitating the learning process. The second aspect is learning from experience, particularly from unsuccessful experiences. This area has been highlighted by entrepreneurship scholars, who have argued the need for further empirical research. The importance of learning from critical incidents is an integral part of the process. The third aspect is the relationship between learning and enacting, which is considered entrepreneurial managing in this study. These dimensions are in tune with Cope's (2005) recent framework of a learning perspective of entrepreneurship, which put forward entrepreneurial preparedness, learning history, learning task, critical incidents and the generative process of entrepreneurial learning as the key components.[3]

The first dimension is entrepreneurial commitment, which is related to self-efficacy (Bandura, 1995) and enduring personal characteristics (Shaver and Scott, 1991) that predispose entrepreneurs to entrepreneurial activity, according to Greenberg and Sexton (1988). Based on the traits-approach of entrepreneurship, this is a rather narrow conceptualisation of entrepreneurial commitment. Whilst we refer to such *behavioural* characteristics in this study, such as their relentless pursuit of business opportunities,[4] we also include the entrepreneurs' reading and construction of circumstances embedded in particular contexts. Much of the literature has moved away from the identification of specific traits to a consideration of skills and competences. For example, entrepreneurial awareness is a type of competence that nascent entrepreneurs might usefully develop during their venturing journey and it includes transforming the business idea to a viable business opportunity with a realisation of the marketability of a new product or service (Shane, 2003; Chell, 2008, 2009). This is deemed as one crucial component of a competence block that entrepreneurs require in a contemporary knowledge-based economy, as suggested by Eliasson (1996 cited in Harrison and Leitch, 2005), who construed entrepreneurs as experimenter managers that continually engage in learning.

Entrepreneurial commitment to cope with the liabilities of newness (Politis, 2005) and associated uncertainty and risk is considered very much linked to entrepreneurial awareness, which is a function of interrelated components, such as formal training and education, tacit knowledge and higher level learning. These form the elements of cultural capital

(Bourdieu, 1986) that the nascent entrepreneur, Rosie, has developed during her business venturing experience. The opportunity to obtain advice from the mentors in the incubator centre generated tremendous value to Rosie in starting the business. Similarly, the relationships with other incubator tenants enabled Rosie to exchange information, find access to appropriate networks, and share resources. Therefore, the incubator context and its external networks have been useful for social capital building because it linked Rosie with various service providers (such as the technology student for the development of the computer version of her game), venture capitalists and other suppliers.

As discussed in Chapter 2, Duff (1994) argues that an incubator adds value by bringing together an array of skills and by selecting individuals who can most successfully tailor their services to the needs of new venture creators. Rosie's case exemplifies this, depicting a nascent entrepreneur positioning herself in a university incubator, where she can exploit and connect information effectively from surrounding networks (Totterman and Sten, 2005). These 'weak ties' through network relations (that is, social capital) have supported the creation of new ties later on.[5] The dialectical transformation between social capital and cultural capital is observed in Rosie's venturing experience. The exchange of relationships, which can be accomplished in various ways leading to the exchange of knowledge and other resources, is fundamental for the social and economic organisation of a new venture, even in the case of solo entrepreneurship, as demonstrated by Rosie's story. Such exchanges form the basis for the entrepreneurial learning process of a solo-entrepreneur.

As indicated in Chapter 5 and exemplified by the case of KBrandArt in Chapter 7, social capital can present a wide range of opportunities and also constraints. In a similar vein, Johannisson et al. (2002) suggest that personal ties combine economic and social concerns, which provide the enterprise with a broad range of opportunities and constraints. For example, in dealing with patenting issues, Rosie felt the need to rely on her mentors' advice. She was, in a way, constrained by relying on this interaction to acquire a specific resource for her new venture, intellectual property.

A further facet of entrepreneurial learning is learning from experience. Rosie continually sought information within a broad domain for an enterprise idea and its associated market contacts (for example, customers, suppliers, designers and competitors) and enterprise field forces (for example, investors, sponsors, national and local government institutions, the university and its incubation centre) based on her networks and limited information sources. She had no prior experience and few benchmarks to access to knowledge and resources, and also to evaluate whether the information or resource she has gathered were appropriate to take the venture forward. This is one of the main differences between the learning of nascent entrepreneurs and experienced ones: experienced entrepreneurs are more likely to search for information and resources based on their past experiences through cognitive-based routines and practices, and information sources that have worked well in the past (Politis, 2005, p. 404).

An integral part of the process of experiential learning is learning from critical incidents. Learning from critical incidents is powerful, as shown in the previous case study about KBrandArt. Similarly, during our interview with Rosie, she was asked to describe and reflect upon the critical incidents she had experienced throughout the business venturing process. She identified three critical incidents: winning the Enterprise Challenge competition, securing the first sponsorship money, and moving into the university's incubation centre. Exploring critical incidents (Chell, 1998) and learning episodes (Rae, 2003; Cope, 2005) around them, can provide us with useful insights into the entrepreneurial learning process. This is after all an iterative process (Minniti and Bygrave, 2001). Rosie identified that winning the Enterprise Challenge competition had given a phenomenal boost to her enterprise activity. It spurred her on her way forward to the realisation of her business start-up dream. The process of learning from the incident includes the importance of developing self-efficacy,[6] alertness to opportunities and moving fast and flexibly to proceed with an idea (submitting the application form for the competition in this situation).

Moving into the university incubator and forming and developing the venture within an incubator context have influenced her business venturing experience tremendously. This was due to the intensity of the exchange of resources (including know-how and know-who), and that of relationships and the resultant process of building up cultural and social capitals that later transform into economic capital, made tangible in the economic activity of enterprise. The discussion in the preceding section hints at her learning experience surrounding this particular critical incident, by demonstrating the ways in which she developed contacts, took lessons in terms of how and with whom to deal with, and in dealing with various aspects of the new venture creation (such as patenting, funding, and legal aspects).

Given the importance of economic capital, the meanings that she attaches to the third critical incident (securing the first sponsorship money) relate to her learning to formulate and carry out strategic moves concerning an important aspect of nascent entrepreneurship, which is funding the new venture. The decision to develop the Gold Coast edition of the business product at the same time as the London edition, and seek sponsorship from local organisations, was a strategic move. This resulted in her successful attempt to secure the first sponsorship from a large local organisation, which had sponsored the Enterprise Challenge competition of the university.

The third and final aspect of Rosie's entrepreneurial learning pertains to the interrelated nature of entrepreneurial learning and enacting, from a social constructionist perspective. Viewing entrepreneurship as a social process, where enterprise arises from social and economic exchange (Holmquist and Lindgren, 2002) as a consequence of performance for different audiences (Anderson, 2005), the link between entrepreneurial learning and enacting is crucial. The nascent entrepreneur, Rosie, is considered here not simply as an economic agent, but also as an individual performing different roles in different contexts (Anderson, 2005). Entrepreneurial learning therefore involves developing insights into improvisation which include interpretation, response and performance in a given situation (Cornelissen, 2004 cited in Anderson, 2005). This calls for a mastery of the process, involving the need to plan for the predictable and to respond to the unpredictable (Anderson, 2005, p. 589).

In Rosie's case, the entrepreneurial process has a dual nature: planned and emerging. Planned and emerging dynamics paradoxically co-exist in her case. Planned aspects of the process mainly derive from the business planning process undergone and the staged writing-up of a business plan as a business student, entering the university's Enterprise Challenge competition, and later developing her business in the context of a university incubator. Emerging aspects outweigh the planned aspects, as depicted by the previous case account, KBrandArt. Seeking funding and forming strategic alliances with the manufacturer and other suppliers and distributors are all emergent processes. Entrepreneurial managing calls for finding ways to take the venture forward by enacting what the nascent entrepreneur is learning as a part of her personal, social and economic becoming, through accomplishing strategic and everyday tasks (Steyaert, 2003), dealing with uncertainties, and changing the equivocal interactions among a number of different actors into non-equivocal interactions of an organisation (Gartner et al., 1992). This can be cited as an example of her improvisation, in the context of a university incubator. It has enabled the generation of specific patterns of interactions that have resulted in Rosie's pursuit of the business opportunity and organisation of the new venture, R-Games, combined with the continuous and creative adjustment to change. This exemplifies the notion of generating *habitus* through entrepreneurial practice, as will be illuminated further in Chapter 9.

The nascent entrepreneurship process that Rosie experienced involves three modes of organising: vision, strategic organising and tactical organising (Lichtenstein et al, 2006).[7] There is no hierarchy between these three modes in the process of nascent entrepreneurship. They constitute

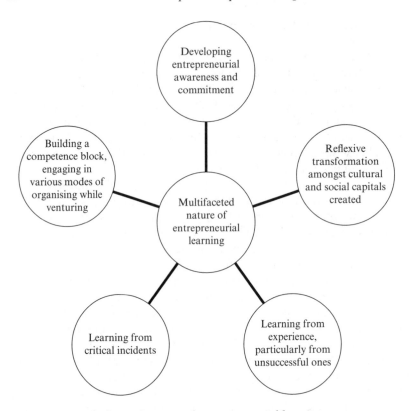

Figure 8.1   Multifaceted nature of entrepreneurial learning

equally important modes of organising. The nascent entrepreneur moves in and out of three different modes concurrently during the process. An example of the *vision* mode of organising includes writing-up the business plan, which led to the Enterprise Challenge award. The *strategic* mode of organising is exemplified by the development of the business concept as a souvenir-game; and the subsequent *tactical* mode involves seeking sponsorship for both London and Gold Coast editions of the game. Given these characteristics of nascent entrepreneurship, the multifaceted nature of entrepreneurial learning, as experienced by Rosie, is shown in Figure 8.1.

Three modes of organising carried out during the business venturing process (Lichtenstein et al., 2006) call for building entrepreneurial competence blocks, such as skills and capability (know-how) and knowledge base, specifically technical and functional (know-what), and networking (know-who) (see also, Chell, Karataş-Özkan and Nicolopoulou, 2007).

These areas also map onto the creation of different forms of capital during the process, including know-who and know-what that are embodied in cultural and symbolic capitals and know-who that is a part of the social capital.

8.4 CONCLUSIONS

In this chapter we have presented the second case account of the research that is Rosie's venturing story leading to the formation of the venture, R-Games. She is a solo nascent entrepreneur, who underwent the venture creation process within the context of the local university's incubator centre. The salient characteristics of her business venturing experience can be explained with reference to the multi-level approach, highlighting the interrelated nature of micro-, meso-, and macro-levels. At the micro-individual level, entrepreneurial motivation is worth mentioning. Her self-realisation to pursue an entrepreneurial career, her willingness and enthusiasm to develop herself and fulfil a sense of achievement are the motivations driving the process. Her entrepreneurial decision-making capacity and capability mark the venturing process. The decisions that she made, for example, in funding the business and refining the business concept (in relation to the core product), embody such characteristics as turning a situation that might be perceived as a problem by others into an opportunity, speediness, flexibility and adaptability, and closeness to the market. Her vision, strategic moves, and tactical moves carry an implicit entrepreneurial outlook, deriving from her determination to succeed and self-efficacy at the individual level.

The meso-relational aspects involve a strategic exchange of relationships with multiple actors in her social circle (for example, business mentors in the incubation centre, financiers, customer groups and suppliers) in order to enact the entrepreneurial activities of creating a new venture, including envisioning new possibilities and future scenarios for her new business. Her entrepreneurial commitment, as described above as a part of the micro-level qualities, and awareness to cope with the complexities and newness of the process, has facilitated the entrepreneurial learning process. The incubator context and its external networks have been useful to build up social capital and cultural capital (in the form of entrepreneurial know-how and tacit knowledge developed as a part of the business mentoring and enterprise training), which are transformed to economic capital, engaging in the economic activity of a new enterprise development. Her entrepreneurial learning experience has been described in the chapter as a multifaceted process, with learning from critical incidents being a significant aspect. Finally, it should be noted that all of the above mentioned processes (that is, entrepreneurial decision making, transformation between various forms of capital, entrepreneurial learning and managing) are embedded in the enterprise culture discourse, with potential or nascent entrepreneurs construed as champions and supported by some institutional forces such as higher education institutions (such as the university incubator) and persistently neglected by the funding institutions. This, at least, is the perspective of the nascent entrepreneur of the case study, Rosie.

NOTES

1. See Tables 6.3 and 6.6 for the research methods and writing-up framework respectively, used in constructing this case account.
2. See Chapter 5 for a fuller discussion of these concepts.
3. These have been delineated in Chapter 4.
4. Here we might more accurately interpret this as 'determined'.
5. Granovetter (1973) refers to 'weak and strong ties'. 'Weak ties' are more remote contacts, but may be the more useful as they deliver new information and knowledge, whereas 'strong ties' are close contacts such as family and friends, and may deliver more familiar knowledge and information.
6. Self-efficacy was first coined and developed by Bandura (1997) and based on his well-established social learning theory (Bandura, 1977). Self-efficacy concerns a person's beliefs in their ability to affect control over their lives, accomplish tasks and master challenges and threats.
7. See also Chapter 4.

9. A multi-layered framework of nascent entrepreneurship from a learning perspective

9.1 INTRODUCTION TO THE CHAPTER

This chapter presents a grounded analysis of the case accounts presented in the preceding Chapters 7 and 8 by encapsulating the key themes that have emerged from the research. A multi-layered framework of nascent entrepreneurship is offered by highlighting learning elements of the process at three levels: micro-level, meso-relational level and macro-level. Bourdieu's theoretical constructs (1977, 1986, 1990, 1993, 1998, 1999, 2003), already applied in organisation studies by taking a multi-level stance by Özbilgin et al. (2005), Özbilgin and Tatli (2005) and Özbilgin (2006), have acted as orienting tools in framing the multi-layered approach, as established in Chapter 5. We should note that these three levels are not mutually exclusive categories: the emphasis is on the interfaces between them. The social construction of the business venturing process is elucidated with reference to a complex and emergent process (Bouchikhi, 1993; Chell 2000), whereby individual nascent entrepreneurs (micro-level) actively and relationally form their new enterprises as a part of a broader venture community (meso-relational level), which is embedded in the macro-field of enterprise culture with its institutions and education programmes (Karatas-Özkan and Murphy, 2006).

The micro-level concepts of dispositions and capitals have served the purpose of analysing and explaining the business venturing process at the individual nascent entrepreneur level. The meso-relational level concept, such as *habitus* and the dynamics that are shaped by, and shape, the *habitus,* has been very instrumental in pulling together the relational, negotiated, situated, agentic and performative characteristics of the business venturing process whereby nascent entrepreneurs act in relation to numerous stakeholders in multiple settings, through strategic exchanges. The micro- and meso- level entrepreneurial activities are embedded in the macro-field of enterprise culture, with its driving forces such as higher education institutions, business development and support programmes, and rapidly growing industries, such as the creative industries, in the context of the current research.

9.2   MICRO-LEVEL QUALITIES: NASCENT ENTREPRENEURS

Nascent entrepreneurs are those who create business opportunities and pursue them by initiating serious entrepreneurial activities that culminate in forming new and viable enterprises (Aldrich, 1999; Chell and Oakey, 2004). The entrepreneurial process, which the participant nascent entrepreneurs go through, is a process characterised by their temporal and contextual constructions of past and present experiences and their imaginations of the future. Discourses about the future are related to the nascent entrepreneurs' past experiences, individual and collective construction of realities pertaining to the current and future state of the business, and the volume of capital that they draw on and aspire to attain. Anderson (2005, p. 596) suggests that 'entrepreneurship is about tomorrow, possible future states of being, so entrepreneurship is "becoming". However each "event" may be new and idiosyncratic, but it needs to have some basis in our existing meaning systems'; and 'all action exists in continuity with the past, which supplies the means of its initiation' (Cassell, 1993 cited in Anderson, 2005). The social constructionist approach taken in this research has enabled these insights to emerge.[1] The key themes that have emanated from the research include the relationship between individual biographies and entrepreneurial learning, the importance of capitals and transformation between capitals, and agentic and performative capacity of nascent entrepreneurs.

9.2.1   Individual Biographies and Entrepreneurial Process from a Learning Perspective

People draw on their background, life stories and interpret them meaningfully to develop their personal theories (Martin and Sugarman, 1996). The process of entrepreneurial learning of the nascent entrepreneurs studied highlights the significance of situations, relationships and people, and endows them with specific meanings, based on the entrepreneurs' personal interpretations of intended business development. Rae (2002, 2003) terms this the 'personal theories of entrepreneurs'. However, he does not fully explain how they are shaped in relation to their own individual biographies, including age, gender and educational affiliation.

For example, Denise (the managing director of KBrandArt), as a young,

25-year-old, dynamic woman, an art and design graduate, the daughter of well-educated parents, developed her understanding and technical knowledge pertaining to business founding and her ability to manage herself and the team. The development of such knowledge and capability drew on her cognitive and relational capacity, as well as her cultural capital (her art and design education and sectoral know-how). In a similar vein, Rosie was a young woman and a mother of two supporting herself as a taxi-driver and studying law and business, at the same time, when she embarked on the journey of business venturing. Her entrepreneurial learning arose from her formal education in law, as well as the training that she received from personnel at the university incubator. This is inextricably linked to sources of informal experiential learning through her creative and problem-solving capacity as she sought to deal with the exigencies of life as a young mother and aspiring entrepreneur.

Bourdieu's (1977, 1990) concept of dispositions is of particular use in explaining the micro-level aspects of nascent entrepreneurship in terms of the importance of individual dispositions in shaping the process of business venturing, and the underlying process of entrepreneurial learning. In his *Outline of Theory of Practice* Bourdieu (1977) introduces the notion of 'dispositions' as an analytical concept that includes cognitive and affective individual attributes, including three layers of meaning: as an outcome of an organising action; the way of being as in habitual existence and action; and finally, a tendency, propensity, or inclination (Özbilgin and Tatli, 2005), as discussed in Chapter 5. The examination of nascent entrepreneurs' dispositions offers greater opportunities than the examination of attitudes in understanding their entrepreneurial motivations, tendencies to start up their own business, and in generating insights into both social and cognitive elements of their entrepreneurial learning.

In the case of KBrandArt, the experience of higher education in art and design with a particular exposure to possibilities to commercialise such activity, creates a context that disposes the potential student entrepreneurs to develop tendencies and preferences towards enterprising activities, which are followed by such entrepreneurial actions as putting the venture team together and attracting some funding. These actions can be demonstrated as exemplary of their engagement in entrepreneurial practice. Similarly, Rosie, the nascent entrepreneur of the R-Games, developed a strong tendency to set up her own business. She was disposed to make her own way up in society through education and entrepreneurial activity. The university context, which is highly influenced by the current discourses of enterprise culture, and is able to facilitate the development of student entrepreneurship, helped her to develop a more realistic and structured approach to starting her own business.

9.2.2   Capitals and Transformation Between Capitals

The capitals that nascent entrepreneurs draw on, and aspire to attain, form another important aspect of the micro-level characteristics of nascent entrepreneurship. Resources that nascent entrepreneurs need to acquire for the business development process are well studied in the entrepreneurship literature from a number of angles (Eisenhardt and Schoonhoven, 1996; Lichtenstein and Brush, 2001; Chell and Oakey, 2004). Capital is a term that is conceptualised by Bourdieu, and used in this research, as a more encompassing term than resource.[2] Nascent entrepreneurs draw on, develop, and attain capital in the process of entrepreneurship. It has both facilitating and constraining characteristics.

Social capital has been defined as the sum of the actual and potential resources that can be deployed through membership in social networks (Bourdieu, 1986). Both case accounts have illustrated facilitating aspects of social capital in the form of the actual or potential resources, which are tied to possession of a lasting network of relationships based on mutual acquaintance and recognition (Bourdieu, 1986, p. 248). The nascent entrepreneurs of the KBrandArt case created contacts in their immediate social circle while they were university students, which was a networking activity that enabled them to build up this social capital. Arguably the social capital is both within them and outwith them. Within them as they actively cognise and effect the relationships, and outwith them as the resource exists independently of them. Their networking activity has taken a more structured and institutionalised form by steering the creation of the INO. The social capital that these nascent entrepreneurs have drawn on from the early days of the venturing process attained during the conception and gestation periods of the process by forming strategic alliances with other creative businesses, RDAs, the local university and governmental organisations through formalised networking activity – has been crucial. The large volume of social capital created has facilitated numerous ways of acquiring useful market information, developing financial and legal resources, and ultimately creating business opportunities. The social capital that they have generated has been instrumental and powerful in their relentless economic and social struggle in the process of business venturing.

At the INO steering group meetings one of the authors also observed constraining aspects of social capital. Social capital has brought about quick and obligatory reciprocity in the form of a perceived need to reciprocate to certain individuals and institutions as a response to their contribution to the development of the INO. An example pertaining to their venturing process is the inclusion of a public sector officer (an enterprise officer from the local council) in the INO as a board member with high levels of authority and decision-making capacity.

In Rosie's case, developing the venture inside the incubator centre of the local university has helped build social and economic capital by securing access to financiers, service providers, suppliers and business mentors. The incubator has provided a context in which the nascent entrepreneur can exploit and connect information from surrounding networks. The cultural capital, which she has developed through her degree studies and mentored training provided by the centre, has been influential in further developing her understanding of the importance of social capital for realising the entrepreneurial process. The transformation between different forms of capital (cultural, social, economic and symbolic) is identified in Rosie's experience, as in the other case study. Constraining aspects of social capital have also been inferred from Rosie's case. For example, she was hampered by over reliance on her mentors in dealing with patenting issues, and some other legal aspects of the venturing process.

In both case accounts, symbolic capital is represented in the form of ownership, power, independence and effecting change in their lives and the community of regional creative industries. This symbolic capital developed over the period. The nascent entrepreneurs reflected on the meaning of their ownership and independence and gained confidence to pursue their entrepreneurial activities. This effectively gave them a sense of power and influence within their milieu and the confidence to take the enterprise forward.

The case accounts support the importance of the notion of capital in nascent entrepreneurship. Bourdieu's (1986) notion of capital is relational and process oriented (Everett, 2002). Capital is created through a multiplicity of relations, such as observed in the incubator centre, INO, new venture, and the education system. For entrepreneurship researchers this means viewing the entrepreneurial process of new venture creation as embedded in a field of relations, one wherein entrepreneurs relentlessly and constantly strive to accumulate capital, which is considered as a form of power for entrepreneurial action. How a combination of different forms of capital at nascent entrepreneurs' disposition (Bourdieu, 1977, 1990) affects their performativity (Butler, 1997; Bell, 1999; Tatli and Özbilgin, 2006) is the concern of next section.[3]

9.2.3 Agentic and Performative Capacity of Nascent Entrepreneurs

One of the liberal philosophies that entrepreneurship is based upon argues for human intentionality and freedom of choice (Bird, 1988; Shaver and Scott, 1991; Pittaway, 2000, 2003, 2005). We argue that there are more complex processes that account for what we term the entrepreneurial process of business venturing, and the interrelated processes of entrepreneurial identity construction and entrepreneurial learning, which are essentially imbued with relational, contextual, temporal-specific, agentic, and performative dynamics. The accounts of nascent entrepreneurs studied during the fieldwork depict agentic and performative capacity as a constitutive and implicit component of entrepreneurial activity. A nascent entrepreneur makes a determined effort to create a new organisation, engaging in social and economic activity, enacting certain roles and performing certain discourses in certain contexts.

We have arrived at this conclusion by applying the social constructionist approach that acknowledges human agency and active perceptual constructions between the members of a society (Chell, 2000, 2008; Nicholson and Anderson, 2005). It was shown through the KBrandArt case account that the nascent entrepreneurs involved pursued a networking activity under a new organisation (in this case the INO) by attracting funding and publicity support from other business owners in the local creative industries and also from governmental organisations. The efforts of the nascent entrepreneurs can be described as, and involve, complex human interactivities. These interactivities are underscored by the processes of legitimacy building in the context of multiple stakeholders, negotiation of meanings, and enacting, promoting and sustaining co-ordinated effort by creating platforms for the exchange of resources.[4] In the case of KBrandArt, this involved building the legitimacy of the new venture, KBrandArt, as the driving force of the new INO initiative and constructing the authencity of the INO itself. Negotiation of meanings included what the INO should seek to achieve, what it should constitute, and how it should be framed strategically, legally and operationally. The exchange of resources was achieved by forming a steering group that comprised a broad spectrum of people in the local creative industries; by holding regular meetings; by commissioning a consultancy project to map out the enterprise activities in the Aurorashire creative industries; and by formalising the networking activity under a charity organisation. These processes triggered debates over the public-private sector divide at some steering group meetings, which one of the authors attended in a research capacity, and some efforts were made to endorse the bottom-up approach that underpinned the creation of the INO. The overall approach was that the needs of the creative industries in the region had been identified by the creative business founders themselves, who pushed the agenda through governmental and non-governmental organisations. This meant performing certain actions and discourses while omitting others. For example, the nascent entrepreneurs felt the need to include somebody from the local city council on the board of the new organisation. Similarly, they sought funding from the local RDA to commission the consultancy project, which again served the purpose of justifying and legitimising the overall activity of creating a new networking organisation for the creative enterprises in the region. In these ways they enacted the entrepreneurial process through promoting, realising and securing power and influence.

Revisiting the conceptualisation of performativity (Butler, 1997; Bell, 1999; Tatli and Özbilgin, 2006),[5] Rosie pursued her business venturing endeavour in interaction with various stakeholders by managing an intricate web of strategic relationships and performing in strategic ways that will enable her to increase the capitals at her disposition. This parallels the aforementioned processes of legitimacy building, negotiation of meanings and strategic exhange of resources with multiple stakeholders. Rosie acquired a significant volume of cultural capital through her law and business studies and enterprise training programme, while developing social capital at the same time through networking. Her entrepreneurial awareness and agentic capacity have increased over time as she has managed to create and transform different forms of capital. She was able to perform in entrepreneurial ways in her search for funding and a manufacturer for her game, drawing on the advice and support that she was getting from her enterprise mentors in the incubator centre. These exemplify what is actually meant by agentic and performative capacity of nascent entrepreneurs as revealed by this study.

The central argument of this section is that nascent entrepreneurship is a social process whereby nascent entrepreneurs create a new venture to actualise their ideas for a product, service or process by relationally and relentlessly pursuing business opportunities; and by developing their agentic and performative capacity as entrepreneurs so that they can engage in strategic exchange of relationships. Agentic and performative capacity is also a distinctive component of entrepreneurial identity.

9.3 MESO-RELATIONAL LEVEL QUALITIES: FORMING VENTURE COMMUNITIES

Nascent entrepreneurship is characterised by a social exchange of relationships. The nascent entrepreneurs that participated in this study have formed or joined broader communities of people, termed venture communities. The meso-relational level qualities of their entrepreneurial experience can be encapsulated in three interconnected themes: business venturing as a process of generative exchange by developing *habitus* through entrepreneurial experience, co-construction of entrepreneurial and organisational identities, and entrepreneurial learning from critical incidents.

9.3.1   Business Venturing as a Process of Generative Exchange: Developing *Habitus* through Entrepreneurial Practice

The academic discourse on the entrepreneurial process of venturing identifies the necessary and sufficient conditions of the business venturing process and leaves untouched the social construction of the variety of characteristics and forms that this process may generate in practice (Chell, 2007). This research has generated insights into the social construction of various forms of nascent entrepreneurship as experienced, and constructed, by the research participants (nascent entrepreneurs, enterprise educators and mentors) and the researchers.

The business venturing process by the nascent entrepreneurs involves processes of sense-making and developing understandings of the market and the views of stakeholders, in addition to refining their own future objectives and rewards. We can discern in the social constructionist writings of Anderson (2003, 2005) an approach that describes the process of entrepreneurship as a process of becoming, which is transitive and about enacting a future. As a part of their entrepreneurial becoming, the nascent entrepreneurs that are presented in the case accounts have engaged in strategic exchanges with numerous actors, including, for example, financiers, suppliers, distribution partners, and the officers of RDAs and local universities. Generative dialogues and formulating models of understandings and actions are fundamental characteristics of such modes of engagement in strategic exchanges.

This research has illustrated that the entrepreneurial process of new venture creation is characterised by developing practical meanings and actions as a result of the spontaneously coordinated interplay (including spontaneous exploitation of contingencies at times) between nascent entrepreneurs' responsive relations to each other (as in the case of KBrandArt) or other relevant stakeholders in the venture community. Their venturing process is grounded in this venture community, and given shape and direction, by patterns of enduring exchanges, which Bourdieu (1977) describes as *habitus*. Rosie's responses and actions, for example, in relation to her mentors in the incubation centre or the financiers she sought for sponsorship, reflect such exchanges and her *habitus*.

These responsive relations do not always present themselves as smooth or straightforward relations without any tensions or contingencies involved. In the venture team meetings in KBrandArt, debates and contradictory arguments have been observed when shaping the direction of the business.[6] The team seemed to take forward the process of developing the venture through 'heedful interrelating' (Weick and Roberts, 1993) and by deciding on actions that are deemed to be the most appropriate responses endowed with meaning and interest.

The analysis of both case accounts shows that the nascent entrepreneurs have developed a feel for the game during the business venturing process.[7] Their entrepreneurial experience is characterised by developing meanings, sharing understandings and pursuing their business ideas through various vehicles in interaction with numerous stakeholders. The experience that we refer to does not consist in a stock of technical knowledge, as some scholars such as Minniti and Bygrave (2001) or Politis (2005) have posited, but rather in a relational posture, which can be defined by the concept of *habitus* whereby the micro-individual and macro-field (structural) conditions existing in a state of interplay (Bourdieu, 1986; Özbilgin et al., 2005) can be explored. As a meso-relational concept, *habitus* offers a more critical alternative to the concept of culture as discussed in Chapter 5. Revisiting Bourdieu's (1977) definition of *habitus*, it is argued that he also connects it to the micro-level of agency (Özbilgin and Tatli, 2005):[8]

> [Habitus is] the strategy generating principle enabling agents to cope with unforeseen and ever-changing situations . . . as system of lasting and transposable dispositions, which integrating past experiences, functions at every moment as a matrix of perceptions, appreciations and actions that made possible the achievement of infinitely diversified tasks (Bourdieu, 1977, p. 72, 95).

This conceptualisation of *habitus* denotes a historically constituted, shared, generative schema of perceptions, appreciations and actions, mediating between structure and agency (Nash, 1999) or connecting structure and agency in a dialectical relationship (Gorton, 2000), which enables the (re) production of social practices by individuals in a social group (Bourdieu, 1985). One can problematise the use of *habitus* in explaining nascent entrepreneurship because the concept of *habitus* implies a regulatory mechanism that is contrary to the workings of entrepreneurs.[9] Entrepreneurship is about creativity or producing new worlds rather than reproducing (Hjort, 2003a; Steyaert, 2005). In other words, entrepreneurs tend to break the mould, work to their own rules and set new precedents. Hence they do not simply reproduce extant social practices. However, nascent entrepreneurs' activities do shape, and are shaped by, the dynamics of meso- and macro-level aspects of the entrepreneurial process, including the market forces of an industry or region and institutional forces of the enterprise culture. Therefore, nascent entrepreneurs engage in a dialogue between established *habitus* and emergent *habitus*.

The learning element of this dialogue for entrepreneurs involves developing practical theories of what works and what doesn't, developed during the course of the entrepreneurial socialisation that they go through as part of the process of business venturing. These practical theories are internalised and transformed into dispositions that generate meaningful practices within a social space, which is the field where entrepreneurs persistently pursue entrepreneurial practices to achieve their objectives. Therefore, it is this understanding of *habitus* that is applied in this research, which recognises the meso-relational aspects of nascent entrepreneurs' engagement in the entrepreneurial activities of starting a business, by drawing on their individual past experiences, current understandings and interactions with a view to enact the future through strategic exchanges with various social actors in the field and developing practical theories from an entrepreneurial learning perspective.

Hence our construction and application of *habitus* denotes and illustrates its strength in illuminating the business venturing process as a generative exchange between the members of a venture community, involving the nascent entrepreneurs formulating and adjusting their responses, strategies and actions during the course of entrepreneurial socialisation. It permits an inquiry into the relational judgements embodied in strategic exchanges and tactics in the course of business venturing. The creation of the INO by the nascent entrepreneurs of KBrandArt and Rosie's involvement in the Enterprise Challenge competition and subsequent decision to set up the new venture in the incubation centre of the local university, are exemplars of such relational judgements.

How do nascent entrepreneurs, relating to *habitus*-based perceptions, meanings and actions in the field of enterprise culture, with its government agents, banks and universities providing business incubation or education programmes and creative industries, construct their entrepreneurial identity and the identity of their organisations? This question is the concern of next section.

9.3.2 Co-construction of Entrepreneurial and Organisational Identities

The identity construction of nascent entrepreneurs involves choices (Pittaway, 2000) that over time lead to entrepreneurial decisions. These choices and decisions are associated with a number of interrelated factors across the cases, including cultural and educational foundations and a multiplicity of issues that affect life's course. The significance of creativity and independence in choosing education, and the experience of creative industries, appear to be important influences in both case accounts. We should also note that there are a plethora of decisions and issues pertaining to personal context that will contribute to the shaping of entrepreneurial decisions and choices. Their entrepreneurial becoming is described as emergent, dynamic and interlinked with the organisational becoming, using Fletcher's (2004) words, that is embedded in their social and historical contexts, as illuminated from a social constructionist standpoint. In reflecting on the KBrandArt case, the organisations that they have created (both KbrandArt and the INO) are used as agents of change to effect change in their lives and their communities. This also applies to the story of Rosie, who actively used her business idea to change her life from being a taxi driver to a successful young entrepreneur who has been featured in national and local television and newspapers. Her entrepreneurial identity is characterised by her entrepreneurial endeavour to break patterns, pursue new directions in life and choose her own way by actualising a business idea in the form of a new enterprise.

The main process involved in the reciprocal production of entrepreneurial identity and business identity is the dialectical enactment of ceremonial and remedial work, which are terms put forward by Gherardi (1994) in gender studies. In the case of Rosie, the distinctive features of ceremonial work include cultivating public relations by attending social events, delivering speeches to enterprise communities including students as a nascent entrepreneur, engaging in strategic exhanges with relevant people in her social milieu, and enhancing the corporate image and personifying the company. The remedial work includes defining the unique selling point of the product that positions it in the market as a souvenir game, and finding alternative sources of funding. In the case study of five nascent entrepreneurs who formed KBrandArt, the ceremonial work includes similar activities of raising the profile of the new venture by taking part in, and winning the Shell Live Award competition, and creating a sectoral networking organisation. The team's aversion to public policies for new enterprise creation in specific sectors, more specifically, providing incubators for nascent entrepreneurs in the creative industries, can be interpreted as remedial practices necessary to ensure that KBrandArt is effectively imbued with an independent corporate image as a creative business, a brand communications agency, which symbolically sustains entrepreneurship.

The case accounts also demonstrate the spatial dimension of entrepreneurial identity as a recurrent theme in the entrepreneurship research (Anderson, 2003; Foss, 2004). The efforts and identity construction processes of the nascent entrepreneurs are shaped by and also shape the current discourses and institutions of enterprise culture. The nascent entrepreneurs studied in this research perform two essential actions of identity formation: identification and differentiation (Melucci, 1982 cited in Bruni, Gherardi and Poggio, 2005). When they talked about themselves as entrepreneurs in the interviews, they tended to emphasise their opportunistic, creative and risk-taking characteristics, presenting themselves as entrepreneurs in the community, comparing themselves to other entrepreneurs. The nascent entrepreneurs in the case of KBrandArt differentiated themselves from other groups (other student/nascent entrepreneurs in the region) by pursuing a business venturing route outside an incubator, focusing on their independent and corporate image. At the interviews, they made frequent reference to the notion of independence as a significant component of an entrepreneurial image and identity. Rosie talked about herself as a self-believer and determined young woman, who led a difficult and challenging life and was ready for further challenge on the way to realising her dream of starting her own company and being very successful. This exemplifies her identification with other entrepreneurs. This dimension is also evident in her comments as she differentiates herself from other student entrepreneurs who took part in the Enterprise Challenge competition. She also differentiates herself from those who have established businesses in the same university incubator centre in which she is located.

9.3.3   Entrepreneurial Learning through Experience and Critical Incidents

Our research findings have revealed that the entrepreneurial process is more complex than its earlier conceptualisations as either a cognitive (Young and Sexton, 1997; Minniti and Bygrave, 2001) or social process (Cope, 2001, 2003, 2005; Rae, 2002) and can be understood from a multi-level perspective that links micro-level learning (personal learning of nascent entrepreneur) to meso- (relational) and macro- (contextual) dimensions. Through a further examination of the case accounts, we argue that entrepreneurial learning has a multifaceted nature that can be explained by paying greater attention to the complexities and subtleties of the process. In the case of KBrandArt, we show that the entrepreneurial learning process involves learning to transform creative artistic practice into a commercially viable business idea, learning to understand the dynamics of the creative industries, forming strategic alliances in the sector, and influencing opinion-formers and policy-makers towards certain initiatives. Learning to raise their profile and legitimise their venturing activity by leading a sectoral collaboration is another aspect of their entrepreneurial learning – learning by doing. Equally, learning to perform certain discourses (constructing a business plan for the Shell Live Award competition, for example, or restructuring the departments of the business and communicating the business concept to clients through a redesigned website) and learning to cope with ever-changing situations, and even fashioning such situations to create favourable social and economic relations, characterise their entrepreneurial learning.

Using the critical incidents technique (Chell, 1998),[10] significant occurrences were examined as catalysts for entrepreneurial learning. In order to gain a richer account of entrepreneurial learning, the participants were encouraged to elaborate on their actions and responses in the context of these incidents and how they see their behaviour changing since then. We note that their construction of criticality – what they considered as critical – cannot be divorced from the *habitus* of the venture community.

We acknowledge the importance of such critical incidents in instigating new forms of behaviour. Further, an integral part of the learning process is the relationship between the reflection on these incidents and subsequent decision making. It is from these incidents that nascent entrepreneurs make transferences to other situations. Of particular interest is the complex relationship between the reflective process of learning episodes and pursuit of entrepreneurial activities during the venturing process as they unfold. All case accounts demonstrate that the generative nature of learning prevails as a result of learning episodes from such incidents. This contributes to entrepreneurial preparedness (Harvey and Evans, 1995; Cope, 2005) of individuals as they accumulate entrepreneurial know-how and competences during the new venture development process. This aids us to understand better the interrelated themes of cumulative learning, stock of knowledge (Minniti and Bygrave, 2001), or learning history in entrepreneurial contexts by unravelling the key learning incidents, relationships between them and how they influence later entrepreneurial actions.

Prior learning informs the entrepreneurial tasks of sustaining and growing the business once the venture is established. In the case of KBrandArt, the nascent entrepreneurs have developed understandings of the creative industries context, national and regional developments pertaining to new enterprise creation, and the nature of their business as a niche marketing business. This has played an appreciable role in shaping the future direction of the business and preparing them to tackle the challenges, by at least contemplating strategies to cope. Also, Rosie's account demonstrates that a nascent entrepreneur's earlier frustrations with financiers, for example, and the lessons drawn from such incidents, influences the attitude and approach taken to external-financing of the business. This would appear to have significant implications for expanding the business.

9.4   MACRO-LEVEL PROPERTIES: FIELD OF ENTERPRISE CULTURE AND CREATIVE INDUSTRIES

The nascent entrepreneurs' experiences of new venture creation and entrepreneurial learning are embedded in the macro-field. Such experiences can be seen as historically contingent constructions that arise out of a discourse including policies, programmes, and texts produced, all interpreted by a broader set of actors in a social context (the members of a venture community as discussed in the earlier section). Furthermore, discursive activities of nascent entrepreneurs often draw strategically from broader societal discourses consisting of enterprise culture and creative industries discourses in this research. The nascent entrepreneurs under study made sense of such discourses in particular ways and made attempts to fashion preferable social relations that would help them enact their entrepreneurial performances. The macro-level qualities of the process of nascent entrepreneurship, as studied in this research, are embodied in two key themes: the perceived institutionalising forces of enterprise culture and those of creative industries.

9.4.1 Perceived Institutionalising Forces of Enterprise Culture

As with entrepreneurship, the term enterprise culture is difficult to conceptualise (Ritchie, 1991), having a series of different meanings and implications (Fairclough, 1991; Morris, 1991; Selden, 1991; Carr and Beaver, 2002; Chell, 2004b, 2007).[11] In the UK the decade of the 1980s was characterised by individualism and the pursuit of personal wealth, with an emphasis put on enterprising qualities of individuals and 'self-employment' – the Thatcherite enterprise culture philosophy. As a part of the popularisation of entrepreneurship as a political ideology that occurred throughout the globe during the 1980s (Huse and Landstrom, 1997; Hjort, 2003b), several political interventions to encourage new business formation and to improve the situation of small businesses, were mounted in the UK by the Conservative government. The shift away from a culture of dependency on the welfare state to one of personal responsibility and self-reliance (Keat, 1991; Wheelock and Baines, 1998; Peters, 2001) was a strong element of what Morris (1991, p. 34) describes as cultural engineering. A nation of self-reliant and enterprising individuals was viewed as the panacea for Britain's social and economic ills (Heelas and Morris, 1991; Cope, 2001).

There have been several critiques of the enterprise culture philosophy and the associated policies and programmes of the Thatcherite era.[12] The re-emergence of enterprise culture rhetoric under New Labour in the post-1997 era marks a different approach to marketing of entrepreneurship, which has highlighted entrepreneurial activity as a socially beneficial activity, dispelling the perception of entrepreneurship as solely an individualistic pursuit of personal wealth (Atherton, 2004; Chell, 2004b, 2007). Major policy programmes have been initiated, elevating high-growth entrepreneurship, mainly science entrepreneurship and more recently social entrepreneurship. Arguably, there exists a political consensus on the importance of entrepreneurship and an increasing acknowledgement of the need to be more focused and to create a more conducive environment for enterprise and entrepreneurship. However, the post-1997 discourse of enterprise culture still emulates an over-loaded notion of enterprise. The differences from that of the Thatcherite era in terms of raising team-enterprise have been noted, and we might add the promotion of enterprise education as an agent of change and development. HEIs have been given a crucial role to play in facilitating entrepreneurial activity. One major facet of the pervasion of enterprise culture is the increase in the numbers of educational institutions teaching entrepreneurship courses and providing incubation programmes (Jack and Anderson, 1999).

Given the preceding summary of the discussion on the enterprise culture in the UK, the case studies and interviews with the enterprise educators and university incubation managers reveal interesting shades of opinion towards collaboration between nascent entrepreneurs and universities. Although some aspects of the structuring forces of enterprise culture have been criticised strongly by the nascent entrepreneurs involved (such as financial and legal support),[13] the importance of working with entrepreneurship academics and educators has been recognised by the research participants. Nascent entrepreneurs in the KBrandArt case interpreted the forces of enterprise culture, mainly university incubators, negatively at the outset and they opted for an independent start-up, endorsing the autonomous and self-reliant image of business start-up in the creative industries. They collaborated with the local university that they graduated from on different levels, such as initiating a sectoral networking organisation and participating in doctoral research that has mirrored some important characteristics of their business venturing experience back to them, and, in a way, facilitated reflection upon their own entrepreneurial endeavour and the learning process attached to it. Therefore, they have become reflective practitioners and are attuned to engaging in both artistic and scientific aspects of the entrepreneurial process, as argued by Jack and Anderson (1999).

It is worth noting a different perception of the mechanisms of enterprise culture by Rosie, the nascent entrepreneur who set up her business in the local university's incubator centre. Her case accentuates the importance of university incubators as conducive environments for networking, facilitating more informed accomplishment of entrepreneurial activities during the business venturing process, and developing entrepreneurial know-how that can help entrepreneurs cope with complex tasks and relationships with various stakeholders (such as financiers, suppliers, mentors, and customers). This draws a parallel with Gibb's (2002b) argument that effective entrepreneurship education and incubation programmes call for the creation of a context that reflects the actual experiences of entrepreneurs.

9.4.1.1 Perceived role of enterprise educators and mentors

The perceived role of enterprise educators and mentors is an important theme that emerged from this research. The second group of research participants,[14] including enterprise educators and university incubator managers, drew attention to giving direction and equipping nascent entrepreneurs with access to knowledge and resources. The following extract from the interview transcript with an incubator manager, who is also an experienced enterprise educator, shows that he advocates the benefits of the notion of nurturing businesses at different stages of the venturing process in an incubator context:

> It is important to surround them with a lot of infrastructure, how to finance, how to get legal information, how to network and ensuring that its infrastructure is actually in place to enable them to move the business forward. And then when they leave the incubator, they understand how a business operates . . . Big problem with incubation, big critique is that it is a very protective environment. They don't want to leave them or when they leave the incubator, they have got to face the harsh world outside and to be able to survive in that harsher environment.

> In the 1990s, in particular, there was a backlash in America. Because Americans were saying that these were too comfortable environments. People do not leave them, when they do leave, they don't survive. I would argue that the trouble with incubators is to make sure that they have prepared for an exit strategy. What you are doing is working with nascent entrepreneurs on an exit strategy. As with a child if a baby is premature, you can't get her or him out and say 'that's it, get on with it'. You nurture the baby. What I am saying is incubation is about nurturing, working with them at different stages of their evolution and development. That links us to what we are trying to do here is to build up links, relationships with SMEs. They don't easily build up relationships with public sector companies.

> Because traditionally, there is a fear of universities, many entrepreneurs, small business managers have a negative feeling, partly because of their fear of the higher education (HE) system and partly because they may enter the business without any formal qualifications whatsoever. For them, HE is a move from reality. The government strategy is to try to get them through things like TCS (Teaching Company Scheme), STEP (Science Technology Enterprise Programme) and to build up links with HE, the business community, and small business community. Trying to get universities to believe in small businesses and trying to get small businesses to believe in universities that they can help them. If we can manage to work with businesses at the pre-formation stage through an incubator, then we can work with them after they exit the

incubator. We won't have any problems trying to attract them in because we have been with them, we have worked with them and we are continuing to work together.

This highlights the increasing importance placed upon changing attitudes of the small business community towards universities in general and enterprise education and training in particular, as a broader rhetoric of collaboration between universities and the business community. Hence, the role of enterprise educators and mentors in such incubation programmes is more focused, with a view to equipping nascent entrepreneurs' with know-how and know-who that is required for the business venturing process. This draws a parallel with what is discussed in Chapter 2, conveying a shift towards facilitating the business development process (Barrow, 2001; Totterman and Sten, 2005), rather than providing a shared office facility in an affordable space as the initiatives of managed workspace (Kirby, 2002) have done. The idea of endowing nascent entrepreneurs with business knowledge and helping them get access to the relevant people, information and other resources is prevailing in the current understanding of incubators and training programmes. The following remark by one of the research participants, who is an enterprise educator, demonstrates this shift quite clearly:

> Incubators are not only basic premises. We have moved forward from the idea of managed workspace. There are two main problems which businesses, start-ups face: one is premises and two is know-how. Initially, incubators were seen as solving the first of the two: a kind of easy-in, easy-out; often links to secretarial support. They were seen as providing low-cost accommodation in quality environments and within a longitudinal frame. You were often given reception facilities and financial service. Gradually, we have begun to recognise that it is important to find a solution to such premises to make them more effective. They have got to be backed by the knowledge support. What we are doing in most quality incubators is that we are combining it with different forms of mentoring, training and working with people to ensure that they understand the principles of doing a business.

University incubators and entrepreneurship education and training can become instrumental in providing a fertile arena for nascent entrepreneurship, provided a critical approach is taken to the development of such programmes informed by research and practice. The way in which nascent entrepreneurs perceive these forces of enterprise culture can be influenced by such hybrid approaches that combine theory and practice (Jack and Anderson, 1999) and tailored to the particular needs at particular stages of their developmental trajectory in the course of the business venturing process.

9.4.2   Perceived Market Forces of Creative Industries

The creative industries are well recognised for their contribution to economic development, regeneration and social inclusion in the UK (Leadbeater and Oakley, 1999; Heartfield, 2000; Brown, Creigh-Tyte and Radin, 2002; NESTA, 2005, 2008c; The Work Foundation, 2007). At the heart of this economic activity lies original creativity, the generation of ideas and their successful delivery to the market. The creative industries have been growing at twice the rate of the rest of the economy in recent years (DCMS, 2007). The distinct contribution of the creative industries was acknowledged in the Creative Industries Task Force Mapping Documents (DCMS, 1998, 2001). The first aforementioned Creative Industries Mapping document (DCMS, 1998) constituted the first attempt to define and measure the contribution of the creative industries to the UK economy and also identify the opportunities and threats they encountered. This document defined the creative industries as 'those industries which have their origin in individual creativity, skill and talent which have a potential for wealth and job creation through the generation and exploitation of intellectual property' (DCMS, 1998, p. 2).

Reflecting on this governmental definition of the creative industries, the term creative industries marks individual creativity combined with arts skills; generation of marketable products having the potential for wealth and job creation; and development of such commercially viable products whose value lies in their intellectual properties. As discussed earlier, such a definition encompasses a vast range of businesses. Therefore, one has to be careful in using the term creative industries due to the range and diversity of what may be labelled as creative businesses (that is a business operating in the creative industries). The businesses that were under scrutiny in this research include a brand communications agency and a souvenir game business with an interactive side developed alongside the core product. These businesses correspond to the process of value creation described for the creative sector in the literature (Bilton and Leary, 2002; Brown, 2004; Raffo et al., 2000). Due to the intangible nature of the products and services, their commercial value is contingent upon how the customer endows them with meanings. An advertising campaign or promotional material may appeal to a particular group of people due to lifestyle reasons and it can change their conception of the products and services advertised and subsequently buying behaviour.

The nascent entrepreneurs studied in the research acknowledged that a fundamental characteristic of the creative sector is a customised approach, which entails a direct connection to the specific market and facilitating a symbolic exchange between the producer and customers. Rae (2003, 2005) uses the term cultural diffusion to illuminate the process of symbolic exchange through which the venture engages the customer as an active participant, not simply as a passive consumer. In the case of R-Games, this meant Rosie, the nascent entrepreneur, trying to refine her game concept as a souvenir game and develop its interactive computer version to be installed in aeroplanes for tourists travelling to London. In the case of KBrandArt, this meant sharpening its business concept by segmenting the market and offering more customised and refined products and services. This affected the venture development process in the later stages, stages that might be described as strategic and tactical according to Lichtenstein et al. (2006). These stages were played out by restructuring the organisation in order to create three key departments, KBrandArt Studios, KBrandArt Interactive and KBrandArt Strategy; and furthermore, recruiting a brand manager to help develop the marketing strategy side of the business. In the participant observation sessions and interviews, the team of nascent entrepreneurs often referred to the creative sector in the UK being characterised by a vast number of freelances or self-employed people who work on an ad-hoc, contractual basis with creative businesses such as themselves. Given this awareness, they have worked with a number of freelances on a variety of projects since the establishment of the venture. However, their decision to employ a full-time permanent employee as a brand manager was a crucial one in reflecting their understanding of successful creative businesses in the sector and taking a longer term strategy in moulding the business.

The initial size and mode of the organisational form of both ventures fits with what is termed a micro-business, reflecting a feature of the creative industries, which is noted by the works of Cunningham (2003, 2005) and Raffo et al. (2000). However, this is not considered to be a distinctive characteristic of these creative businesses in this research, as most start-ups of this nature would be similarly micro-businesses. A longer term study would shed light on this aspect in respect of how these ventures fit in with the overall characteristics of the creative sector, including growth rate and size.

What is crucial is how these nascent entrepreneurs perceive the current discourses of creative industries and fashion their actions in establishing favourable exchanges of social and economic relationships through networking. As noted in Chapters 7 and 8, participation in selected networks, influencing opinion-formers and being talked about in the right way, are crucial, learned aspects of entrepreneurial working in the creative industries (Leadbeater and Oakley, 1999). The nascent entrepreneurs who set up KBrandArt opted for not forming the venture inside the local university incubator facilities for creative industries due to their perception of an entrepreneurial creative venture being independent, autonomous and self-sufficient. Furthermore, two of the nascent entrepreneurs, Denise and Adam, put in determined effort and considerable time initiating a sectoral networking organisation, the INO, which evolved from a series of loose connections amongst people in the creative industries in the region to create a structured organisation with its own website, board, mission statement, activities and membership structure. The INO was perceived to have the potential to unlock creativity and enterprise and to influence the creation of an entrepreneurial culture by fostering partnerships, collaboration and the exchange of ideas. These are considered as defining market forces in the creative industries. Moreover, it is important to shape the attitudes and perceptions of people who work in the creative industries towards being more enterprising and entrepreneurial; creating new markets; expanding production chains; encouraging diversity and delivering business support and even financial assistance. These nascent entrepreneurs demonstrate some entrepreneurial qualities by responding to such dynamics within the macro-field in which their business venturing process is embedded. It is a reflexive process: they do shape such dynamics and they are shaped by them.

In concluding this section on the perceived market forces of creative industries, it is important to note the interface of macro- and meso-level dynamics on the need for political, economic and strategic support for the creative industries. If it is the case that nascent entrepreneurs often rely on formal or informal networks to transform their creative work to commercial viability through value-adding entrepreneurial activities, a thorough understanding of their needs and, subsequently, tailored support programmes are fundamentally important, while maintaining the integrity of their creative work. The manager of the incubator facility used the metaphor 'Bauhaus synergy' to signify networking and the generative exchange of relationships in the creative industries' environment, by establishing a link between creativity and enterprise. This he suggested entails a careful approach to the development of enterprise support programmes for potential or nascent entrepreneurs in the creative industries:

> There is a community of practitioners which feed off each other's creativity. I use the term 'Bauhaus Synergy'. When turning this building into a real incubator, we shouldn't jeopardise this creative environment. We should remain in this luxurious position to maintain the space for that creative inheritance. Our job is to increase the support available so that they can voluntarily access and develop a structured view about commercialising their work; and they can get closer to funding bodies and training bodies as well.

9.5 MOVING TOWARDS A MULTI-LAYERED UNDERSTANDING OF NASCENT ENTREPRENEURSHIP

A social constructionist approach enables us to take into consideration different stakeholders during the business venturing process and address their needs more effectively. Social constructionist approaches offer a view of the way in which social order and transformation is rooted in joint sense-making and identity-construction. These social processes precede and underpin accounts of organisational development and changing business models as the result of the interplay of markets, culture, large institutionalising forces or networking, relationships and personal entrepreneurial learning and managing (Downing, 2005, p. 188). Therefore, they should be examined at these intersecting levels of micro-, meso- and macro- (Karatas-Özkan and Murphy, 2006, p. 119). A multi-layered understanding of nascent entrepreneurship from a learning perspective integrates such dimensions of the process. The key themes are summarised in Figure 9.1.

The social construction of nascent entrepreneurship is explicated with reference to a dynamic and emergent process, which is imbued with the interplay of micro-meso-macro-level qualities of the process of business

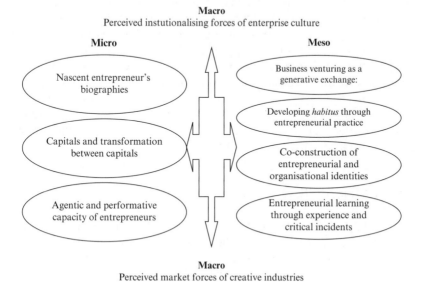

Figure 9.1   A multi-layered conceptualisation of nascent entrepreneurship

venturing. Nascent entrepreneurs (micro-level) disposed to start-up their own businesses, relentlessly and relationally pursue their business ideas and form their new enterprises by drawing on a combination of different forms of capital (such as cultural and social capital), with the objective to attain other forms of capital like economic and symbolic capital. Their agentic and performative capacity as entrepreneurs in transforming capital to each other and engaging in strategic exchanges with the social actors in the field are important facets of the business venturing process. They are explained by meso-relational level qualities, such as developing *habitus* through entrepreneurial practice, co-construction of entrepreneurial and organisational identities, and entrepreneurial learning through experience and critical incidents. All of these processes are embedded in the macro-field of enterprise culture with its institutional forces, such as government agents, banks and higher education institutions; and in the creative industries with its market forces (Karataş-Özkan, 2006; Chell, 2008). The venturing process is shaped by, and shapes, the macro-field of enterprise culture.

These insights generated by using Bourdieu's conceptual tools make possible the integration into entrepreneurship research of a new perspective that acknowledges the interplay of the multiple layers of the entrepreneurial process, moving beyond individual or collective understandings of entrepreneurship. The entrepreneurial process should no longer be studied through the narrow prism of solo entrepreneurship or team entrepreneurship. The same applies to researching entrepreneurial learning, which should be explored through a multi-level approach rather than taking an individual, team or firm level approach. The way we research, write and teach entrepreneurship should be based on such conceptualisations of entrepreneurship so that creating a new venture – the art side of it – can be learnt, while skill-sets and the foundations for entrepreneurial managing, can be developed by focusing on the analytical aspects without interfering in the crafting process (Jack and Anderson, 1999). Entrepreneurial managing is just as much art as it is science.

9.6   CONCLUSIONS

In this chapter we have sought to take the analysis of the case accounts to another level, that of interpretation according to Wolcott (1994), by revisiting Bourdieu's orienting tools at micro-, meso-, macro-levels. We have offered a multi-layered framework of nascent entrepreneurship. Nascent entrepreneurship is conceptualised from a multi-layered perspective by taking into account the interplay of micro-, meso- and macro-level qualities of the process. The key argument is that individual nascent entrepreneurs (micro-level) actively and relationally form their new ventures as a part of a broader venture community (meso-relational level), which is embedded in the macro-field of enterprise culture with its institutions and education programmes.

NOTES

1. As discussed in Chapter 5 in relation to the works of Berger and Luckmann (1966), Martin and Sugarman (1996), Gergen (1985, 1994, 1999), Chell (2000, 2008) and Nicholson and Anderson (2005).
2. See Chapter 1 and the discussion in Chapter 5.
3. See Butler, 1997, for the introduction of the concept of performativity; see Bell, 1999, for a discussion on the application of the concept in organisation studies; see Tatli and Özbilgin, 2006, for the application in the area of diversity management.
4. This can be linked to Gidden's structuration theory, which addresses such legitimacy building activities as a part of dynamics between agents and structures.
5. Performativity is a function of interrelated components including the volume of capital under the nascent entrepreneurs disposition, and the form of legitimised action in relation to *habitus* and field. See Chapter 5 for a more detailed discussion of these concepts.
6. See discussion in Chapter 7.
7. Chell, 2008: 190-1 used the phrase 'form of life' based on Wittgenstein's metaphoric language to describe forms of life as games enacted according to social rules absorbed and understood during social intercourse.
8. See Chapter 5 in this volume.
9. This is also related to Martin and Sugarman's (1996) thesis of getting beyond the social determinism of socio-historical structures as implicit in some forms of social constructionism.
10. See Chapter 6.
11. See Chapter 2.
12. See Chapter 2.
13. These forces include RDAs, universities, national and local government, non-governmental institutions providing business support programmes, incubation programmes, and various other enterprise initiatives.
14. See Table 6.1 for the research questions and different group of participants to address the questions.

10. Conclusions and implications for research, policy and practice

10.1 CONCLUDING REMARKS

Entrepreneurship is a nebulous concept, a collection of taken-for-granted assumptions (Hjort, 2003; Steyaert and Hjort, 2003; Gartner, 2004; Steyaert, 2005), which are tacitly and explicitly informed by the logic of practice, in Bourdieu's (1990, 1998) terms. We assume that we share a common understanding of the concept through socialisation or tacit knowledge through social education. Entrepreneurship (both as a discipline and practice) provides a conceptual framework that transcends the dichotomy of agency-structure, which exists within a paradigm of what is knowable, foreseeable and observable (Steyaert, 2005). In this book, we have demonstrated nascent entrepreneurship as a socially constructed process, which means that it is historically, geographically and discursively specific. We do not make any claims that the nature of the findings are generalisable as the case studies are only examples. However, they are very rich and vivid examples of nascent entrepreneurship and the insights that they reveal may be evidence of testable propositions that suggest underlying theory.

The social construction of the business venturing process is elucidated in this book with reference to a complex and emergent process whereby individual nascent entrepreneurs (micro-level) actively and relationally form their new enterprises as a part of a broader venture community (meso-relational level), which is embedded in the macro-field of enterprise culture with its institutions and education programmes. The social constructionist literature on entrepreneurship shows considerable interest in process-relational aspects of business venturing and is receptive to inter-relationships between process, social interactions, language and discourse in shaping entrepreneurial outcomes (Steyaert, 1998, 2003, 2004, 2005; Anderson, 2003, 2005; Fletcher and Tansley, 2003; Fletcher and Watson, 2003; Nicholson and Anderson, 2005). This study is not about the evaluation of the entrepreneurial process or about finding out what actually happened during the process and how it affected entrepreneurial performance (Anderson, 2005), rather it has sought to explore how the nascent entrepreneurs narrated their entrepreneurial experience and how they, and we, viewed this experience from a learning perspective.

The research accounts, mainly the case studies, illustrate that in practice the business venturing process contains both emergent and planned elements, in approach and content. The study illustrates the importance of creativity and how nascent entrepreneurs create new business opportunities by actualising implicit possibilities into new contexts (Steyaert, 1998). By drawing on one's earlier experiences and capital that has been generated (cultural, social, economic or symbolic capital), nascent entrepreneurs engage in a transformative process. This process is characterised by the interaction of structural and agentic forces at multiple levels.

We argue that one needs to reconsider the underlying motivations for entrepreneurial endeavours at the micro-individual level (that is the nascent entrepreneurs' level). The intrinsic motivation of entrepreneurs is not only wealth creation but also their felt need to position themselves in society as creators and owners and change agents. This requires acknowledgement of human will-power and belief for personal and social change, which can also be viewed as an existential challenge. Such efficacious beliefs reinforce the view that the process of nascent entrepreneurship is absorbed by perceiving and construing social contexts and as such it is inherently a process of learning, which is characterised by social as well as cognitive learning. Following Bandura (1990) in his seminal work *The Social Foundations of Thought and Action*, social learning is rooted in experience and involves people developing attitudes, beliefs, values and actions relationally with others and consistent with their objectives and projects at hand. In our research, the entrepreneurial act of starting a new venture has been the project of the participant nascent entrepreneurs. This project has entailed developing different forms of capital (Bourdieu, 1984) as well as cognitive schema for entrepreneurial action. Chell (2009) has recently examined the innovative characteristics of young people and emphasised such cognitive elements of learning. The process of innovation, and the learning experience that underpins it, is clearly cognitive in that it draws on individuals' experience and ability to translate and transform their knowledge and ideas into something novel that will be valued by others (Chell, 2009, p. 10). In the case of nascent entrepreneurship, an additional dimension is to make an impact in the economy and society by creating economic and social wealth.

At the meso-level, we have highlighted the agentic and performative capacity of nascent entrepreneurs as a constitutive and implicit aspect of entrepreneurial activity in this book. The analysis of case accounts has shown that nascent entrepreneurs make a determined effort to create a new enterprise. They do this by engaging in social and economic activity with certain forms of capital that they have developed and by engineering situations and relationships that allow them to enact their entrepreneurial role. One of the interesting findings from the research is that performativity is a function of micro-, meso-, and macro-level concepts, including the volume of capital inherent in the nascent entrepreneurs' disposition, and the form of legitimised action in relation to *habitus* and field. The participant nascent entrepreneurs in the study have pursued their entrepreneurial endeavour in interaction with various stakeholders, by managing an intricate web of strategic relationships and performing certain discourses in strategic ways that will allow them to enhance the capital at their disposition. The transformation between different forms of capital has been a significant part of the process. The strength of such a transformation lies in its potential to shape and strengthen entrepreneurial identity, which is closely linked to organisational identity developed in the creative industries context.

We have sought to explore the entrepreneurial experiences of the participants from a learning perspective which we have combined with a recognition of the need to move beyond the cognitive approaches to entrepreneurial learning (Cope, 2003, 2005; Rae, 2002, 2004, 2006). Social constructionist or constructivist approaches have been advocated in exploring the learning process of entrepreneurs and subsequent teaching programmes. Binks, Starkey and Mahon (2006) highlight the need to understand nascent entrepreneurs' development of human and social capital over the simple cognitive assimilation of skills and/or knowledge. Flowing from a social constructionist premise, and moving beyond the current social constructionist explanations of entrepreneurial learning (Cope, 2003, 2005; Rae, 2002, 2004, 2006), entrepreneurial learning can be understood from a multi-level perspective that links micro-level learning (the personal learning of a nascent entrepreneur) to meso- (relational) and macro- (contextual) dimensions, combining a number of sub-themes. As illustrated in Figure 9.1, the sub-themes include developing capital, agentic and performative capacity, and dispositions at micro-individual level; learning to enact business venturing as a strategically generative process, learning through experience and critical incidents, and learning to form an entrepreneurial identity aligned with the organisational identity developed at the meso-relational level. These sub-processes of entrepreneurial learning are all embedded in the macro-field of enterprise culture. Through a further examination of the case accounts, it is argued that entrepreneurial learning has a multifaceted nature that can be explained by paying greater attention to complexities and subtleties of the process, by analysing the above mentioned sub-processes carefully.

The participant nascent entrepreneurs in this study, who have drawn on their personal repertoire of life experiences, capital, and agentic and performative capacity, have constructed meanings and understandings, pertaining to the entrepreneurial activities in which they were engaged, through experience and critical incidents. Concurrently, they have developed entrepreneurial actions of creating, recognising and acting on opportunities, which include creating resources, forming strategic alliances, entrepreneurial decision making and enaction (Gartner et al., 1992; Anderson, 2005). Entrepreneurs' construction of the realities of the new world that they are creating cannot be divorced from the *habitus* of the venture community – a strategy-generating schema that is actively developed in the social interaction of nascent entrepreneurs with numerous stakeholders in the field.

Practical meanings and actions emerge as a result of the spontaneously co-ordinated interplay of nascent entrepreneurs' responsive relations with relevant stakeholders in the venture community. Practical theories (Rae and Carswell, 2001) of what works and what doesn't are developed during the course of entrepreneurial socialisation, which contributes to the development of *habitus*. These practical theories are internalised and transformed into dispositions that generate meaningful and strategic relationships and practices within a social space that is the field.

The learning process of nascent entrepreneurs can be best encapsulated by the notion of entrepreneurial becoming (Anderson, 2005) – described as an emergent and dynamic process and interwoven with organisational becoming (Fletcher, 2002, 2003). This suggests to us a multi-level framework within which we conceive of the co-construction of entrepreneurial and organisational identities. The reciprocal production of entrepreneurial identity and business identity is imbued with a dialectical enactment of ceremonial and remedial work, which are terms borrowed from Gheardi (1994) in her research in gender studies. As discussed in Chapter 9, both the ceremonial and remedial work include strong elements of entrepreneurial learning. The ceremonial work of cultivating public relations, raising the profile of the business through new initiatives and activities, and forming strategic alliances calls for developing entrepreneurial skills and competences such as creativity, independent and generative thinking and opportunity creation. Remedial work of, for example, engineering solutions to perceived problems, fashioning adverse interactions in ways that would serve a positive purpose during the venturing process, involves learning to cope with these situations and developing contingencies.

At the macro-level, as a part of the enterprise culture, the role of higher education is fundamental in providing an environment for nascent entrepreneurs where they can get support and guidance in the early stages of their venturing process; have access to knowledge, information and other resources through situated-learning and mentoring via entrepreneurship courses; and benefit from incubation schemes in order to enhance their understanding of setting up a business and improving their networking activity. Some might view the incubators as restraining the essence of a creative business. An attempt to gauge the advantages and disadvantages of critical independence and collaboration through an incubation scheme, by looking at the issue from a nascent entrepreneur's perspective indicate the need to retain the creative integrity of their work. From the perspective of incubation managers and enterprise educators that are involved in the development of such initiatives, programmes should be designed to address this particular need of potential or nascent entrepreneurs in the creative industries. Therefore, incubator spaces and training programmes should serve the purpose of enabling them to get access to relevant people, information, funding and training opportunities to commercialise their creative work.

A multi-layered understanding of nascent entrepreneurship from a learning perspective challenges the perceived tension in the academic and policy environments, particularly in the university incubators, between the pursuit of creative practice and the preparation of nascent entrepreneurs for the entrepreneurial process. The two are not necessarily incompatible. This view proposes that addressing the enterprise side of art and design practice does not devalue creativity. It enhances it by providing a context for the transfer of creativity to commercial success. In line with the arguments of numerous scholars in the field, this calls for rethinking the conventional models for business incubation programmes and entrepreneurship and enterprise training. The agenda for higher education should be reconceived by taking a holistic approach with an understanding of nascent entrepreneurs' motivations and needs through an appreciation of the nature of capital, including cultural, social and financial capital, which they hold and are willing to attain (the micro-level issues). Organisational issues, such as new enterprises that they create, entrepreneurial practice that is developed as a part of a broader venture community that includes agents from RDAs, universities and stakeholders in the market should be also better understood (meso-relational level). Finally, macro-forces of enterprise culture, which drive the development and implementation of numerous business support programmes should be taken into consideration in reshaping and implementing the higher education agenda.

10.2   CONTRIBUTION TO THE ONGOING SCHOLARLY WORK AND IMPLICATIONS FOR FUTURE RESEARCH

Recently there has been a proliferation of studies in the subject domains of nascent entrepreneurship and entrepreneurial learning in which it has been evident that a multi-level approach has not been adopted. This is disappointing as the development of entrepreneurial understanding takes place at a number of different levels – being an entrepreneur and making sense of one's immediate experience and learning from it, whilst absorbing information and lessons by becoming a part of venture communities, embedded in the socio-cultural and economic milieu. The current study has aimed to address this gap in our understanding. By cutting across the boundaries of levels of analysis – the nascent entrepreneur, the venture team, the nascent entrepreneur and associated actors, the macro-field of enterprise culture – we offer an explanation of a complex web of human interactivities involved in nascent entrepreneurship. The social constructionist paradigmatic approach has enabled us to examine critically nascent entrepreneurship and its underlying processes of entrepreneurial learning and managing in detail. The convergence of two interrelated research trends offers timely momentum in studying nascent entrepreneurs' experiences of learning and managing An increasing recognition of qualitative approaches to research in general (Denzin and Lincoln, 1998, 2000; M.M. Gergen and K.J. Gergen, 2000) and the growing appreciation of narrative and discursive approaches to entrepreneurship in particular (Hjort and Steyaert, 2003; Hjort, 2004; Hosking and Hjorth, 2004; Anderson, 2005), which are often underpinned by social constructionist, critical theorist or postmodernist perspectives, provides fertile ground for entrepreneurship scholars to generate insights into the real lives of entrepreneurs.

The social constructionist approach has been one of the latest waves of entrepreneurship research. Our book contributes to this movement of the discipline, by studying the processes of social construction surrounding nascent entrepreneurship from a learning perspective. We will see more examples of this nature in the near future, as it happens in other disciplines such as organisation studies. Through a combination of theories (social constructionist approaches to entrepreneurship and the use of relational frameworks through the works of Bourdieu, Özbilgin and his co-workers) and explicating the intricacies of theoretical frameworks, we have attempted to contribute to the entrepreneurship discipline as:

> a fertile middle space, a heterotopic space for varied thinking, a space that can connect to many forms of theoretical thinking and where many thinkers can connect to, a so-called inter-discipline or rhizome that breaks with the idea that science is linear, progressive and cumulative (Steyaert, 2005, p. 3).

The need for such insightful research in entrepreneurship studies is acknowledged by Gartner, Davidsson and Zahra (2006) who invite entrepreneurship scholars to engage in further dialogues that combine various theoretical and disciplinary perspectives.

Concerning our subject domain of nascent entrepreneurship, such dialogue could take place in research which offers a longitudinal study of the learning experience of nascent entrepreneurs, particularly at times of crises, in the period following the initial stages of new venture creation. This would shed further light on the dynamics of the process and illuminate the focal areas of nascent entrepreneurs' learning processes. Through such a longitudinal research that tracks participants over time, it would be possible to investigate the links between their entrepreneurial learning and the decisions taken at both tactical and strategic levels that potentially impact on the growth and performance of the new ventures.

Multi-layered understanding of nascent entrepreneurship has potential to be applied in further research, in other industry settings and in other sub-domains of entrepreneurship research, such as female entrepreneurship and ethnic entrepreneurship. More specifically, there is some merit in examining micro-, meso- and macro-dimensions of the entrepreneurial process that such groups of entrepreneurs go through, placing an emphasis on gender and ethnicity dimensions.

10.3 IMPLICATIONS FOR PRACTITIONERS, ACADEMIC-PRACTITIONER COLLABORATION, AND POLICY MAKERS

The stories of the KBrandArt team and Rosie are instructive for those nascent entrepreneurs that are considering setting up a business outside or inside an incubator setting respectively, and as a way to understand how different strategies in pursuing business opportunities and garnering resources can be used. The KBrandArt case is also redolent of how social exchanges impact on the entrepreneurial story and the venture. The facilitating and constraining aspects of social capital are worth considering in engaging in networking activity and engineering ties with stakeholders in the venture community.

Nascent entrepreneurs have a great deal to learn not only from the insights generated by a study of this nature, but also from the research process itself and the information through its fieldwork. Nascent entrepreneurs need to view their own experiences as a process. To facilitate this, a fertile dialogue between entrepreneurship academics and nascent entrepreneurs can be created. Nascent entrepreneurs can use and integrate the input of researchers, as they have done these cases through a management report and discussions about the research outcomes. Corporations have been known to work with academics for years. It is timely to argue that nascent entrepreneurs should understand the synergistic power of, and mutual benefits from, working with academics and researchers in order to integrate their thinking and their frameworks in the process of new venture creation. By the same token academics should explore ways of translating their theoretical understanding into comprehensible messages for the benefit of practitioners. Here the key is the language being adopted and the need to find a common language whereby the interactivities between the two parties may be enhanced.

Entrepreneurship and enterprise educators and business mentors form another group of practitioners to which we aim to relate through this book. The learning process of nascent entrepreneurs has been examined in an in-depth manner in this research and it has been concluded that entrepreneurial learning is a complex and heuristic process that calls for a combination of networking skills and specific technical and practical knowledge. This is in order to explore business ideas and create a viable business opportunity, learn how to garner resources, learn to manage yourself and others as the venture grows, and learn inter-related functions of the business (such as marketing, finance and operations) (Chell, Karatas-Özkan and Nicolopoulou, 2007). The complex nature of the process and inter-relatedness of several learning activities should be well understood by educators and mentors in the area of entrepreneurship so that they can cater for the variety of needs of nascent entrepreneurs in different industries and in different phases of their new venture creation process. As a consequence, effective methods of teaching and mentoring may be devised. Based on the insights from real life case accounts, practitioners of entrepreneurship teaching and business mentoring may develop the content and methods of education programmes in the way that will equip potential or nascent entrepreneurs with access to knowledge and other resources (such as people, networks of people, legal advice) and help nascent entrepreneurs understand the emergent and complex nature of the entrepreneurial process. In this way, they will be aware of challenges and may devise ways to overcome them, as argued by many others such Ronstadt (1987), Jack and Anderson (1999) and Cope (2003).

These are the areas where the academic-practitioner collaboration lies. The development of education and business support programmes informed by research of this nature will benefit the members of a venture community, including nascent entrepreneurs, enterprise officers and mentors of local governmental institutions or RDAs (through programmes of training the trainers). At the policy-making level, policy needs to be informed by current thinking on relevant issues pertaining to nascent entrepreneurship in the creative industries and entrepreneurial learning. This research has added to this thinking by generating relevant insights and issues arising from nascent entrepreneurs' perceptions of the dynamics of enterprise culture and creative industries.

References

Ackroyd, S. and J. Hughes (1992), *Data Collection in Context*, 2nd edition, New York, NY: Longman.

Albert, P. (1986), *Enterprise Incubators – An Initial Diagnosis*, Revue Francaise de Gestion, Sep–Oct.

Albert, P. and L. Gaynor (2001), 'Incubators growing up, moving out: a review of the literature', available at http://www.ceram.fr (accessed on 18 November 2002).

Aldrich, H. (1999), *Organizations Evolving*, Thousand Oaks, CA: Sage Publications.

Aldrich, H. and C. Zimmer (1986), 'Entrepreneurship through social networks', in Sexton, D. and Smilor, R.W. (eds), *Art and Science of Entrepreneurship*, Cambridge, MA: Ballinger Publishing Co, pp. 3–23.

Allen, D. and E. Bazan (1990), 'Value added contributions of Pennsylvania's business incubators to tenant firms and local economies', State College, Pennsylvania, Appalachian Regional Commission and the Pennsylvania Department of Commerce.

Allen, D. and R. McCluskey (1990), 'Structure, policy, services and performance in the business incubator industry', *Entrepreneurship Theory and Practice*, **15**(2), 61–77.

Alcoff, L. and E. Potter (1993), (eds), *Feminist epistemologies*, New York: Routledge.

Aldrich, H. (1999), *Organizations Evolving*, London: Sage Publications.

Aldrich, H. and C.M. Fiol (1994), 'Fools rush in? The institutional context of industry creation', *Academy of Management Review*, **19**(4), 645–670.

Allinson, C.W., E. Chell and J. Hayes (2000), 'Intuition and entrepreneurial behaviour', *European Journal of Work and Organisational Psychology*, **9**(1), 31–43.

Argyris, C. and D.A. Schon (1975), *Theory in practice: Increasing professional effectiveness*, San Francisco: Jossey-Bass.

Allinson, C.W., E. Chell and J. Hayes (2000), 'Intuition and entrepreneurial behaviour', *European Journal of Work and Organisational Psychology*, **9**(1), 31–43.

Alstete, J.W. (2002), 'On becoming an entrepreneur: an evolving typology', *International Journal of Entrepreneurial Behaviour and Research*, **8**(4), 222–234.

Alvesson, M. and S. Deetz (1996), 'Critical theory and postmodernism approaches to organisation studies', in S.R. Clegg, C. Hardy and W.R. Nord (eds), *Handbook of Organization Studies*, Thousand Oaks, CA: Sage Publications, pp. 191–217.

Alvesson, M and S. Deetz (2000), *Doing Critical Management Research,* London: Sage Publications.

Alvesson, M. and Skoldberg, K. (2000), *Reflexive methodology: New vistas for qualitative research towards a reflexive methodology*, London: Sage Publications.

Ambrosini, V. and C. Bowman (2001), 'Tacit knowledge: some suggestions for operationalisation', *Journal of Management Studies*, **38**(6), 811–829.

Anderson, A.R. (2003), 'Enacted metaphor: the theatricality of the entrepreneurial process', Paper addressed at the Entrepreneurial Dramas Track of the European Academy of Management (EURAM) Conference, 3–5 April, University of Bocconi, Milan.

Anderson, A.R. (2005), 'Enacted metaphor: the theatricality of the entrepreneurial process', *International Small Business Journal*, **23**(6), 587–603.

Anderson, A.R. and S. Jack (2002), 'The articulation of social capital in entrepreneurial networks: a glue or lubricant', *Entrepreneurship and Regional Development*, **14**(3), 193–210.

Anderson, V. and D. Skinner (1999), 'Organisational learning in practice: how do small businesses learn to operate internationally?', *Human Resource Development International*, **2**(3), 235–258.

Angrosino, M.V. and M.D. Perez (2000), 'Rethinking observation from method to context', in N.K. Denzin and Y.S. Lincoln (eds.), *Handbook of Qualitative Research*, 2nd edition, Thousand Oaks, CA: Sage Publications, 673–702.

Anheier, H.K., J. Gerhards and F.P. Romo (1995), 'Forms of capital and social structure in cultural fields: examining Bourdieu's social topography', *The American Journal of Sociology*, **100**(4), 859–903.

Atherton, A. (2004), 'Unbundling enterprise and entrepreneurship: from perceptions and preconceptions to concept and practice', *International Journal of Entrepreneurship and Innovation*, **5**(2), 121–127.

Atkinson, P. and A. Coffey (1997), 'Analysing documentary realities', in Silverman, D. (ed.), *Qualitative Research: Theory, Method and Practice*, London: Sage Publications, 45–62.

Attwood, R. (2009), 'BIS remit "too broad" for one select committee', *Times Higher Education*, 12 June 2009.

Ayas, K. and N. Zeniuk (2001), 'Project based learning: building communities of reflective practitioners', *Management Learning*, **32**(1), 61–76.

Bandura, A. (1986), *The Social Foundations of Thought and Action*, Englewood-Cliffs, NJ: Prentice Hall.

Bandura, A. (1995) (ed.), *Self-efficacy in Changing Societies*, New York: Cambridge University Press.

Barnard, H. (1990), 'Bourdieu and ethnography: reflexivity, politics and praxis', in Harker, R., Mahar, C. and Wilkes, C. (eds.), *An Introduction to the Work of Pierre Bourdieu*, London: Macmillan, 58–85.

Barrow, C. (2001), *Incubators: A Realist's Guide to the World's New Business Accelerators*, Chichester: John Wiley and Sons Ltd.

Baum, J.R. and E.A. Locke (2004), 'The relationship of entrepreneurial traits, skill, and motivation to subsequent venture growth', *Journal of Applied Psychology*, **89**(4), 587–598.

Bayliss, V. (2001), 'Work in the knowledge driven economy', *Industry and Higher Education*, **15**(1), 13–29.

Becker, G.S. (1975), *Human Capital*, New York: National Bureau of Economic Research.

Belbin, R.M. (1981), *Management Teams: Why They Succeed or Fail*, New York: Wiley.

Belbin, R.M. (2000), *Beyond the Team*, Oxford: Heinemann.

Bell, V. (1999), 'Performativity and belonging: an introduction', *Theory, Culture and Society*, **16**(2), 11–10.

BERR (2008), *Enterprise: Unlocking the UK's Talent*, Department for Business, Enterprise and Regulatory Reform, London.

Berger, P. and T. Luckmann (1966), *The Social Construction of Reality: A Treatise in The Sociology of Knowledge*, New York: Doubleday and Co.

Bhave, M.P. (1994), 'A process model of entrepreneurial venture creation', *Journal of Business Venturing*, **9**, 223–242.

Bilton, C. and R. Leary (2002), 'What can managers do for creativity? Brokering creativity in the creative industries', *International Journal of Cultural Policy*, **8**(1), 49–64.

Binks, M., K. Starkey and C. Mahon (2006), 'Entrepreneurship education and the business school', *Technology Analysis and Strategic Management*, **18**(1), 1–18.

Bird, B. (1988), 'Implementing entrepreneurial ideas: the case for intention', *Academy of Management Review*, **13**(3), 442–453.

Bird, B.J. (1989), *Entrepreneurial Behaviour*, London: Scott Foresman.

Birley, S. and S. Stockley (2000), 'Entrepreneurial teams and venture growth', in Sexton, D.L. and Landstrom, H. (eds), *Handbook of Entrepreneurship*, Oxford: Blackwell, pp. 107–127.

BIS (2009), Department for Business Innovation and Skills press release available at http://www.berr.gov.uk/aboutus/pressroom/page51711.html (accessed on 27 June 2009).

Bishop, K., D.D. Crown and K.M. Weaver (2001), 'Viewing entrepreneurs as learning individuals and related implications for entrepreneurial training', Working paper, University of Alabama.

Blair, T. (1988), 'The third way', Speech by the UK Prime Minister Tony Blair to the French National Assembly, Paris, 24 March.

Blumer, H. (1969), *Symbolic Interactionism: Perspective and Method*, London: Prentice Hall.

Bogdewic, S.P. (1999), 'Participant observation', in Crabtree, B.F. and Miller, W.L. (eds), *Doing Qualitative Research*, 2nd edition, Newbury Park: Sage Publications, 47–70.

Bouchikhi, H. (1993), 'Constructivist framework for understanding entrepreneurship performance', *Organization Studies*, **14**(4), 549–570.

Boud, D., R. Cohen and D. Walker (1993), 'Introduction: understanding learning from experience', in Boud, D., Cohen, R. and Walker, D. (eds), *Using Experience for Learning*, Buckingham: SRHE and Open University Press.

Bourdieu, P. (1977), *Outline of a Theory of Practice*, Cambridge: Cambridge University Press.

Bourdieu, P. (1985), 'The social space and the genesis of groups', *Social Science Information*, **24**(2), 195–220.

Bourdieu, P. (1986), 'The forms of capital', in Richardson, J.G. (ed.), *Handbook of Theory and Research for the Sociology of Education*, New York: Greenwood, 241–258.

Bourdieu, P. (1990), *The Logic of Practice*, Stanford: Stanford University Press.

Bourdieu, P. (1993), *Sociology in question*, London and Thousand Oaks, CA: Sage Publications.

Bourdieu, P. (1998), *Practical Reason*, Cambridge: Polity Press.

Bourdieu, P. (1999), 'Understanding', in Bourdieu, P. (ed.), *The Weight of the World: Social Suffering in Contemporary Society*, Cambridge: Polity Press, 607–626.

Bourdieu, P. (2000), *Pascalian Meditations*, Cambridge: Polity Press.

Bourdieu, P. (2003), 'Participant objectivation', *Journal of the Royal Anthropological Institute*, **9**, 282–294.

Bourdieu, P. and L. Wacquant (1992), *An Invitation to Reflexive Sociology*, Cambridge: Polity Press.

Bouveresse, J. (1999), 'Rules, dispositions, and the *habitus*', in R. Shusterman (ed.) *Bourdieu: A Critical Reader*, Oxford: Blackwell, 45–63.

Bouwen, R. and C. Steyaert (1990), 'Construing organisational texture in young entrepreneurial firms', *Journal of Management Studies*, **27**(6), 637–650.

Brantlinger, E. (1997), 'Using ideology: cases of non-recognition of the politics of research and practice in special education', *Review of Educational Research*, **67**, 425–459.

Brennan, M.C. and P. McGowan (2006), 'Academic entrepreneurship: an exploratory case study', *International Journal of Entrepreneurial Behaviour and Research*, **12**(3), 144–164.

Brown, A.D. (2000), 'Making sense of inquiry sensemaking', *Journal of Management Studies*, **37**(1), 45–75.

Brown, P. (2004), *Performing Arts Entrepreneurship*, Lancaster: University of Lancaster: Palatine Publications.

Brown, J.S. and P. Duguid (1991), 'Organisational learning and communities-of-practice: toward a unified view of working, learning and innovation', *Organization Science*, **2**(1), 40–57.

Brown, J.S. and P. Duguid (2001), 'Knowledge and organisation: a social practice perspective', *Organization Science*, **12**, 198–213.

Brown, C., S. Creigh-Tyte and C. Radin (2002), 'UK creative industries: their growth during the 1990s and prospects for the 21st century', Paper addressed at ACEI 2002 Conference, Rotterdam, 13–15 June.

Bruni, A., S. Gherardi and B. Poggio (2005), *Gender and Entrepreneurship: An Ethnographical Approach*, London and New York: Routledge.

Brush, C., I.M. Duhaime, W.B. Gartner, A. Stewart, J.A. Katz, M.A. Hitt, S.A. Alvarez, G.D. Meyer and S. Venkataraman (2003), 'Doctoral education in the field of entrepreneurship', *Journal of Management*, **29**(3), 309–331.

Bruyart, C. and P. Julien (2000), 'Defining the field of research in entrepreneurship', *Journal of Business Venturing*, **16**, 165–180.

Bryman, A. (2001), *Social Research Methods*, New York: Oxford University Press.

Buchanan, D., D. Boddy and J. McCalman (1988), 'Getting in, getting out and getting back', in Bryman, A. (ed.), *Doing Research in Organisations*, London: Routledge, 54–67.

Burr, V. (1995), *An Introduction to Social Constructionism*, London: Routledge.

Burrell, G. and G. Morgan (1979), *Sociological Paradigms and Organisational Analysis*, London: Heinemann.

Burrows, R. (ed.) (1991), *Enterprise Culture: Critical Analysis*, London: Routledge.

Burrows, R. and J. Curran (1991), 'Not such a small business: reflections on the rhetoric, the reality and the future of the enterprise culture', in Cross, M. and Payne, G. (eds), *Work and the Enterprise Culture*, London: Falmer Press.

Butler, J. (1997), *Excitable Speech: A Politics of the Performative*, New York: Routledge.

Bygrave, W.D. and C.W. Hofer (1991), 'Theorizing about entrepreneurship', *Entrepreneurship Theory and Practice*, **16**(2), 13–22.

Bygrave, W.D. (1993), 'Theory building in the entrepreneurship paradigm', *Journal of Business Venturing*, **8**, 255–280.

Bygrave, W.D. and M. Minniti (2000), 'The social dynamics of entrepreneurship', *Entrepreneurship Theory and Practice*, **24**(3), 25–36.

Calas, M. and L. Smircich (1999), 'Past postmodernism? Reflections and tentative directions', *Academy of Management Review*, **24**(4), 649–671.

Campbell, D. (2000), *The Socially Constructed Organisation*, London: Karnac Books.

Carland, J.W., F. Hoy, W.R. Boulton and J.A.C. Carland (1984), 'Differentiating entrepreneurs from small business owners: a conceptualization', *Academy of Management Review*, **9**, 354–359.

Carr, P. and G. Beaver (2002), 'The enterprise culture: understanding a misunderstood concept', *Strategic Change*, **11**, 105–113.

Carter, N.M., W.B. Gartner, K.G. Shaver and E.J. Gatewood (2003), 'The career reasons of nascent entrepreneurs', *Journal of Business Venturing*, **18**, 13–39.

Cassell, C. (1993), *The Giddens Reader*, London: Macmillan.

Cassell, C. (2005), 'Creating the interviewer: identity work in the management research process', *Qualitative Research,* **5**(2), 167–179.

Castells, M. (2000), 'Materials for an exploratory theory of the network society', *British Journal of Sociology*, **51**(1), 5–24.

Charmaz, K. (2000), 'Grounded theory: objectivist and constructivist methods', in Denzin, N.K. and Lincoln, Y.S. (eds), *Handbook of Qualitative Research*, 2nd edition, Thousand Oaks, CA: Sage Publications, 509–535.

Chaston, I., B. Badger and E. Sadler-Smith (1999a), 'Small firm organisational learning: comparing the perceptions of need and style among UK support service advisors and small firm managers', *Journal of European Industrial Learning*, **23**(1), 36–43.

Chaston, I., B. Badger and E. Sadler-Smith (1999b), 'Organisational learning: research issues and application in SME sector firms', *International Journal of Entrepreneurial Behaviour and Research*, **5**(4), 191–203.

Chell, E. (1985), 'The entrepreneurial personality: a few ghosts laid to rest?', *International Small Business Journal*, **3**(3), 43–54.

Chell, E. (1997), 'The social construction of the entrepreneurial personality', Paper addressed at the British Academy of Management Conference, London.

Chell, E. (1998), 'The critical incident technique', in Symon, G. and Cassell, C. (eds), *Qualitative Methods and Analysis in Organisational Research*, London: Sage Publications, 51–72.

Chell, E. (2000), 'Towards researching "the opportunistic entrepreneur": a social constructionist approach and research agenda', *European Journal of Work and Organisational Psychology*, **9**(1), 63–80.

Chell, E. (2001), *Entrepreneurship: Globalisation, Innovation and Development*, London: Thomson Learning.

Chell, E. (2004a), IfE Business Plan, Institute for Entrepreneurship, University of Southampton.

Chell, E. (2004b), 'Social enterprise and entrepreneurship: towards a convergent theory of the entrepreneurial process', Paper addressed at the workshop on social capital and its relevance to entrepreneurship, Lancaster University Management School, 19 November.

Chell, E. (2004c), 'Critical incident technique', in Lewis, B.M., Bryman, A. and Fuiting, L.T. (eds), *The Sage Encyclopaedia of Social Science Research Methods*, Sage Publications, Thousand Oaks, CA, 218–219.

Chell, E. (2007), 'Social enterprise and entrepreneurship: towards a convergent theory of the entrepreneurial process', *International Small Business Journal*, **25**(1), 5–26.

Chell, E. (2008), *The Entrepreneurial Personality: A Social Construction*, 2nd edition, London and New York: Routledge.

Chell, E. (2009), 'The identification and measurement of innovative characteristics of young people: development of the youth innovation skills measurement tool', Research Report, NESTA, London, July 2009.

Chell, E. and L. Pittaway (1998a), 'The social constructionism of entrepreneurship', Paper addressed at the 21st ISBA National Small Firms Conference: Celebrating the small business, Durham University, 18–20 November.

Chell, E. and L. Pittaway (1998b), 'A study of entrepreneurship in restaurant and café industry: exploratory work using the critical incident technique as a methodology', *International Journal of Hospitality Management*, **17**(1), 23–32.

Chell, E. and H. Rhodes (1999), 'The development of a methodology for researching vertical relations in small and medium sized enterprises', British Academy of Management Proceedings, Manchester, 170–186.

Chell, E. and S. Baines (2000), 'Networking, entrepreneurship and micro-business behaviour', *Entrepreneurship and Regional Development*, **12**, 195–215.

Chell, E. and K. Allman (2003), 'Mapping the motivations and intentions of technology orientated entrepreneurs', *R & D Management*, **33**(2), 117–134.

Chell, E. and R. Oakey (2004), 'Knowledge creation, its transfer, and the role of science enterprise education: a research agenda', *Innovation*, **6**(3), 444–458.

Chell, E. and P. Tracey (2005), 'Relationship building in small firms: the development of a model', *Human Relations*, **58**(5), 577–616.

Chell, E., J.M. Haworth and S.A. Brearly (1991), *The Entrepreneurial Personality: Concepts, Cases and Categories*, London: Routledge.

Chell, E., M. Karataş-Özkan and K. Nicolopoulou (2007), 'Social entrepreneurship education: policy, core themes, and developmental competencies', *International Journal of Entrepreneurship Education*, **5**, 143–162.

Chia, R. (1996a), 'The problem of reflexivity in organisational research: towards a postmodern science of organisation', *Organization*, **3**(1), 31–59.

Chia, R. (1996b), *Metaphors and metaphorization in organisational analysis: Thinking beyond the thinkable*, London: Sage Publications.

CISD (2002), Create@Derby: a creative industries strategy for Derby, Draft 2.5, May.

Comedia (2003), *The Creative Industries in the East Midlands*, EMDA.

Cook, S.D.N. and D. Yanow (1993), 'Culture and organisational learning', *Journal of Management Inquiry*, **2**(4), 373–390.

Cope, J. (2001), 'The entrepreneurial experience: towards a dynamic learning perspective of entrepreneurship', unpublished PhD thesis, University of Lancaster.

Cope, J. (2003), 'Entrepreneurial learning and critical reflection: discontinuous events as triggers for "higher-level" learning', *Management Learning*, **34**(4), 429–450.

Cope, J. (2005), 'Toward a dynamic learning perspective of entrepreneurship', *Entrepreneurship Theory Practice*, **29**(4), 373–397.

Cope, J and G. Watts (2000), 'Learning by doing – an exploration of experience, critical incidents and reflection in entrepreneurial learning', *International Journal of Entrepreneurial Behaviour and Research*, **6**(3), 104–124.

Cornelissen, J.P. (2004), 'What are we playing at? Theatre, organisation and the use of metaphor', *Organization Studies*, **25**(5), 705–726.

Centre for Policy Studies (CPS) (1987), Internal CPS Document.

Creswell, J.W. (1998), *Qualitative Inquiry and Research Design: Choosing among Five Traditions*, Thousand Oaks, CA: Sage Publications.

Croll, P. (2004), 'Observation schedule', in Lewis, B.M., Bryman, A. and Fuiting, L.T. (eds), *The Sage Encyclopaedia of Social Science Research Methods*, Thousand Oaks, CA: Sage Publications, 751–752.

Cronbach, L.J. (1975), 'Beyond the two disciplines of scientific psychology', *American Psychologist*, **30**, 116–127.

Cunliffe, A.L. (2003), 'Reflexive inquiry in organizational research: questions and possibilities', *Human Relations*, **56**(8), 983–1003.

Cunliffe, A. (2004), 'On becoming a critically reflexive practitioner', *Journal of Management Education*, **28**, 407–426.

Cunningham, S. (2003), 'From cultural to creative industries: theory, industry and policy implications', eprints.qut.edu.au, available at www. scholar.google.com (Date of access: 14 June 2004).

Cunningham, S. (2005), 'Creative enterprises', in Hartley, J. (ed.), *Creative Industries*, Oxford: Blackwell, 282–298.

Curtis, P. (2009), 'Dismantling DIUS could cost millions', *Guardian*, 10 June 2009.

Czarniawska, B. (1997), *Narrating the Organisation: Dramas of Institutional Identity*, Chicago: University of Chicago Press.

Czarniawska, B. (1998), *A Narrative Approach to Organisation Studies*, Thousand Oaks, CA: Sage Publications.

Czarniawska-Joerges, B. and R. Wolff (1991), 'Leaders, managers, entrepreneurs on and off the organizational stages', *Organization Studies*, **12**(4), 529–546.

Czarniawska, B. and K. Genell (2002), 'Gone shopping? Universities on their way to the market', *Scandinavian Journal of Management*, **18**, 455–474.

Danserau, F., F.J. Yammarino and J.C. Kohles (1999), 'Multiple levels of analysis: from a longitudinal perspective: some implications for theory building', *Academy of Management Review*, **24**(2), 346–357.

Davidsson, P. (2003), 'The domain of entrepreneurship research: some suggestions', in J. Katz and D. Shepherd (eds), *Advances in Entrepreneurship, Firm Emergence and Growth: Cognitive Approaches to Entrepreneurship Research*, **6**, Oxford: Elsevier/JAI Press, 315–372.

Davidsson, P. (2004), *Researching Entrepreneurship*, New York: Springer.

Davidsson, P. (2005), 'The entrepreneurial process as a matching problem', in Proceedings of Academy of Management Conference, August, Hawaii.

Davidsson, P. and J. Wiklund (2001), 'Levels of analysis in entrepreneurship research: current research practice and suggestions', *Entrepreneurship Theory Practice*, **25**(4), 81–99.

Davidsson, P. and B. Honig (2003), 'The role of social and human capital among nascent entrepreneurs', *Journal of Business Venturing*, **18**, 301–331.

Dawson, P. (1994), *Understanding Organisational Change*, London: Sage Publications.

Dawson, P. (1997), 'In at the deep end: conducting processual research on organisational change', *Scandinavian Journal of Management*, **13**(4), 389–405.

Dawson, P. (2003), *Reshaping Change: A Processual Perspective*, London: Routledge.

Department of Culture, Media and Sport (DCMS) (1998), First mapping document: creative industries, Department for Culture, Media and Sport, Creative Industries, London.

Department of Culture, Media and Sport (DCMS) (2001), Second mapping document: creative industries, Department for Culture, Media and Sport, Creative Industries, London.

Department of Culture, Media and Sport (DCMS) (2003), Creative industries – fact file, Department for Culture, Media and Sport, London.

Department of Culture, Media and Sport (DCMS) (2007), *Creative Industries Economic Estimates Statistical Bulletin October 2007*, London: DCMS.

Deakins, D. (1996), *Entrepreneurship and Small Firms*, Maidenhead: McGraw-Hill.

Deakins, D. and M. Freel (1998), 'Entrepreneurial learning and the growth process in SMEs', *The Learning Organisation*, **5**(3), 144–155.

De Cock, C., J. Fitchett and C. Volkmann (2005), 'Constructing the new economy: a discursive perspective', *British Journal of Management*, **16**, 37–49.

Deetz, S. (1996), 'Describing differences in approaches to organisation science: rethinking Burrell and Morgan and their legacy', Organization Science, **7**(2), 191–207.

Delmar, F. and P. Davidsson (2000), 'Where do they come from? Prevalence and characteristics of nascent entrepreneurs', *Entrepreneurship and Regional Development*, **12**, 1–23.

Denzin, N.K. (1989), *The Research Act: A Theoretical Introduction to Sociological Methods*, 3rd edition, Englewood Cliffs, NJ: Prentice Hall.

Denzin, N.K. (1994), 'The arts and politics of interpretation', in Denzin, N.K. and Lincoln, Y. (eds), *Handbook of Qualitative Research*, Thousand Oaks, CA: Sage Publications, 500–515.

Denzin, N.K. (2001), *Interpretive Interactionism*, 2nd edition, Thousand Oaks, CA: Sage Publications.

Denzin, N.K. and Y.S. Lincoln (1998), 'Entering the field of qualitative research', in Denzin, N.K. and Lincoln, Y.S. (eds), *Strategies of Qualitative Inquiry*, Thousand Oaks, CA: Sage Publications, 1–34.

Denzin, N.K. and Y.S. Lincoln (2000), 'Introduction: the discipline and practice of qualitative research', in Denzin, N.K. and Lincoln, Y.S. (eds), *Handbook of Qualitative Research*. 2nd edition, Thousand Oaks, CA: Sage Publications, 1–28.

Descartes, R. (1960), *Discourse on method and meditations*, Library of Liberal Arts, Indianapolis, IN (Original work published in 1637, 1641).

Dexter, B. (2003), 'Career progression and the first line manager', Unpublished PhD Thesis, Derby: University of Derby.

DfES (2003), 'Realising our potential', Government White Paper, London.

Drakopoulou-Dodd, S.D. and A.R. Anderson (2001), 'Understanding the enterprise culture: paradigm, paradox and policy', *International Journal of Entrepreneurship and Innovation*, **2**(1), 13–26.

Downing, S. (2005), 'The social construction of entrepreneurship: narrative and dramatic processes in the co-production of organizations and identities', *Entrepreneurship Theory and Practice*, **29**(2), 185–204.

Douglas, D. (2005), 'The human complexities of entrepreneurial decision making: a grounded case considered', *International Journal of Entrepreneurial Behaviour and Research*, **11**(6), 422–435.

David Powell Associates Ltd (DPA) (2002), 'Creative and cultural industries: an economic impact study for South East England', SEECC and SEEDA.

Drass, K.A. (1980), 'A computer programme for the analysis of qualitative data', *Urban Life*, **9**, 332–353.

Driver, M. (2002), 'Learning and leadership in organisations: toward complementary communities of practice', *Management Learning*, **33**(1), 99–126.

Department of Trade and Industry (DTI) (1998), 'Our competitive future: building the knowledge driven economy', Command Paper 4176, London: The Stationery Office.

Department of Trade and Industry (2001), 'Opportunities for all in a world of change', Competitiveness White Paper, London: Department of Trade and Industry.

Dooley, L. and D. Kirk (2007), 'University-industry collaboration: getting the entrepreneurial paradigm onto academic structures', *European Journal of Innovation and Management*, **10**(3), 316–332.

Duff, A. (1994), 'Best practice in incubator management', AUSTEP Strategic Partnering Pty. Ltd., Article available at http://members.iinet.net.au/~aduff/bestpracrpt.pdf (Date of access: 10 December 2002).

Du Gay, P. (2004), 'Against "Enterprise" (but not against "enterprise", for that would make no sense)', *Organization*, **11**(1), 37–57.

Dubini, P. and H. Aldrich (1991), 'Personal and extended networks are central to the entrepreneurial process', *Journal of Business Venturing*, **6**, 305–313.

Easterby-Smith, M., R. Snell and S. Gherardi (1998), 'Organisational learning: diverging communities of practice', *Management Learning*, **29**(3), 259–272.

Easterby-Smith, M. and D. Malina (1999), 'Cross-cultural collaborative research: towards reflexivity', *Academy of Management Journal*, **42**(1), 76–86.

Easterby-Smith, M., M. Crossan and D. Nicolini (2000), 'Organisational learning: debates past, present and future', *Journal of Management Studies*, **37**(6), 783–796.

Easterby-Smith, M., R. Thorpe and A. Lowe (2002), *Management Research: An Introduction*, 2nd edition, London: Sage Publications.

Eisendardt, K.M. and C.B. Schoonhoven (1996), 'Resource-based view of strategic alliance formation: strategic and social effects in entrepreneurial firms', *Organization Science*, **7**, 136–150.

Eliasson, G. (1996), *The Pharmaceutical and biotechnological competence block*, Royal Institute of Technology, Department of Industrial Economics and Management.

Enterprise Panel (1996), 'Growing Success: Helping companies to generate wealth and create jobs through business incubation', Midland Bank plc, London.

Evans, S. (2002), 'Introduction to creative industries', available at http://www.creativeclusters.co.uk/modules/eventsystem (accessed on 10 January 2005).

Everett, J. (2002), 'Organisational research and the praxeology of Pierre Bourdieu', *Organisational Research Methods*, **5**(1), 56–80.

Fairclough, N. (1991), 'What might we mean by "enterprise discourse"?', in Keat, R. and Abercrombie, N. (eds) *Enterprise Culture*, London and New York: Routledge, 38–57.

Financial Times (1999), 'Golden opportunity for industry to lift off: the enterprise culture Byers believes low inflation and the removal of red tape can encourage business flair', 15 November, 3.

Fielding, N.G. and J.L. Fielding (1998), *Computer Analysis and Qualitative Research*, Thousand Oaks, CA: Sage Publications.

Finlay, L. (2002), 'Negotiating the swamp: the opportunity and challenge of reflexivity in research practice', *Qualitative Research*, **2**(2), 209–230.

Fiol, C.M. and M.A. Lyles (1985), 'Organisational learning', *Academy of Management Review*, **10**(4), 803–813.

Flanagan, J.C. (1954), 'The critical incident technique', *Psychological Bulletin*, **51**(4), 327–358.

Fletcher, D. (1997), 'Organisational Networking, Strategic Change and the Family Business', Unpublished doctoral thesis, Nottingham Trent University.

Fletcher, D. (2002), 'In the company of men: a reflexive tale of cultural organizing in a small organisation', *Gender, Work and Organization*, **9**(4), 398–419.

Fletcher, D. (2003), 'Framing organizational emergence: discourse, identity and relationship', in Steyaert, C. and Hjorth, D. (eds), *New Movements in Entrepreneurship*, Cheltenham: Edward Elgar, pp. 125–142.

Fletcher, D. and C. Tansley (2003), 'A biographical account of "entrepreneurial responsiveness", theatre management and performance', paper addressed at the Entrepreneurial Dramas Track of the European Academy of Management (EURAM) Conference, 3–5 April, University of Bocconi, Milan.

Fletcher, D. and T. Watson (2003), 'Making it otherwise for us – otherwise for them: Drama, dialogue and enterprise creation', paper addressed at Entrepreneurial Dramas track of the European Academy of Management (EURAM) Conference, 3–5 April, University of Bocconi, Milan.

Flew, T. (2002), 'Beyond ad hocery: defining creative industries', paper presented to Cultural Sites, Cultural Theory, Cultural Policy at the Second International Conference on Cultural Policy Research, Te Papa, Wellington, New Zealand, 23–26 January.

Forster, N. (1994), 'The analysis of company documentation', in Cassell, C. and Symons, G. (eds), *Qualitative Methods in Organisational Research*, London: Sage Publications, pp. 147–166.

Foss, L. (2004), 'Going against the grain . . . Construction of entrepreneurial identity through narratives', in D. Hjort and Steyaert (2004) (eds), *Narrative and Discursive Approaches in Entrepreneurship*, Cheltenham: Edward Elgar, pp. 80–104.

Gartner, W.B. (1985), 'A framework for describing the phenomenon of new venture creation', *Academy of Management Review*, **10**(4), 696–706.

Gartner, W.B. (1988), '"Who is an entrepreneur?" is the wrong question', *American Journal of Small Business*, **12**(4), 11–32.

Gartner, W.B. (1990), 'What are we talking about when we talk about entrepreneurship', *Journal of Business Venturing*, **5**(1), 15–28.

Gartner, W.B. (2004), 'The edge defines the (w)hole: saying what entrepreneurship is (not)', in Hjort, D. and Steyaert (2004) (eds), *Narrative and Discursive Approaches in Entrepreneurship*, Cheltenham: Edward Elgar, 245–254.

Gartner, W.B., B.J. Bird and J.A. Starr (1992), 'Acting as if: differentiating entrepreneurial from organizational behaviour', *Entrepreneurship Theory and Practice*, **16**(3), 13–31.

Gartner, W.B., N.M. Carter and G.E. Hills (2003), 'The language of opportunity', in Steyaert, C. and Hjorth, D. (eds), *New Movements in Entrepreneurship*, Edward Elgar, Cheltenham, pp. 103–124.

Gartner, W.B., P. Davidsson and S.A. Zahra (2006), 'Are you talking to me? The nature of community in entrepreneurship scholarship', *Entrepreneurship Theory and Practice*, **30**(3), 321–331.

Garton, M. (2000), 'Overcoming the structure-agency divide in small business research', *International Journal of Entrepreneurial Behaviour and Research*, **6**(5), 276–292.

Gavron, R., M. Cowling, G. Holtham and A. Westall (1998), *The Entrepreneurial Society*, London: IPPR.

Geertz, C. (1973), 'Deep play: notes on the Balinese cockfight', in Geertz, C. (ed.), *The Interpretation of Cultures*, New York: Basic Books, 412–453.

Gergen, K.J. (1985), 'The social constructivist movement in modern psychology', *American Psychologist*, **40**, 266–275.

Gergen, K.J. (1992), 'Organisation theory in the postmodern era', in Reed, M. and Hughes, M. (eds), *Rethinking Organisation*, London: Sage Publications, 207–226.

Gergen, K.J. (1994), *Realities and Relationships,* Cambridge: Harvard University Press.

Gergen, K.J. (1999), *An Invitation to Social Construction*, London: Sage Publications.

Gergen, M.M. (1994), 'The social construction of personal histories: gendered lives in popular autobiographies', in Sarbin, T.R. and Kitsuse, J.I. (eds), *Constructing the Social*, London: Sage Publications, 19–44.

Gergen, K.J. and M.M. Gergen (1983), 'Narratives of the self', in Sarbin, T.R. and Scheibe, K.E. (eds), *Studies in Social Identity*, New York: Praeger Publishers.

Gergen, K.J. and M.M. Gergen (eds) (1984), *Historical Social Psychology*, Lawrence Erlbaum.

Gergen, K.J. and T.J. Thatchenkery (1996), 'Organization science as social construction: postmodern potentials', *Journal of Applied Behavioural Science*, **32**(4), 356–377.

Gergen, K.J. and M.M. Gergen (1991), 'Toward reflexive methodologies', in F. Steier (ed.), *Research and Reflexivity*, London: Sage Publications.

Gergen, K.J. and M.M. Gergen (2000), 'Qualitative inquiry: tensions and transformations', in Denzin, N.K. and Lincoln, Y.S. (eds), *Handbook of Qualitative Research*, 2nd edition, Thousand Oaks, CA: Sage Publications, 1025–1046.

Gherardi, S. (1994), 'The gender we think, the gender we do in our everyday organizational lives', *Human Relations*, **47**, 591–610.

Gherardi, S. (1999), 'Learning as problem driven or learning in the face of mystery', *Organisation Studies*, **20**(1), 101–124.

Gherardi, S. and D. Nicolini (2000), 'Practice-based theorizing on learning and knowing in organizations: an introduction', *Organization*, **7**(2), 211–223.

Gherardi, S. and D. Nicolini (2002), 'Learning in a constellation of interconnected practices: canon or dissonance?', *Journal of Management Studies*, **39**(4), 420–436.

Gibb, A. (1987), 'Enterprise culture and its meaning and implications for education and training', Bradford: MCB University Press.

Gibb, A. (1997), 'Small firms' training and competitiveness: building on the small business as a learning organisation', *International Small Business Journal*, **15**(3), 13–29.

Gibb, A. (2001), 'Creating conducive environments for learning and entrepreneurship: living with, dealing with and enjoying uncertainty and complexity', address to the first conference of the Entrepreneurship Forum, Naples, 21–24 June.

Gibb, A. (2002a), 'In pursuit of a new "enterprise" and "entrepreneurship" paradigm for learning: creative destruction, new values, new ways of doing things and new combinations of knowledge', *International Journal of Management Reviews*, **4**(3), 233–269.

Gibb, A. (2002b), 'Creating conducive environments for learning and entrepreneurship', *Industry and Higher Education*, **16**(3), 135–148.

Giddens, A. (1984), *The Constitution of Society: Outline of the Theory of Structuration*, Cambridge: Polity Press.

Giddens, A. (1990), 'Structuration theory and sociological analysis', in J. Clark, C.Modgil, S. Modgil (eds), *Anthony Giddens: Consensus and Controversy*, London: Falmer Press, pp. 297–315.

Giddens, A. (1991), *Modernity and Self-Identity*, Cambridge: Polity Press.

Gioia, D.A. and E. Pitre (1990), 'Multi-paradigm perspectives on theory building', *Academy of Management Review*, **15**(4), 584–602.

Glaser, B.G. (1992), *Basics of Grounded Theory Analysis: Emergence versus Forcing*, Mill Valley, CA: Sociology Press.

Glaser, B.G. and A.L. Strauss (1967), *Discovery of Grounded Theory: Strategies for Qualitative Research*, Chicago: Aldine.

Gold, R.L. (1958), 'Roles in sociological field observations', *Social Forces*, **36**, 217–223.

Goss, D. (2005), 'Schumpeter's legacy? Interaction and emotions in the sociology of entrepreneurship', *Entrepreneurship Theory and Practice*, **29**(2), 205–218.

Granovetter, M. (1973), 'The strength of weak ties', *American Journal of Sociology*, **78**(6), 1360–1380.

Granovetter, M. (1983), 'The strength of weak ties: a network theory revisited', *Sociological Theory*, **1**, 201–233.

Grant, P. and L.J. Perren (2002), 'Small businesses and entrepreneurial research: metatheories, paradigms and prejudices', *International Small Business Journal*, **20**(2), 185–209.

Gray, C. (1998), *Enterprise and Culture*, London: Routledge.

Gray, B., M. Bougon and A. Donnellon (1985), 'Organizations as constructions and deconstructions of meaning', *Journal of Management*, **11**(1), 83–95.

Greenberger, D.B. and D.L. Sexton (1988), 'An interactive model for new venture creation', *Journal of Small Business Management*, **26**(3), 107–118.

Greenwood, D. and M. Levin (2001), 'Re-organizing universities and "knowing how": university restructuring and knowledge creation for the 21st century', *Organization*, **8**(2), 433–440.

Guba, E.G. (1978), 'Toward a methodology of naturalistic inquiry in educational evaluation', CSE Monograph Series in Evaluation, No.8, Centre for the Study of Evaluation, University of California, Los Angeles.

Guba, E.G. and Y.S. Lincoln (1981), *Effective Evaluation*, San Francisco: Jossey-Bass.

Guba, E.G. and Y.S. Lincoln (1989), *Fourth Generation Evaluation*, Newbury Park, CA: Sage Publications.

Guillemin, M. and L. Gillam (2004), 'Ethics, reflexivity and ethically important moments in research', *Qualitative Inquiry*, **10**(2), 261–280.

Haar, D. and D.M. Hosking (2004), 'Evaluating appreciative inquiry: a relational constructionist perspective', *Human Relations*, **57**(8), 1017–1036.

Hague, D. and K. Oakley (2000), 'Spin-offs and start-ups in the UK universities', Committee of Vice Chancellors and Principles, London.

Hannon, P., A. Atherton and P. Chaplin (2002), 'Supporting incubation through the public sector at the sub-regional level in a peripheral location', paper addressed at 25th ISBA National Small Business and Entrepreneurship Conference, University of Brighton, 13–15 Nov.

Hammersley, M. and P. Atkinson (1995), *Ethnography: Principles in Practice*, 2nd edition, London: Routledge.

Harker, R., C. Mahar and C. Wilkes (1990), *An Introduction to the Work of Pierre Bourdieu: The Practice of Theory*, New York: Saint Martin's Press.

Harris, R.G. (2001), 'The knowledge-based economy: intellectual origins and new economic perspectives', *International Journal of Management Reviews*, **3**(1), 21–40.

Harryson, S.J. (2008), 'Entrepreneurship through relationships navigating from creativity to commercialisation', *R & D Management*, **38**(3), 290–310.

Harrisson, R.T. and C.M. Leitch (2005), 'Entrepreneurial learning: researching the interface between learning and the entrepreneurial context', *Entrepreneurship Theory and Practice*, **29**(4), 351–371.

Hart, M., H. Stevenson and J. Dial (1995), 'Entrepreneurship: a definition revisited', in *Frontiers of Entrepreneurship research*, Massachusetts: Babson Park.

Hartshorn, C. (2002), 'Learning from the life-world of the entrepreneur', paper presented at the Cambridge-MIT Institute Innovative Learning Methods Workshop, 20 March.

Harvey, M. and R. Evans (1995), 'Strategic windows in the entrepreneurial process', *Journal of Business Venturing*, **10**, 331–347.

Haslam, S.A., T. Posmen and N. Ellmers (2003), 'More than a metaphor: organisational life makes organisational life possible', *British Journal of Management*, **4**(4), 357–372.

Hassard, J. (1991), 'Multiple paradigms and organisational analysis: a case study', *Organisation Studies,* **12**(2), 275–99.

Hassard, J. and M. Kelemen (2002), 'Production and consumption in organisational knowledge: the case of the "paradigms" debate', *Organization*, **9**(2), 331–355.

Heartfield, J. (2000), *Great Expectations: The Creative Industries in the New Economy*, London: Design Agenda.

Heelas, P. and P. Morris (1991), *The values of enterprise culture*, London: Harper & Collins Academic.

Hegel, G.W.F. (1874), *The Logic: Encyclopaedia of the Philosophical Sciences*, 2nd edn, London: Oxford University Press.

Higher Education Funding Council of England (HEFCE) (2002), 'Higher Education Institutions (HEI) and Business & Community', at http://www.hefce.ac.uk (accessed on 28 November 2002).

Hertz, R. (1997), *Reflexivity and Voice*, Thousand Oaks, CA: Sage Publications.

Hesmondhalgh, D. and A.C. Pratt (2005), 'Cultural industries and cultural policy', *International Journal of Cultural Policy*, **11**(1), 1–13.

Hjort, D. (2003a), 'Transformative insinuations: an entrepreneurial drama of desiring and creating new worlds', Paper addressed at the Entrepreneurial Dramas Track of the European Academy of Management (EURAM) Conference, University of Bocconi, Milan, 3–5 April.

Hjort, D. (2003b), *Rewriting Entrepreneurship*, Liber-Abstrakt, Copenhagen Business School Press, Copenhagen.

Hjort, D. (2004), 'Towards genealogic storytelling in entrepreneurship', in Hjort, D. and Steyaert (2004) (eds), *Narrative and Discursive Approaches in Entrepreneurship*, Cheltenham: Edward Elgar, 210–232.

Hjorth, D. and C. Steyaert (2003), 'Entrepreneurship beyond (a new) economy: creative swarms and pathological zones', in Steyaert, C. and Hjorth, D. (eds), *New Movements in Entrepreneurship*, Cheltenham: Edward Elgar, 286–303.

Hjort, D., U. Johansson and L. Svengren (2004), 'The industrial designer as an entrepreneurial force', paper presented at the EURAM conference, St Andrews, UK.

Hobbes, T. (1651/1962), *Leviathan (or the matter, form and power of a commonwealth ecclesiastical and civil)*, New York: Collier Books.

Hodkinson, P. (1999), 'Use of habitus, capital and field in understanding young people's career decision making', in M. Grenfell and M. Kelly (eds), *Pierre Bourdieu: Language, Culture and Education*, Berne: Peter Lang, 259–269.

Holden, J. (2005), *Valuing Culture in the South East*, London: Demos.

Holland, R. (1999), 'Reflexivity', *Human Relations*, **52**(4), 463–484.

Holman, D. and R. Thorpe (2003), 'Management and language: the manager as a practical author', in D. Holman and R. Thorpe (eds), *Management and Language: The Manager as a Practical Author*, London: Sage Publications, pp. 1–11.

Holmquist, C. (2003), 'Is the medium really the message? Moving perspective from the entrepreneurial actor to entrepreneurial action', in Steyaert, C. and Hjort, D. (eds), *New Movements in Entrepreneurship*, Cheltenham: Edward Elgar Publishing, pp. 73–85.

Holmquist, C. and M. Lindgren (2002), 'Interactive entrepreneurship: from the acting individual to the interacting individuals', paper presented at the Second Movements in Entrepreneurship Workshop, Stockholm, 23–26 May.

Holstein, J.A. and J.F. Gubrium (1994), 'Constructing family: descriptive practice and domestic order', in Sarbin, T.R. and Kitsuse, J.I. (eds), *Constructing the Social*, London: Sage Publications, 232–250.

Honig, B. (2001), 'Learning strategies and resources for entrepreneurs and intrapreneurs', *Entrepreneurship Theory and Practice*, **26**(1), 21–35.

Hosking, D.M. and R. Bouwen (2000), 'Organisational learning: relational-constructionist approaches: an overview', *European Journal of Work and Organisational Psychology*, **9**(2), 129–132.

Hosking, D. and S. Fineman (1990), 'Organising processes', *Journal of Management Studies*, **27**(6), 583–604.

Hosking, D.M. and G. Green (1999), 'The processes of social construction: some implications for research and development', *Concepts and Transformation*, **4**(2), 1–12.

Hosking, D.M. and I.E. Morley (1991), *A Social Psychology of Organising*, Chichester: Harvester Wheatsheaf.

Hosking, D. and C. Ramsey (2000), 'Research, intervention and change: a constructionist contribution to process', research paper, RP0004, Aston Business School, Aston University, Birmingham.

Hosking, D.M. and D. Hjort (2004), 'Relational constructionism and entrepreneurship: some key notes', in D. Hjort and Steyaert (2004) (eds), *Narrative and Discursive Approaches in Entrepreneurship*, Cheltenham: Edward Elgar, 255–268.

Hughey, A.W. (2003), 'Higher education and the public, private and non-profit sectors', *Industry and Higher Education*, **17**(4), 251–268.

Huse, M. and H. Landstrom (1997), 'European entrepreneurship and small business research: methodological openness and contextual differences', *International Studies of Management and Organization*, **27**(3), 3–27.

Huysman, M. (2000), 'An organisational learning approach to the learning organisation', *European Journal of Work and Organisational Psychology*, **9**(2), 133–145.

Hytti, U. and C. O'Gorman (2004), 'What is "enterprise education"? An analysis of the objectives and methods of enterprise education programmes in four European countries', *Education and Training*, **46**(1), 11–23.

Inns, D. (2002), 'Metaphor in the literature of organisational analysis: a preliminary taxonomy and a glimpse at a humanities-based perspective', *Organization*, **9**(2), 305–333.

Jack, S.L. and A.R. Anderson (1999), 'Entrepreneurship education within the enterprise culture: producing reflective practitioners', *International Journal of Entrepreneurial Behaviour and Research*, **5**(3), 110–125.

Jack, S.L., S.D. Drakopoulou-Dodd and A.R. Anderson (2004), 'Social structures and entrepreneurial networks: the strength of strong ties', *International Journal of Entrepreneurship and Innovation*, **5**(2), 107–120.

Jack, S., S. Drakopoulou-Dodd, and A. Anderson (2008), 'Change and the development of entrepreneurial networks over time: a processual perspective', *Entrepreneurship and Regional Development*, **20**(2), 125–159.

Jack, S.L. and A.R. Anderson (2002), 'The effects of embeddedness on the entrepreneurial process', *Journal of Business Venturing*, **17**, 467–487.

Jackson, N. and P. Carter (1991), 'In defense of paradigm incommensurability', *Organization Studies*, **12**, 109–127.

Jarillo, J.C. (1989), 'Entrepreneurship and growth: the strategic use of external resources', *Journal of Business Venturing*, **4**, 133–147.

Jarvis, C. (2004), 'Knowledge really is route to success', *Times Higher Education Supplement*, 24/31 December, 1.

Jennings, R. (1992), *Pierre Bourdieu*, London: Routledge.

Jennings, P.L., L. Perren and S. Carter (2004), 'Guest editors' introduction: alternative perspectives on entrepreneurship research', *Entrepreneurship Theory and Practice*, **29**(2), 145–152.

Johannisson, B. (1990), 'Community entrepreneurship – cases and conceptualisation', *Entrepreneurship and Regional Development*, **2**, 71–88.

Johannisson, B. (1995), 'Paradigms and entrepreneurial networks: some methodological challenges', *Entrepreneurship and Regional Development*, **7**, 215–232.

Johannisson, B. (1998), 'Personal networks in emerging knowledge-based firms: spatial and functional patterns', *Entrepreneurship and Regional Development*, **10**, 297–312.

Johannisson, B. (2002), 'Walking the promised land – enacting and researching entrepreneurship', paper presented at the Second Movements in Entrepreneurship Workshop, Stockholm, May.

Johannisson, B., K.N. Alexanderson and K. Semeseth (1994), 'Beyond anarchy and organisation: entrepreneurs in contextual networks', *Entrepreneurship and Regional Development*, **6**, 329–356.

Johannisson, B. and M. Monsted (1997), 'Contextualising entrepreneurial networking – the case of Scandinavia', *International Studies of Management and Organization*, **27**(3), 109–136.

Johannisson, B., M. Ramirez-Pasillas and G. Karlsson (2002), 'The institutional embeddedness of local inter-firm networks: a leverage for business creation', *Entrepreneurship and Regional Development*, **14**, 297–315.

Johnson, W.C. (2003), 'University relations: the HP model', *Industry and Higher Education*, **17**(6), 39.

Johnson, P. and J. Duberley (2000), *Understanding Management Research: An Introduction to Epistemology*, London: Sage Publications.

Johnson, P. and J. Duberley (2003), 'Reflexivity in management research', *Journal of Management Studies*, **40**(5), 1279–1303.

Junker, B. (1960), *Fieldwork*, Chicago: University of Chicago Press.

Kamm, J.B., J.C. Shuman, J.A. Seeger and A.J. Nurick (1990), 'Entrepreneurial teams in new venture creation', *Entrepreneurship Theory and Practice*, **14**(4), 7–24.

Karataş-Özkan, M. (2006), 'The social construction of nascent entrepreneurship: dynamics of business venturing process from an entrepreneurial learning perspective', unpublished PhD thesis, University of Southampton, Southampton.

Karataş-Özkan, M. and W.D. Murphy (2002a), 'Emerging approaches to organisational analysis: a social constructionist proposal to entrepreneurial learning in organisations', paper addressed at the 17th Annual ERU Conference, Cardiff University, 9–11 September.

Karataş-Özkan, M. and W.D. Murphy (2002b), 'The dynamics of entrepreneurial learning and managing', work-in progress paper addressed at the 25th ISBA National Small Firms Policy and Research Conference, University of Brighton, 12–15 November.

Karataş-Özkan, M., W.D. Murphy and D. Rae (2005), 'University incubators in the UK', *International Journal of Entrepreneurship and Innovation*, February, 401–421.

Karataş-Özkan, M. and W.D. Murphy (2006), 'Venturing as a relational process', in O. Kyriakidou and M.F. Özbilgin (eds), *Relational Perspectives in Organizational Studies: A Research Companion*, Cheltenham and Northampton, MA: Edward Elgar, 112–137.

Katzko, M.W. (2002), 'Construction of social constructionism', *Theory and Psychology*, **12**(5), 671–683.

Keat, R. (1991), 'Introduction: starship Britain or universal enterprise?' in Keat, R. and Abercrombie, N. (eds), *Enterprise Culture*, London and New York: Routledge, 1–17.

Keeble, D. and F. Wilkinson (1999), 'Collective learning and knowledge development in the evolution of regional clusters of high-technology SMEs in Europe', *Regional Studies*, **33**(4), 295–303.

Kets de Vries, M.F.R. and D. Miller (1987), 'Interpreting organisational texts', *Journal of Management Studies*, **24**(3), 233–247.

King, N. (1994), 'The qualitative interview', in Cassell, C. and Symon, G. (eds), *Qualitative Methods in Organisational Research*, London: Sage Publications, 14–36.

Kirby, D.A. (2002), *Entrepreneurship*, Maidenhead: McGraw-Hill.

Kitson, M., J. Howells, R. Braham and S. Westlake (2009), *The Connected University*, London: NESTA.

Kolb, D. (1984), *Experiential Learning*, Englewood Cliffs, NJ: Prentice-Hall.

Kuhn, T. (1970), *The Structure of Scientific Revolutions*, 2nd edition, Chicago: Chicago University Press.

Kumar, U. and V. Kumar (1997), 'Incubating technology: best practices', prepared for the Federal Partners in Technology Transfer (Canada), Fall, Report at http://www.scietech.gc.ca/fprtt.kumar (accessed on 18 February 2003).

Kvale, S. (1996), *Interviews*, Thousand Oaks, CA: Sage Publications.

Kvale, S. (2006), 'Dominance through interviews and dialogues', *Qualitative Inquiry*, **12**, 480–500.

Lambert, R. (2003), 'Lambert review of business-university interaction: summary of consultation responses and emerging issues', report commissioned by HM Treasury.

Lave, J. and E. Wenger (1991), *Situated Learning: Legitimate Peripheral Participation*, Cambridge, MA: Harvard University Press.

Lawson, N. (1984), *The British Experiment*, Fifth Mais Lecture, London: HM Treasury.

Layder, D. (1993), *New Strategies in Social Research*, Cambridge: Polity Press.

Layder, D. (1994), *Understanding Social Theory*, London: Sage Publications.

Leadbeater, C. and K. Oakley (1999), *The Independents: Britain's New Cultural Entrepreneurs*, London: Demos.

Learned, K.E. (1992), 'What happened before the organisation? A model of organisation formation', *Entrepreneurship Theory and Practice*, **17**(1), 39–48.

Lechner, C. and M. Dowling (2003), 'Firm networks: external relationships as sources for growth and competitiveness of entrepreneurial firms', *Entrepreneurship and Regional Development*, **15**, 1–26.

Lesser, E. and K. Everest (2001), 'Using communities of practice to manage intellectual capital', *Ivey Business Journal*, **65**(4), 37–42.

Lichtenstein, B.B., and C.G. Brush (2001), 'How do "resource bundles" develop and change in new ventures? A dynamic model and longitudinal exploration', *Entrepreneurship Theory and Practice*, **25**(3), 37–59.

Lichtenstein, B.B., K.J. Dooley and G.T. Lumpkin (2006), 'Measuring emergence in the dynamics of new venture creation', *Journal of Business Venturing*, **21**, 153–175.

Lincoln, Y.S. and E.G. Guba (1985), *Naturalistic Inquiry*, London: Sage Publications.

Lincoln, Y.S. and E.G. Guba (1986), 'But is it rigorous? Trustworthiness and authenticity in naturalistic evaluation', in Williams, D.D. (ed.), *New Directions for Program Evaluation 30*, San Francisco: Jossey-Bass, 73–84.

Lincoln, Y.S. and E.G. Guba (2000), 'Paradigmatic controversies, contradictions, and emerging confluences', in Denzin, N.K. and Lincoln, Y.S. (eds), *Handbook of Qualitative Research*, 2nd edition, Thousand Oaks, CA: Sage Publications, 163–188.

Lindh de Montoya, M. (2004), 'Driven entrepreneurs: a case study of taxi owners in Caracas', in Hjort, D. and Steyaert (2004) (eds), *Narrative and Discursive Approaches in Entrepreneurship*, Cheltenham: Edward Elgar, 57–79.

Lockett, A., A. Vohora and M. Wright (2002), 'Universities as incubators without walls', *International Journal of Entrepreneurship and Innovation*, **3**(4), 245–256.

Lofland, J. and L.H. Lofland (1995), *Analysing Social Settings: A Guide to Qualitative Observation and Analysis*, 3rd edition, Belmot, CA: Wadsworth Publishing.

Low, M.B. and I.C. MacMillan (1988), 'Entrepreneurship: past research and future challenges', *Journal of Management Studies*, **14**(2), 139–161.

Lowe, A. (2004), 'Methodology choices and the construction of facts:

some implications from the sociology of scientific knowledge', *Critical Perspectives on Accounting*, **15**, 207–231.

Luna, M. and J.L. Velasco (2003), 'Bridging the gap between firms and academic institutions', *Industry and Higher Education*, **17**(5), 313–324.

MacBeth, D. (2001), 'On reflexivity in qualitative research', *Qualitative Inquiry*, **7**(1), 35–68.

Mahroum, S. (2008), *UK Global Innovation – Engaging with New Countries, Regions and People*, London: NESTA.

Malach-Pines, A., A. Sadeh, D. Dvir and O. Yafe-Yanai (2002), 'Entrepreneurs and managers: similar yet different', *International Journal of Organizational Analysis*, **10**(2), 172–190.

Mangham, I.L. and A. Pye (1991), *The Doing of Management*, Oxford: Blackwell.

Marshall, C. and G.B. Rossman (1995), *Designing Qualitative Research*, 2nd edition, Thousand Oaks, CA: Sage Publications.

Marshall, C. and G.B. Rossman (1995), *Designing Qualitative Research*, 3rd edition, Thousand Oaks, CA: Sage Publications.

Martin, J. and J. Sugarman (1996), 'Bridging social constructionism and cognitive constructionism: a psychology of human possibility and constraint', *Journal of Mind and Behaviour*, **17**(4), 291–320.

Mason, J. (1996), *Qualitative Research*, London: Sage Publications.

Mason, J. (2002), *Qualitative Researching*, London: Sage Publications.

Matlay, H. (2000), 'Industry-higher education collaborations within small business clusters: evidence from UK case studies', *Industry and Higher Education*, **14**(6), 38–55.

Mather, R. (2002), 'Gergen's social constructionism', *Theory and Psychology*, **12**(5), 695–699.

McCracken, G. (1988), *The Long Interview*, Newbury Park, CA: Sage Publications.

Melucci, A. (1982), *L'invenzione del presente*, Bologna: Il Mulino.

Mennell, S. (1994), 'The formation of we-images: a process theory', in C. Calhoun (ed.), *Social Theory and the Politics of Identity*, Oxford: Blackwell, 170–198.

Merleau-Ponty, M. (1963), *The Structure of Behaviour*, translated by Smith C., London: Routledge.

Merz, G.R., P.B. Weber and V.B. Laetz (1994), 'Linking small business management with entrepreneurial growth', *Journal of Small Business Management*, **32**, 4, 48–60.

Mian, S.A. (1997), 'Assessing and managing the university technology business incubator: an integrative framework', *Journal of Business Venturing*, **12**, 251–285.

Miles, M.B. and A.M. Huberman (1994), *Qualitative Data Analysis: An Expanded Sourcebook*, Thousand Oaks, CA: Sage Publications.

Minniti, M. and W. Bygrave (2001), 'A dynamic model of entrepreneurial learning', *Entrepreneurship Theory and Practice*, **25**(3), 5–17.

Mora Valentin, E.M. (2000), 'University-industry cooperation: a framework of benefits and obstacles', *Industry and Higher Education*, **14**(3), 165–172.

Morgan, G. (1980), 'Paradigms, metaphors and puzzle solving in organisation theory', *Administrative Science Quarterly*, **25**(4), 605–622.

Morgan, G. (1997), *Images of Organization*, London: Sage Publications.

Morgan, G. and L. Smircich (1980), 'The case for qualitative research', *Academy of Management Review*, **5**(4), 491–500.

Morris, N. (2002), 'Tower power: academics' commitment to the wealth creation mission', *Industry and Higher Education*, **16**(6), 33–49.

Morris, P. (1991), 'Freeing the spirit of enterprise: the genesis and development of the concept of enterprise culture', in R. Keat and N. Abercrombie (eds), *Enterprise Culture*, London and New York: Routledge, pp. 1–17.

Mowery, D. (2001), 'Trends in patenting, licensing and the role of equity at selected US universities', presentation to the National Academies Board on Science, Technology and Economic Policy Committee on Intellectual Property Rights in the Knowledge-Based Economy, 17 April.

MSC (1987), MSC press release, November.

Nash, R. (1999), 'Bourdieu, habitus and educational research', *British Journal of Sociology of Education*, **20**(2), 175–187.

Neergard, H. (2003), 'The process of entrepreneurship: a managerial and organizational journey', in C. Steyaert and D. Hjorth (eds), *New Movements in Entrepreneurship*, Cheltenham: Edward Elgar, pp. 160–176.

National Endowment for Science Arts and Technology (NESTA) (2005), 'Creating value: How the UK can invest in new creative businesses', NESTA research report, London: NESTA.

NESTA (2005), 'Creating value: how the UK can invest in new creative businesses', NESTA research report, London: NESTA.

NESTA (2008a), 'Developing entrepreneurial graduates', NESTA report in collaboration with the Council for Industry and Higher Education, London: NESTA.

NESTA (2008b), 'Business Incubation in Challenging Times', London: NESTA.

NESTA (2008c), 'Beyond the creative industries: making policy for the creative economy', policy briefing, BCI/20, London: NESTA.

Nicholson, L. and A.R. Anderson (2005), 'News and nuances of the entrepreneurial myth and metaphor: linguistic games in entrepreneurial sense-making and sense-giving', *Entrepreneurship Theory and Practice*, **29**(2), 153–172.

Nicolaidis, C.S. and G. Michalopoulos (2004), 'Education, industry and the knowing-doing gap: a knowledge management perspective of business education', *Industry and Higher Education*, **18**(2), 101–110.

Nicolini, D. and M.B. Meznar (1995), 'The social construction of organisational learning: conceptual and practical issues in the field', *Human Relations*, **48**(7), 727–746.

Oakley, K. (2004), *Developing the evidence base for support of cultural and creative activities in the South East*, SEEDA.

O'Connor, E. (1997), 'Discourse at our disposal: stories in and around the garage can', *Management Communication Quarterly*, **10**(4), 395–432.

O'Connor, J. (1999), 'The definition of cultural industries', unpublished paper, Manchester Institute for Popular Culture, available at http://mmu.ac.uk/h-ss/mipc/iciss/home2.htm (accessed on 10 January 2004).

O'Connor, J. (2002), 'Public and private in the cultural industries', unpublished paper, Manchester Institute for Popular Culture, available at http://www.teichenberg.at/essentials/O_Connor2.pdf (accessed on 10 January 2004).

O'Connor, E. (2004), 'Storytelling to be real: narrative, legitimacy building and venturing', in Hjort, D. and Steyaert (2004) (eds), *Narrative and Discursive Approaches in Entrepreneurship*, Cheltenham: Edward Elgar, 105–124.

Ogbor, J.O. (2000), 'Mythicizing and reification in entrepreneurial discourse: ideology-critique of entrepreneurial studies', *Journal of Management Studies*, **37**(5), 605–635.

Olson, P.D. (1985), 'Entrepreneurship: process and abilities', *Entrepreneurship Theory and Practice*, **10**(1), 25–32.

Owen-Pugh, V. (2002), 'The elite British basketball club as a "community of practice": a critique of Lave and Wenger's model of situated learning', paper addressed at the ERU conference, Cardiff University Business School, 9–11 September.

Özbilgin, M. (2006), 'Relational methods in organisation studies', in Kyriakidou, O. and Özbilgin, M. (eds), *Relational Perspectives in Organization Studies*, Cheltenham: Edward Elgar, 244–264.

Özbilgin, M. and A. Tatli (2005), 'Book review essay: understanding Bourdieu's contribution to organisation and management studies', *Academy of Management Review*, **30**(4), 855–877.

Özbilgin, M. and F. Küskü and N. Erdogmus (2005), 'Explaining influences on career "choice": the case of MBA students', *International Journal of Human Resource Management*, **16**(11), 2000–2028.

Parker, S.C. (2006), 'Learning about the unknown: how fast do entrepreneurs adjust their beliefs?', *Journal of Business Venturing*, **21**, 1–26.

Patton, M.Q. (1990), 'Humanistic psychology and qualitative research: shared principles and processes', *Person-Centered Review*, **5**(2), 191–202.

Patton, M.Q. (2002), *Qualitative Research and Evaluation Methods*, 3rd edition, Thousand Oaks, CA: Sage Publications.

Payne, S.L. (2000), 'Challenges for research ethics and moral knowledge construction in the applied social sciences', *Journal of Business Ethics*, **26**(4), 307–318.

Penn, D.W., W. Angwa, R. Forster, G. Heydon and S.J. Richardson (1998), 'Learning in smaller organisations', *The Learning Organisation*, **5**(3), 128–137.

Perren, L.J. and P. Grant (2000), 'The evolution of management accounting routines in small businesses: a social construction perspective', *Management Accounting Research*, **11**(4), 391–411.

Perren, L.J. and P. Jennings (2005), 'Government discourses on entrepreneurship: issues of legitimisation, subjugation and power', *Entrepreneurship Theory and Practice*, **29**(2), 173–184.

Peskett, R. (1987), 'Analysing the production of meeting talk', in Mangham, I.L. (ed.), *Organization Analysis and Development: A Social Construction of Organizational Behaviour*, Chichester: John Wiley & Sons, 47–60.

Peters, M. (2001), 'Education, enterprise culture and the entrepreneurial self: a Foucauldian perspective', *Journal of Educational Inquiry*, **2**(2), 58–71.

Pike, K. (1954), *Language in Relation to a Unified Theory of the Structure of Human Behaviour*, Vol 1, University of California, Summer Institute of Linguistics, published in 1967, Mouton, the Hague, Netherlands.

Pinnington, A., T. Morris and C. Pinnington (2003), 'The relational structure of improvisation', *International Studies of Management and Organisation*, **33**(1), 10–33.

Pittaway, L. (2000), 'The social construction of entrepreneurial behaviour', unpublished PhD thesis, University of Newcastle upon Tyne, Newcastle upon Tyne.

Pittaway, L. (2003), 'Paradigms as heuristics: a review of the philosophies underpinning economic studies in entrepreneurship', Working Paper No 2003/053, Lancaster University Management School, Lancaster.

Pittaway, L. (2005), 'Philosophies in entrepreneurship: a focus on economic theories', *International Journal of Entrepreneurship and Innovation*, **11**(3), 201–221.

Pittaway, L. and J. Cope (2006), 'Stimulating entrepreneurial learning: assessing the utility of experiential learning designs', *Management Learning*, forthcoming.

Politis, D. (2005), 'The process of entrepreneurial learning: a conceptual framework', *Entrepreneurship Theory and Practice*, **29**(4), 399–424.

Pratt, A. (2004), 'Mapping the cultural industries: regionalisation, the example of South East England', in A.J. Scott and D. Power (eds), *The Cultural Industries and the Production of Culture*, London: Routledge, pp. 45–63.

Putnam, R.D. (1993), *Making Democracy Work: Civic Traditions in Modern Italy*, Princeton: Princeton University Press.

Rae, D. (2002), 'Entrepreneurial emergence: a narrative study of entrepreneurial learning in independently owned media businesses', *International Journal of Entrepreneurship and Innovation*, **3**(1), 53–59.

Rae, D. (2003), 'Entrepreneurial identity and capability: the role of learning', unpublished PhD thesis, Nottingham Trent University, Nottingham.

Rae, D. (2004a), 'Entrepreneurial learning: a practical model from the creative industries', *Education and Training*, **46**(8–9), 492–500.

Rae, D. (2004b), 'Practical theories from entrepreneurs' stories: discursive approaches to entrepreneurial learning', *Journal of Small Business and Enterprise Development*, **11**(2), 195–202.

Rae, D. (2005), 'Mid-career entrepreneurial learning', *Education and Training*, **47**(8–9), 562–574.

Rae, D. (2006), 'Entrepreneurial learning: a conceptual framework for technology-based enterprise', *Technology Analysis and Strategic Management Journal*, **18**(1), 39–56.

Rae, D. and M. Carswell (2000), 'Using a life-story approach in researching entrepreneurial learning: the development of a conceptual model and its implications in the design of learning experiences', *Education and Training*, **42**(4–5), 220–227.

Raffo, C., A. Lovatt, M. Banks and J. O'Connor (2000), 'Teaching and learning entrepreneurship for micro and small businesses in the cultural industries', *Education and Training*, **42**(6), 356–365.

Ram, M. and D. Smallbone (2003), 'Policies to support ethnic minority enterprise: the English experience', *Entrepreneurship and Regional Development*, **15**, 151–166.

Ramsey, C. (2005), 'Narrative: from learning in reflection to learning in performance', *Management Learning*, **36**(2), 219–235.

Reason, P. (1994), *Participation in Human Inquiry*, London: Sage Publications.

Reinharz, S. (1997), 'Who am I? The need for a variety of selves in the field', in Hertz, R. (ed.), *Reflexivity and Voice*, Thousand Oaks, CA: Sage Publications, 3–20.

Reuber, A.R. and E.M. Fischer (1993), 'The learning experiences of entrepreneurs', in Churchill, N.C.E.A. (ed.), *Frontiers of Entrepreneurship Research*, Wellesby, MA: Babson Centre.

Reynolds, P. (1994), 'Reducing barriers to understanding new firm gestation: prevalence and success of nascent entrepreneurs', unpublished paper presented at the meeting of the Academy of Management, Dallas, TX.

Reynolds, P. and S.B. White (1997), *The Entrepreneurial Process: Economic Growth, Men, Women and Minorities*, Westport, CN: Quorum Books.

Rhodes, C. and A.D. Brown (2005), 'Writing responsibly: narrative fiction and organisation studies', *Organization*, **12**(4), 467–491.

Ritchie, J. (1991), 'Enterprise cultures', in R. Burrows (ed.), *Deciphering the Enterprise Culture*, London: Routledge, pp. 12–34.

Rizardo, O. (2004), 'The cognitive origins of Bourdieu's habitus', *Journal for the Theory of Social Behaviour*, **34**(4), 375–401.

Ronstadt, R. (1987), 'The educated entrepreneurs: a new era of entrepreneurial education is beginning', *American Journal of Small Business*, **11**(4), 37–53.

Rosen, M. (1991), 'Coming to terms with the field: understanding and doing organizational ethnography', *Journal of Management Studies*, **28**(1), 1–24.

Roulston, K., K. deMarrais and J.B. Lewis (2003), 'Learning to interview in the social sciences', *Qualitative Inquiry*, **9**, 643–668.

Ryan, G.W. and H.R. Bernard (2000), 'Data management and analysis methods', in N.K. Denzin and Y.S. Lincoln (eds), *Handbook of Qualitative Research*, Thousand Oaks, CA: Sage Publications, 769–802.

Sarbin, T.R. and J.I. Kitsuse (1994), *Constructing the Social*, London: Sage Publications.

Small Business Service (SBS) (2002), 'Small business and government: the way forward', London: DTI.

Small Business Service (SBS) (2004), 'A government action plan for small business: making the UK the best place in the world to start and grow a business – the evidence base, London: DTI.

Schatzki, T.R. (1997), 'Practices and actions: a Wittgensteinian critique of Bourdieu and Giddens', *Philosophy of the Social Sciences*, **27**(3), 283–308.

Schumpeter, J.A. (1934), *The Theory of Economic Development*, Cambridge: Harvard University Press.

Schutz, A. (1967), *Phenomenology of the social world*, translated by G.

Walsh and F. Lehnert, with an introduction by G. Walsh, Evanston, IL: Northwerstern University Press.

Schwandt, T.A. (2000), 'Three epistemological stances for qualitative inquiry: Interpretivism, hermeneutics, and social constructionism', in Denzin, N.K. and Lincoln, Y.S. (eds), *Handbook of Qualitative Research*, 2nd edition, Thousand Oaks, CA: Sage Publications, 189–213.

SEECC (2002), 'Creative and cultural industries: an economic impact study for South East England', research report by David Powell Associates Ltd, SEECC and SEEDA.

SEEDA (2005), 'Creative industries: key questions on regional impact, the view from South East England', SEEDA.

Segal Quince and Wicksteed (2000), *The Cambridge Phenomenon revisited*, Cambridge: SQW.

Selden, R. (1991), 'The rhetoric of enterprise', in R. Keat and N. Abercrombie (eds), *Enterprise Culture*, London and New York: Routledge, 58–71.

Sexton, D., N.B. Upton, L.E. Wacholtz and P.P. McDougall (1997), 'Learning needs of growth-oriented entrepreneurs', *Journal of Business Venturing*, **12**, 1–8.

Shane, S. (2004), *Academic Entrepreneurship: University Spinoffs and Wealth Creation*, Cheltenham: Edward Elgar.

Shane, S. and S. Venkataraman (2000), 'The promise of entrepreneurship as a field of research', *Academy of Management Review*, **25**(1), 217–226.

Shaver, S. and L.R. Scott (1991), 'Person, process, and choice: the psychology of new venture creation', *Entrepreneurship Theory and Practice*, **16**(2), 23–42.

Shotter, J. (1993a), *Conversational Realities*, London: Sage Publications.

Shotter, J. (1993b), *Cultural Politics of Everyday Life*, Buckingham: Open University Press.

Shotter, J. (1995), 'The manager as a practical author: a rhetorical-responsive, social constructionist approach to social organisational problems', in D.M. Hosking, H.P. Dachler and K.J. Gergen (eds), *Management and Organisation: Relational Alternatives to Individualism*, Avebury.

Shotter, J. and A.L. Cunliffe (2003), 'Managers as practical authors: everyday conversation for action', in D. Holman and R. Thorpe (eds), *Management and Language*, London: Sage Publications, 15–37.

Shusterman, R. (1999), 'Introduction: Bourdieu as philosopher', in R. Shusterman (ed.), *Bourdieu: A Critical Reader*, Oxford: Blackwell, pp. 1–13.

Siisiainen, M. (2000), 'Two concepts of social capital: Bourdieu vs. Putnam', paper presented at ISTR Fourth International Conference on 'The Third Sector: For What and for Whom?', Dublin, Ireland, 5–8 July.

Silverman, D. (2005), *Doing Qualitative Research*, 2nd edition, London: Sage Publications.

Smilor, R.W. and M.D. Gill (1986), *The New Business Incubator – Linking Talent, Technology, Capital and Know-How*, DC Heath and Company.

Smircich, L. (1983), 'Concepts of culture and organizational analysis', *Administrative Science Quarterly*, **28**(3), 339–358.

Smith, R. and A.R. Anderson (2004), 'The devil is in the *e-tale*: forms and structures in the entrepreneurial narratives', in D. Hjort and Steyaert (2004) (eds), *Narrative and Discursive Approaches in Entrepreneurship*, Cheltenham: Edward Elgar, pp. 125–143.

Spinosa, C., F. Flores and H.L. Dreyfus (1997), *Disclosing new worlds: Entrepreneurship, Democratic Action, and the Cultivation of Solidarity*, Cambridge: MIT Press.

Spradley, J.P. (1979), *The Ethnographic Interview*, New York: Holt, Rinehart and Winston.

Spradley, J.P. (1980), *Participant Observation*, New York: Holt, Rinehart and Winston.

Stacey, R.D. (2001), *Complex Responsive Processes in Organisations: Learning and Knowledge Creation*, Routledge: London.

Stake, R.E. (1994), 'Case study', In Denzin, N.K. and Lincoln, Y.S. (eds), *Handbook of Qualitative Research*, Thousand Oaks, CA: Sage Publications, pp. 236–447.

Stake, R.E. (1995), *The Art of Case Study Research*, Thousand Oaks, CA: Sage Publications.

Stake, R.E. (1998), 'Case studies', in Denzin, N.K. and Lincoln, Y.S. (eds), *Strategies of Qualitative Inquiry*, Thousand Oaks, CA: Sage Publications, pp. 86–109.

Sternberg, J.S. and T.I. Lubart (1999), 'The concept of creativity: prospects and paradigms', in Sternberg, R.J. (ed.), *Handbook of Creativity*, New York: Cambridge University Press, pp. 3–15.

Steffy, B.D. and A.J. Grimes (1992), 'Personnel/organisational psychology: a critique of the discipline', in M. Alvesson and H. Wilmott (eds), *Critical Management Studies*, London: Sage Publications, pp. 181–201.

Stevenson, H.H. and D.E. Gumpert (1985), 'The heart of entrepreneurship', *Harvard Business Review*, **63**(2), 85–94.

Stevenson, H. and J.C. Jarillo (1990), 'A paradigm of entrepreneurship: entrepreneurial management', *Strategic Management Journal*, **11**, 17–27.

Stewart, A. (1989), *Team Entrepreneurship*, Newbury Park, CA: Sage Publications.

Steyaert, C. (1998), 'A qualitative methodology for process studies of entrepreneurship: creating local knowledge through stories', *International Studies of Management and Organisation*, **27**(3), 13–33.

Steyaert, C. (2003), 'The prosaics of entrepreneurship: narration, drama and conversation', paper addressed at the Entrepreneurial Dramas track of the European Academy of Management (EURAM) Conference, University of Bocconi, Milan, 3–5 April.

Steyaert, C. (2004), 'The prosaics of entrepreneurship', in D. Hjort and C. Steyaert (2004) (eds), *Narrative and Discursive Approaches in Entrepreneurship*, Cheltenham: Edward Elgar, 8–21.

Steyaert, C. (2005), 'Entrepreneurship: in between what? On the 'frontier' as a discourse of entrepreneurship research', *International Journal of Entrepreneurship and Small Business*, **2**(1), 2–16.

Steyaert, C. and R. Bouwen (1997), 'Telling stories of entrepreneurship – towards a narrative-contextual epistemology for entrepreneurial studies', in Donckels, R. and Miettinen, A. (eds), *Entrepreneurship and SME Research: On Its Way to the Next Millennium*, Aldershot: Ashgate Publishing Ltd, pp. 47–61.

Steyaert, C., R. Bouwen and B.V. Looy (1996), 'Conversational construction of new meaning configurations in organisational innovation: a generative approach', *European Journal of Work and Organizational Psychology*, **5**(1), 67–89.

Steyaert, C. and D. Hjorth (2003), 'Creative movements of entrepreneurship', in Steyaert, C. and Hjorth, D. (eds), *New Movements in Entrepreneurship*, Cheltenham: Edward Elgar, pp. 3–19.

Steyaert, C. and J. Katz (2004), 'Reclaiming the space of entrepreneurship in society: geographical, discursive and social dimensions', *Entrepreneurship and Regional Development*, **16**, 179–196.

Strauss, A. and J. Corbin (1990), *Basics of Qualitative Research: Techniques and Procedures for Developing Grounded Theory*, 1st edition, Thousand Oaks, CA: Sage Publications.

Strauss, A. and J. Corbin (1998), *Basics of Qualitative Research: Techniques and Procedures for Developing Grounded Theory*, 2nd edition, Thousand Oaks, CA: Sage Publications.

Swan, J., H. Scarbrough and M. Robertson (2002), 'The construction of "communities of practice" in the management of innovation', *Management Learning*, **33**(4), 477–496.

Swartz, D. (1997), *Culture and Power: The Sociology of Pierre Bourdieu*, Chicago: University of Chicago Press.

Swedberg, R. (2000), *Entrepreneurship: The Social Science View*, Oxford: Oxford University Press.

Tatli, A. and M. Özbilgin (2006), 'Diversity manager's change agency', paper addressed at the European Academy of Management

Conference, BI Norwegian School of Management, Oslo, 16–20 May 2006.

Taousanidis, N. (2002), 'New challenges for European higher education', *Industry and Higher Education*, **16**(5), 289–305.

Taylor, J. and M. Karatas-Özkan (2008), 'Knowledge exchange relationships between higher education institutions and stakeholders in business sector in the developed and developing economies: towards a research agenda for a comparative study', paper addressed at the Conference 'Governance and Management Models in Higher Education – A Global Perspective', Coimbria, Portugal, 3–5 September 2008.

Taylor, D.W. and R. Thorpe (2004), 'Entrepreneurial learning: a process of co-participation', *Journal of Small Business and Enterprise Development*, **11**(2), 203–211.

Thorpe, R., J. Gold, R. Holt and J. Clarke (2006), 'Immaturity: the constraining of entrepreneurship', *International Small Business Journal*, **24**(3), 232–250.

The Work Foundation (2007), 'Staying ahead: the economic performance of the UK's creative industries', London: The Work Foundation.

Tornatzky, L., G. Louis, Y.Batts, N.E. McCrea, M.S. Lewis and L.M. Quittman (1996), *The Art and Craft of Technology Business Incubation – Best Practices, Strategies and Tools from more than 50 programs*, Washington, DC: National Business Incubation Association.

Totterman, H. and J. Sten (2005), 'Start-ups: business incubation and social capital', *International Small Business Journal*, **23**(5), 487–511.

Tsoukas, H. (2002), 'Introduction: knowledge-based perspectives on organisations: situated knowledge, novelty and communities of practice', *Management Learning*, **33**(4), 419–426.

Ucbasaran, D., P. Westhead and M. Wright (2001), 'The focus of entrepreneurial research: contextual and process issues', *Entrepreneurship Theory and Practice*, **25**(4), 57–82.

Ucbasaran, D., M. Wright and P. Westhead (2003), 'A longitudinal study of habitual entrepreneurs: starters and acquirers', *Entrepreneurship & Regional Development*, **15**, 207–228.

Ucbasaran, D., P. Westhead, M. Wright, A. Lockett and A. Lei (2001), 'The dynamics of entrepreneurial teams', *Frontiers of Entrepreneurship Research*, Babson College, Babson Park, MA, available at www.babson.edu/entrep/fer/Babson2001/X/XA/XA/x-a.htm (accessed on 14 March 2003).

UKBI (2002), UKBI Annual Business Incubation Survey, disseminated at the UKBI 4th International Conference: Business Incubation: The Fundamentals of Economic Prosperity, Edinburgh, 24–26 November.

Van Hoorebeek, M. (2005), 'Government policy and university technology transfer practices in the UK', *International Journal of Technology Transfer and Commercialisation*, **4**(4), 500–517.

Van Raaij, E.M. and W.A. Weimer (2003), 'Providing industry with education that meets business standards', *Industry and Higher Education*, **17**(2), 91–101.

Van der Haar, D. and D.M. Hosking (2004), 'Evaluating appreciative inquiry: a relational constructionist perspective', *Human Relations*, **57**(8), 1017–1036.

Varamaki, E. and J. Vesalainen (2003), 'Modelling different types of multilateral co-operation between SMEs', *Entrepreneurship & Regional Development*, **15**, 27–47.

Vyakarnam, S., R.C. Jacobs and J. Hadelberg (1999), 'Exploring the formation of entrepreneurial teams: the key to rapid growth business?', *Journal of Small Business and Enterprise Development*, **6**(2), 153–165.

Wacquant, L.J.D. (1992), 'Towards a socio-praxeology: the structure and logic of Bourdieu's sociology', in Bourdieu, P. and Wacquant, L. (eds), *An Invitation to Reflexive Sociology*, Cambridge: Polity Press, pp. 1–47.

Wagner, J. (2004), 'Nascent Entrepreneurs', Discussion Paper No. 1293, Institute for the Study of Labour, Bonn: University of Lueneburg.

Walsh, D. (2004), 'Doing ethnography', in C. Seale (ed.), *Researching Society and Culture*, London: Sage Publications, 225–238.

Warren, L. (2004a), 'Negotiating entrepreneurial identity: communities of practice and changing discourses', *International Journal of Entrepreneurship and Innovation*, **5**(1), 25–35.

Warren, L. (2004b), 'The case of Airwave Sounds plc.', *International Journal of Entrepreneurship and Innovation*, **5**(2), 129–137.

Warren, L. and J. Stephens (2004), 'From classroom to community of practice', *International Journal of Entrepreneurship Education*, **2**(3), 329–350.

Watson, T.J. (1994a), *In Search of Management: Culture Chaos and Control in Managerial Work*, London: Routledge.

Watson, T.J. (1994b), 'Managing, crafting and researching: words, skills and imagination in shaping management research', *British Journal of Management*, **5**, 77–87.

Watson, T. (1995), 'Rhetoric, discourse and argument in organizational sense-making: a reflexive tale', *Organization Studies*, **16**(5), 805–821.

Watson, T.J. (1997), 'Languages within languages: a social constructionist perspective on multiple managerial discourses', in F. Bargiela-Chiappini and S. Harris (eds), *The Languages of Business: An International Perspective*, Edinburgh: Edinburgh University Press, pp. 211–248.

Watson, T.J. (2001a), 'Negotiated orders in organisations', *International*

Encyclopaedia of Social and Behavioural Science, Amsterdam: Elsevier, 10965–10968.

Watson, T.J. (2001b), *In Search of Management*, 2nd edition, London: Thomson Learning.

Watson, T.J. (2002), *Organising and Managing Work: Organisational, Managerial and Strategic Behaviour in Theory and Practice*, Harlow: FT Prentice Hall.

Watson, T.J. (2003), 'Strategists and strategy making: strategic exchange and the shaping of individual lives and organizational futures', *Journal of Management Studies*, **40**(5), 1305–1323.

Webb, J., T. Schirato, and G. Danaker (2002), *Understanding Bourdieu*, London: Sage Publications

Webster, G. (2003), 'Corporate discourse and the academy', *Industry and Higher Education*, **17**(2), 85–90.

Weick, K.E. (1979), *The Social Psychology of Organising*, New York: Random House.

Weick, K.E. (1995), *Sensemaking in Organizations*, Thousand Oaks, CA: Sage Publications.

Weick, K.E. and K.H. Roberts (1993), 'Collective mind in organizations: heedful interrelating on flight decks', *Administrative Science Quarterly*, **38**, 357–381.

Weick, K.E. (1998), 'Introductory essay: improvisation as a mindset for organisational analysis', *Organization Science*, **9**(5), 543–555.

Wenger, E. (1998), *Communities of Practice: Learning, Meaning and Identity*, Cambridge: Cambridge University Press.

Wenger, E.C. and W.M. Snyder (2000), 'Communities of practice: the organisational frontier', *Harvard Business Review*, 139–145.

Westhead, P. and M. Wright (1998), 'Novice, portfolio and serial founders: are they different?', *Journal of Business Venturing*, **13**, 173–204.

Wheelock, J. and S. Baines (1998), 'Dependency or self-reliance? The contradictory case of work in UK small business families', *Journal of Family and Economic Issues*, **19**(1), 53–73.

Wickham, P.A. (2004), *Strategic Entrepreneurship*, 3rd edition, Harlow: FT Prentice Hall.

Wilmott, H. (1993), 'Breaking the paradigm mentality', *Organization Studies*, **14**, 681–719.

Wolcott, H.F. (1994), *Transforming Qualitative Data: Description, Analysis and Interpretation*, Thousand Oaks, CA: Sage Publications.

Wright, M., K. Robbie and C. Ennew (1995), 'Serial entrepreneurs', in W.D. Bygrave, B. Bird, S. Birley. N.C. Churchill, F. Hoy, R. Keeley, and W.E. Wetzel (eds), *Frontiers of Entrepreneurship Research*, Wellesley, MA: Babson College, pp. 158–171.

Wright, M., S. Birley and S. Mosey (2004), 'Entrepreneurship and university technology transfer', *Journal of Technology Transfer*, **29**(3–4), 235–246.

Wright, M., B. Clarysse, P. Mustar and A. Lockett (2008), *Academic Entrepreneurship in Europe*, Cheltenham: Edward Elgar.

Yin, R.K. (1994), *Case Study Research: Design and Methods*, Applied Social Research Methods, Vol. 5, Thousand Oaks, CA: Sage Publications.

Young, J.E. and D.L. Sexton (1997), 'Entrepreneurial learning: a conceptual framework', *Journal of Enterprising Culture*, **5**(3), 223–248.

Zafirovski, M. (1999), 'Probing into the social layers of entrepreneurship: outlines of the sociology of enterprise', *Entrepreneurship and Regional Development*, **11**, 351–371.

Appendices

APPENDIX 1:   EXAMPLE TO AN INTERVIEW GUIDE

Interview with Rosie (Nascent Entrepreneur of the Venture, R-Games)

- **Business venturing process:**
  Personal goals/objectives
  Personal motivation
  Entrepreneurial activities engaged in
  Support/advice
  Problems/challenges
  Entrepreneurial decisions
  Being an entrepreneur: what is it about?
  Networking/relationships
  Future of the business/entrepreneur: any image?

- **Entrepreneurial learning:**
  Reflections on the start-up process
  Failures/successes
  Lessons learned
  Social learning
  Educational background/training
  Impact on future actions
  Critical incidents

- **Context**
  Support mechanisms
  Obstacles
  Incubator environment
  Characteristics of the industry/market

APPENDIX 2:   LIST OF CODES

Theme	Sub-theme	Code
Business venturing process (BVP)	Personal biography (PB)	BVP-PB
	Entrepreneurial motivation (EM)	BVP-EM
	Dispositions (D)	BVP-D
	Forms of 'capital' drawn on/created (C)	BVP-C
	Transformation between capitals (TC)	BVP-TC
	Business opportunity (BO)	BVP-BO
	Start-up activities (SA)	BVP-SA
	Decision making (DM)	BVP-DM
	Managing relationships (MR)	BVP-MR
	Managing different functions of the business (MDF)	BVP-MDF
	Forming strategic alliances (FSA)	BVP-FSA
	Obtaining support/advice (OSA)	BVP-OSA
	Problems and challenges (PC)	BVP-PC
	Creativity dimension (CD)	BVP-CD
	Future goals/direction (FGD)	BVP-FGD
Entrepreneurial learning (EL)	Social learning (SL)	EL-SL
	Critical incidents (CL)	EL-CL
	Constructing entrepreneurial identity (CEL)	EL-CEL
	Learning by experience (LE)	EL-LE
	Generative exchange (GE)	EL-GE
	Developing agentic and performative capacity (AC)	EL-APC
	Practical theory/what works (PT)	EL-PT
	Sense-making (SM)	EL-SM
	Negotiation of meanings (NM)	EL-NM
	Legitimising the business (LB)	EL-LB
	Contextual learning (CxL)	EL-CxL
	Changing equivocal interactions to non-equivocal ones (CEIN)	EL-CEIN
	Educational background/training (EBT)	EL-EBT
Context (C)	Enterprise/business support programmes (EBP)	C-EBP
	University incubators (UI)	C-UI
	Dynamics of 'creative industries' (CI)	C-CI
	Entrepreneurship/enterprise courses (EEC)	C-EEC
	Socio-economic and political dimensions (SEP)	C-SEP

APPENDIX 3:   INTERVIEW DATA SUMMARY SHEET

Case: R-Games

Research participant: Rosie
(Her mentor, Ralph, visited her during the interview and contributed to the discussion).

Interview date/venue: 25 August 2004; R-Games offices, local university's incubator centre.

Interview agenda: interview guide used (see Appendix VI), outlining the key topics in relation to research questions (and implicitly levels of analysis-micro-meso-macro). The interview guide was explained to the participant at the outset of the interview.

Interview transcript: produced on 31 August 2004 (see Appendix VII for the full transcript of this interview).

Brief summary of salient themes:
Her personal biography:

- Educational background/current status: law and business degree
- Mother of two children
- 30 years old
- Previous work experience at her brother's advertising firm
- Taxi-driver

Venturing process:

- Entrepreneurial motivation/disposition towards wealth creation (personal wealth/recognition/autonomy/being her own boss)
- Developing the business opportunity
- Refining the business concept towards souvenir game
- Start-up activities (legal and technical aspects)
- Setting up the venture in the local university's incubator
- Dealing with different functions of the business (starting a business: multi-dimensional process)
- Importance of funding
- Networking: using contacts (weak ties mainly)
- Organising activities on various levels (strategic/tactical and daily)
- Future: a successful, rich business woman/a global business

Entrepreneurial learning:

- Gaining self-confidence
- Self-determination/entrepreneurial commitment
- Learning from failures/experience
- Defining success
- Critical incidents: winning the EC competition,
    - Moving into the incubator
    - Winning the first sponsorship money
- Managing relationships: social capital
- Raising entrepreneurial awareness throughout the process

APPENDIX 4: OBSERVATION DATA SUMMARY SHEET

KbrandArt

Venture team meeting (board meeting)/ 4 Sep 2003 (5:30–7:30)
Venue: KBrandArt offices

Participants:
Norman (N, a new member of the team working on brand positioning), Denise (D), Adam (A), Paul (P) and Luke (L) and Mine (M). Charles was not attending because he was in Ireland.

Agenda:
- Brand positioning process, vision and values
- Funding: £ Alert

(These two items were on the meeting agenda sheet that Denise distributed to the team members including myself).

Denise opened the meeting with her concern of better organising the business (venture) at this transition stage by referring to the need for more meetings. Then she introduced Norman's agenda regarding brand repositioning for that evening.

Record of the meeting talk:
Norman: (introduces and explains the goal) Well, I have some form of internal document which sets out how we should talk about ourselves. What we do. How we do. Just looking at the process, Production's proposition is much clearer and clearly based in production in video whereas Studios' is basically in media. I see a number of issues here that you need to clarify. It is challenging but we should decide. I started to say 'We' now. Going down that route, you should tell me 'hang on we are not confident' and we should find the way you feel most comfortable (talking to everybody).
L: That's why you are here to push us.
N: Yeah (soft laugh) First of all, I'm not sure what KBrandArt Studios does. Or KBrandArt generically. We are going out there and what do you stand for. We have got to be consistent in that respect. Consistency in how we present ourselves to the market offerings is must. Then creating value strategically and creatively is the key issue in brand positioning. Production arm is very important and it is based in certain areas

and it does underline your expertise. So, we can say we do these. All this brand communication stuff. But we have got the production arm as well.

Denise gave an example from the XYZ Building Society. How they can realise that by providing the technical side as well. Norman asks a question around the name 'Studios' to everybody:

N: What about Studios? Are you all comfortable with the name KBrandArt Studios?

A: Well, not really and we discussed this before but it is about the website, isn't it?

D: You can still have the domain name.

N: I wouldn't be worried about the domain name. What we are, what we are offering through what is the key issue to clarify.

L: KBrandArt becomes the solution to the creative consultancy and productions is the technical side of it.

N: Where does the 'studios' fit then? I'm inclined to have KBrandArt and KBrandArt Productions.

A: KBrandArt does employ a range of activities.

D: But it doesn't cover the strategic studio.

A: It doesn't exclude it. At the moment, it doesn't imply it. When I am going to a meeting, I'm saying I'm from KBrandArt Studios because it is longer. Better than saying just KBrandArt. Then the implication is I'm from a media company or what?

D: The trouble to me is KBrandArt clearer?

N: Adam is right. The name 'KBrandArt Studios' poses a problem in people's minds. Something more strategic I'm after. I'm just thinking if it could work against us.

D: The whole future is very much on the people who have. I mean the clients . . . (not sure of what she is saying . . . looking at the piece of paper in front of her)

N: Well, future seems to me lies in agency type of consultancy rather than studios. I don't think Studios implies that.

A: Lots of things happened in the Studios. So I don't want to ditch Studios but it might mean that it is mainly around the production. What about is the strategy production and creation underneath? (directing the question to Norman)

N: That's one of the things that I am coming to. We are not going to solve it here and then.

D: I've got to think in my head about how it communicates better (seems confused and worried, turns to Adam and explains). We should have 'KBrandArt' as the main name, Brands Communications Agency. Everything you produce is brand communications, a website or a video.

A: (replies) Not exclusively. Everything we do is brand oriented.

N: I think it is the issue of whether the name poses obstacles. Yes, everything we do is brand oriented but . . . (interrupted by Paul)

P: (joins in the conversation, usually quiet and does not talk much at the meetings unless he is spoken to or he feels his intervention is necessary.) The question is should the name have to be explicit in that respect . . . (asking to N)

N: OK! If you take the name issue away for the moment, the thing is how much equity it does have. Are we going to lose anything? Can we inject something into it? Does the word 'Studios' pose obstacles to where we want to be seen. (pause) The next issue is it is all about brand communication.

L: Well. Let's stick to the issue. What is brand? (asking Norman)

N: There is a wide interpretation of what a brand is. So, I would describe us as a brand communication agency . . .

L: (not convinced and asking again) From what you're saying I don't get what your definition of brand is . . .

D: (seems to be bored with all this conceptual talk, as A puts it at times when we have informal talks, and D asks Norman) How do you define it then?

L: I don't know . . . Brand is about everything that touches the consumer . . .

A: (talking to everybody, looking at Denise) Your corporate identity in a way. Clients want us to produce campaigns of the highest creative standard to achieve their brand positioning or strengthening . . . whatever . . .

N: (replying in a reaffirming way) Yeah but the other thing is to deliver what you suggest. I mean the issue is to melt production side with the strategy side. So, rather than talking about disciplines like video, website, motion graphics or print design we need to also talk about marketing activities: advertising, PR, live events, digital marketing . . . Talking about those things support the fact that you guys are actually delivering the strategy side. We need to start talking about those things. Because what people want to see you are competent in this area. Two elements here: first, how we describe ourselves is the main issue . . . (interrupted by Denise)

D: It is about selling a package that people can relate to. (Denise reminded that they had this discussion a year ago but at that stage they weren't sure about what they were: advertising agency or a brands agency).

N: Why we need to be talking about advertising and direct marketing as well is because we are moving to the brand communications side. We are more than a creative production firm . . .

L: Are we? (asking to everybody) I am not quite sure.

D: (replying to L) We should be . . . When N talked about the emphasis on the brands agency, I thought we might lose some of our advertising customers but we need to consider from whom we can get proper projects. Production side will continue . . .

N: Absolutely . . . It doesn't deny it at all.

L: Calling it KBrandArt Productions is like a cult that combines . . .

He draws and shows his figure to people around the table:

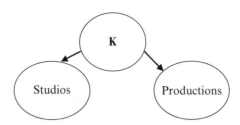

He explains this by going through the figure.

N: I'd like to go through this positioning process for Productions and Studios as well.

L: Yeah, I'd like to be more involved in the website side as well. I'm working with John, freelance person I'm bringing in.

N: (asking L) Who is he? (D answers)

D: Roger's brother.

N: Oh yes, I came across him. That's great.

D: He is quite experienced.

L: Yeah. He will share some of his ideas.

D: Yes. Why not. If we are happy, we can carry on working with him.

N: The other thing we don't do here is that the research. We need to know what clients or other people think of us. I have got a research guy. I mean a PR guy locally. I could bring him in . . .

N: As long as you have got somebody and you ask the right questions it is fine. Getting an absolutely crystal understanding of what the client wants and is committed to is the hardest thing. Once you get it, you can work on what stuff to bring in.

A: Well, yes it is about listening to business requirements, asking questions and finding answers. But they (clients) also want the project to be executed on time . . . (interrupted by Denise)

D: Fast, efficiently and affordably.

N: Yeah. A creative and sophisticated approach. What I'm up to here is to make sure you guys get comfortable with what the description of the business is. And you are confident in talking about it. I've also played around with vision and you know what we are trying to achieve here. I don't know what ambitions you set out guys when you set up KBrandArt.

D: (reinforcing the need to answer Norman's question) Yeah. I'm really interested in hearing your personal objectives guys . . . Why did we start KBrandArt? Just the personal reasons I'm interested in. (asking L, P and A)

P: I think we originally wanted to do creative work and we thought the best way is to turn what we already started to a business. Less constraint than working for somebody . . . That was the initial thought. I think!

D: (a soft laugh-replying) Less constraint? Hmm . . . yeah. More stress I would say . . .

L: (joins in) High ambitions. I think we wanted to become a bigger production agency . . . We saw KBrandArt and then we saw different scenarios within the KBrandArt world. And plans came quite quickly, didn't they?

D: I think we've gone through a massive learning curve. Learning of what is realistic, doable! Moving from a comfort zone to something wow . . .. (All laughter) We've come to a point that the whole thing (she refers to the organisation) has become a family life. Now I feel that it's got stagnant. I feel talking to each other is like talking to ourselves and not listening to . . . So I feel that we have to do something about this.

They discussed that they should stay in the corporate market because Denise believes that it is more reliable.

L: (adds to what Denise is saying) Yeah. It is good to push yourself. Yes, the music industry is not reliable but we liked the certain element of it and produced some good stuff. If we can use the mix of music and visual, that's great.

D: You have been talking for the last five minutes: music market, corporate market, digital and video . . . it sounds very confusing. It is very confusing to hear it so we have to do something about it to communicate clearly what we are doing here. We have to be clear. I mean clear objective of where we want to go eventually . . . (asking everybody) It is getting the balance right, I think. It's the tough thing! Meanwhile, we have to run the business and . . . (interrupted by Norman):

N: . . . bring the money in . . .

D: Absolutely . . .

L: Production side is critical to me. We need to look at the jobs and map out what we need to carry on doing and improve on.

N: (asking to L) At what level?

L: What do you mean?

N: I mean do we sell ourselves as the production company, as the graphics or video? You've got to be careful about the message. People will think about how you can manage such a diverse range of activities. You have to have a 'credible package'. (Norman linked this to long-term objectives of the business and business planning)

D: (responding to N) It is easier for you to talk about all this . . . Management, long-term objectives . . . But again this family thing! How are we going to outsource the management? Yes, you tell us all this business planning stuff but just the practical side of it? I don't know how we will implement all these . . . Certainly, we see you as the first step.

N: Yes. There needs to be some sort of business attitude in place. And it is a developmental process. I mean we are talking about stages. What drives a business is brand. What I do here is to help you to communicate your brand and make that relationship with clients stronger. What we are offering is brand communications and what we are trying to do here for ourselves in KBrandArt is brand strengthening communication. It is about adding value and getting away from business bullshits.

D: (responding to N) Certainly we need to get away from that 'cliché' stuff.

N: (responding to D) This is a bit more than that. Things that I talk about . . . Hmmm . . . The equation is complex . . . I am sorry for not being very explicit. I can see I've caused some confusion here . . . What I am trying to say is what we strive to do is to build a strong relationship between the client's brands and its target audience. That's just my sort of take on it. It might be wrong, right. So again what matters is what you guys think about it . . . (talking to everybody).

A: Sorry! I'm beginning to switch off a bit . . .

D: Norman, maybe repeat what you've just said.

N: Right! Perhaps it is easier to think about it in terms of benefits to clients. Taking Aurorashire as an example. That video engaged in every aspect of branding, knowing the customer . . .

L: (asking to N) So what we want to get across to clients? Engage with them. Everything from a single frame to a whole CD-Rom or video is about strengthening the relationship with clients.

N: (adding to L) the other thing is you should talk about why you are unique. (N talked about portfolio work, business driven benefits . . . etc.) I'll stop here. I'm conscious of the time but we should run another session next week. We should have a clear idea of how we talk about ourselves. We will take it from there . . .

D: Charles is very good at planning the website out and implementing it.

Norman's mobile phone rang and he apologised and left the room to answer his phone.

D: So, the next item on the agenda is website.

They discussed ideas about the website. How appealing it should be and technical details . . . N came back to the meeting room.

A: Sort of reinforcing the message . . .
N: Yes but you need to let people know what you are doing.
D: You have to digest it first and then sell it to others . . .

A reminded the next item on the agenda. As the meeting lasted longer, A appeared to be rather uncomfortable and impatient.

A: Yes, next: legal issues? (asking Denise)
D: Yes, shareholders stuff. I'm sorting that out. We may need to meet in my house next week to finalise a couple of things. Sorry Norman! That's a bit of ownership issue and we should discuss it ourselves.
N: Fine! Absolutely . . .

D turns to the next item. She usually has agenda items written on an A4 sheet and gives it to the others at the beginning of the meeting. Next item: Funding £ Alert This is how it is put on that sheet.

D: We will get 40% of the development fund from Business Development Agency. This is Objective 2 Area stuff . . .

She asked their wish list on the equipment because they are getting some money from regional business support agencies: 50% funding on equipment. The other item on the agenda: Live jobs: They are talking about client X.

N: What should be our next step?
D: I'm just thinking if we should set ourselves a target, do some research on?
N (answers): Shall we consider a presentation emphasising the local elements?
D: I think that would be better. So any volunteers to work on this? (asking everybody)

It was only Norman who raised his hand and they all laughed. At the end, they agreed that N and A will work together. A was rather reluctant though.

Denise went through other agenda items quickly and asked the team if there were any other key things to go through. 'Priority things' she called. She explained how she should sort out particular things. Next item: INO feedback. Denise said she would provide her feedback on the INO consultancy report/document.

D: It is extensive and it ticks the right boxes in terms of funding, mapping out the industry but as a document, as a practical document to us, it needs to be more informative. (She didn't ask if anybody else would like to read it and comment on it).

N had left the meeting room just before D moved on to the INO report. He was working in his cubicle and D asked if they were quite positive about Norman who started for a week now.
L: Very positive . . .
P: Early days . . .
A: No comments . . .

The meeting ended with a discussion on ongoing projects and related tasks. Denise asked me if I could stay in the room for a while and share my opinions about a marketing campaign pitch that they would prepare in response to the brief that they received from the local university. We had a short conversation and I provided her some information about the university's recent student/staff facilities (e-learning platform etc.) and restructuring of the departments. I answered her questions and accepted her invite to the brainstorming session that was scheduled for the following week.

Researcher's Initial Thoughts/Ideas:

This is one of the most crucial meetings that I attended. It is mainly about refining the business concept, which is an integral part of the entrepreneurial process. It is also a powerful illustration of social construction between a team of nascent entrepreneurs. The way in which they interact with each other and construct meanings/understandings (and agree on actions at times) during an active engagement in the strategic matters of the business is a salient aspect of this meeting. Furthermore, the nascent entrepreneurs reflected on their personal objectives/motivations to set up this venture, collectively. This was very interesting and illuminating.

Initial Analysis: Key Themes Emerging from the Observation Data:

Page Salient points	Themes/aspects
1 Consistency in how we present ourselves to the market offerings is must. Then creating value strategically and creatively is the key issue in brand positioning.	*VENTURING PROCESS:* REFINING THE BUSINESS CONCEPT/ MARKET PERCEPTION
Production arm is very important.	*LEARNING PROCESS:* DIFFERENT FUNCTIONS OF BUSINESS
2 KBrandArt becomes the solution to the creative consultancy and productions is the technical side of it.	*VENTURING PROCESS:* INDIVIDUAL/COLLECTIVE DEFINITION OF THE BUSINESS
2 The whole future is very much on the people who have. I mean the clients . . . Well, future seems to me lies in agency type of consultancy rather than studios. I don't think Studios implies that.	*VENTURING PROCESS:* TRANSITIVE PROCESS/ ENACTING A FUTURE
3 L: Well. Let's stick to the issue. What is brand? N: . . . There is a wide interpretation of what a brand is. So, I would describe us as a brand communication agency . . .	*VENTURING PROCESS:* SOCIAL CONSTRUCTION OF MEANINGS
L: From what you're saying I don't get what your definition of brand is . . . D: How do you define it then? L: I don't know . . . Brand is about everything that touches the consumer . . .	*LEARNING PROCESS:* NEGOTIATING MEANINGS EQUIVOCAL INTERACTIONS

Page Salient points   **Themes/aspects**

A: Your corporate identity in
a way.

3   N: As long as you have got   *VENTURING PROCESS:*
         somebody and you ask the   DYNAMICS OF CREATIVE
         right questions it is fine.   INDUSTRIES
         Getting an absolutely crystal   CUSTOMISED APPROACH
         understanding of what the
         client wants and is committed
         to is the hardest thing. Once
         you get it, you can work on
         what stuff to bring in.
         A: Well, yes it is about listen-
         ing to business requirements,
         asking questions and finding
         answers. But they (clients)
         also want the project to be
         executed on time . . .
         D: Fast, efficiently and   *LEARNING PROCESS:*
         affordably.   LEGITIMISING THE
         N: Yeah. A creative and   BUSINESS
         sophisticated approach. What   DEVELOPING CONFIDENCE
         I'm up to here is to make sure   AGENTIC CAPACITY
         you guys get comfortable with
         what the description of the
         business is. And you are confi-
         dent in talking about it.

3-4   N: I've also played around   *VENTURING PROCESS:*
         with vision and you know   ENTREPRENEURIAL
         what we are trying to achieve   MOTIVATION
         here. I don't know what ambi-   OBJECTIVES
         tions you set out guys when   DISPOSITIONS
         you set up KBrandArt?   AUTONOMY/
         D: Yeah . . . I'm really inter-   INDEPENDENCE
         ested in hearing your personal
         objectives guys . . . Why did
         we start KBrandArt? Just the
         personal reasons I am inter-
         ested in.

Page Salient points	**Themes/aspects**

P: I think we originally wanted to do creative work and we thought the best way is to turn what we already started to a business. Less constrained than working for somebody . . . That was the initial thought. I think!
D: Less constraint? Hmm . . . yeah. More stress I would say . . .

L: (joins in) High ambitions. I think we wanted to become a bigger production agency . . . We saw KBrandArt and then we saw different scenarios within the KBrandArt world. And plans came quite quickly, didn't they?

VENTURING PROCESS:
IDENTIFYING THE
OPPORTUNITY
PLANS/GARNERING
RESOURCES

4   D: I think we've gone through a massive learning curve. Learning of what is realistic, doable! Moving from a comfort zone to something wow! . . ..
We've come to a point that the whole thing (she refers to the organisation) has become a family life. Now I feel that it's got stagnant. I feel talking to each other is like talking to ourselves and not listening to . . . So I feel that we have to something about this.

LEARNING PROCESS:
SETTING REALISTIC GOALS
FACING CHALLENGES
MANAGING
RELATIONSHIPS
RESOLVING ISSUES/
PROBLEMS

Index